The New York Times
GUIDE TO
REFERENCE
MATERIALS

REVISED EDITION

by MONA McCORMICK

𝕿𝖍𝖊 𝕹𝖊𝖜 𝖄𝖔𝖗𝖐 𝕿𝖎𝖒𝖊𝖘
GUIDE TO
REFERENCE
MATERIALS

REVISED EDITION

𝕿𝖎𝖒𝖊𝖘
BOOKS

Owing to limitations of space, all acknowledgments of permission to reprint material will be found on pages 219–222.

Library of Congress Cataloging in Publication Data

McCormick, Mona.
  The New York Times guide to reference materials.

  Bibliography: p. 218.
  Includes index.
  1. Reference books—Bibliography.   2. Information retrieval.   3. Report writing.   I. New York Times.
II. Title.   III. Title: Guide to reference materials.
Z1035.1.M17   1985   011'.02   84-40109
ISBN 0-8129-1127-X

Designed by Janis Capone

Manufactured in the United States of America

9 8 7 6 5 4 3 2

First Edition

For Ben

CONTENTS

Introduction to the Revised Edition

This guide was first published in hardcover as *Who-What-When-Where-How-Why-Made Easy* by Quadrangle Books (1971). The paperback edition by Popular Library was titled *The New York Times Guide to Reference Materials* (1971) and it was updated (1977). This is a Second Edition completely revised and with much new material added.

The flood of information is even more overwhelming today than it was at the time of the first edition of this guide. But the good news is that there are even better ways to get and organize information. There are new research tools that are more complete, efficient, and accurate and more up-to-date because they are produced quickly. So, after all, the information explosion is still a challenge we can meet. And certainly information is very important to our lives, helping us to make informed decisions, to learn and to understand.

Some things are the same for this new edition. It is intended to assist students and general readers in their search for information by offering a strategy for searching and an *introduction* to basic reference sources.

This is not, therefore, a comprehensive list of all good books in various fields. But with an understanding of the basic books and procedures described here, a reader should be able to extend the search beyond the scope of this work. For *The New York Times Guide to Reference Materials*, in addition to listing basic sources, is designed to indicate the wide range of material available. The bibliography on page 218 offers titles for further study.

The method of this guide is to give an inkling or sample of the kind of information found in various sources. Descriptions will not dwell on the technical arrangement because that is best learned when a reader has a book in hand and has a motive for using it. Emphasis and treatment for each work vary according to probable use.

There is a new emphasis in this edition on the critical evaluation of information. "Don't believe everything you read" has never been better advice. Because there is so much information, it can get diluted and distorted as it is passed through various media, sifted from primary source to secondary source, abstracted, summarized, and computerized. It's like the old game of telephone: The message hissed from child's ear to child's ear came out totally different at the end of the line.

Sections are arranged to lead the reader through a search for information, an evaluation of that material, and, finally, the organization and communication of conclusions and new ideas.

Readers, I hope, will pick up the clue here that libraries, reference sources, and research strategies are not overwhelming and mysterious but are exciting and rewarding and at their service.

PART I

FINDING INFORMATION

CHAPTER 1   *SEARCH STRATEGY*

Any search for information no matter how "high" or "low" the purpose—whether it is baseball statistics or philosophy—is valid because it is a search for truth . Everyone needs information for different reasons at different times; we need it as students, workers, executives, parents, friends. Information can add to our pleasure, aid us in our work, help us make informed decisions. In an agricultural age, land was power; in the Industrial Revolution, technology was power; ours seems to be the age of information, when the ability to gather and communicate information is power. In this society there is so much information that the process of finding what is revelant to a particular question requires a systematic approach or the task of finding, evaluating, and communicating information can be overwhelming.

A search strategy offers an orderly way of sifting through information for material pertinent to the question and for the *best* material to answer the question. Ideally the search begins with a questioning mood, not just a question. To search means to explore, to follow ideas wherever they lead, to examine carefully, penetratingly. If, however, you are a student with a specific assignment on a topic you're feeling lukewarm about, all is not lost. A search strategy is even more important and comforting in your case, and if you have at least a tiny bit of intellectual curiosity, you may even end up interested. Try to think of the task as a rehearsal for a time in the future when you have a question of your own to answer. Part of education is to have the *experience* of learning so the process can continue throughout life, whether or not it's in a formal school setting. Knowing how to find and evaluate information will be useful throughout life.

The following is a suggested search strategy to organize the hunt. The major steps are:

1. Overview
2. Bibliographies/Research Guides

3. Subject Headings
4. Library Catalogs to Locate Books
5. Indexing and Abstracting Services to Locate Periodical Articles
6. Special Sources
7. Evaluation

OVERVIEW

Before anyone begins an investigation of any topic, especially an unfamiliar topic, it is best to get a brief overview in a general or special-subject encyclopedia. This provides a good idea of what's involved in the topic, what the major and minor elements are, and whether or not the topic needs to be broadened or narrowed. It also offers an introduction to the specific language of the subject and definitions of terms and, in that way, suggests appropriate subject headings for use later on in library catalogs and indexing and abstracting services.

BIBLIOGRAPHIES/RESEARCH GUIDES

A bibliography is simply a list of books or articles by an author or on a subject. In most books, encyclopedias, and scholarly articles, there is a bibliography at the end of the discussion. These usually list outstanding works on the subject and will constitute a good beginning for finding the best material. There is also an index to bibliographies by subject. Each major work found during the search will contain a bibliography, so references build as the inquiry continues. They also converge; readers will begin to recognize the authorities in a field as their names repeatedly appear in bibliographies. In large subject areas there are guides to research in the field that outline research methods and name the important reference books in various subdivisions of the topic. Library catalogs also show subheadings ("Bibliography" and "Study and Teaching," for example) that lead to bibliographies and research guides.

SUBJECT HEADINGS

Those who catalog books use a uniform word or phrase to bring together in the catalog materials with a common topic. There are lists one can check to determine the correct headings and related headings on a topic. Indexes and abstracting services also use subject headings, and for that reason familiarity with the language and subordinate themes of a subject is important.

LIBRARY CATALOGS TO LOCATE BOOKS

Basic to research is an understanding of how to use library catalogs to find books by author, title, and subject. Today other materials, such as recordings and films, are also located through the library catalog. It tells where a book can be found in the library (via the call number) and gives a lot of other information about a book or author. The call number leads to a section in the bookshelves that may have other books on the subject. Browse the stack area then to see what else might be useful.

INDEXING AND ABSTRACTING SERVICES TO LOCATE PERIODICAL ARTICLES

Indexes and abstracts are used to find articles in magazines and scholarly journals, also called serials or periodicals. An index gives only the citation (author, title of article, title of periodical, volume, pages, and date of the publication). An abstract gives the citation and a brief summary of the article. The searcher then seeks out the magazine or journal to read the full article. Indexes and abstracts are essential in a field requiring "current awareness" because books take time to publish and distribute.

SPECIAL SOURCES

Tracking a subject will frequently suggest other materials to check, such as government documents, annual reviews of the literature, directories, etc., which will prove invaluable. And don't forget people. If an expert is available, ask that person about the subject and for recommendations on the best reference books in the field.

EVALUATION

Finally, a researcher must sift through the material gathered and deal critically as well as creatively with it. One must identify the most important information and test it for authority, accuracy, relevance, and completeness.

All the elements of the search strategy are given expanded treatment throughout this guide. A first, quick run through steps one through five will give you an idea of how much is "out there." For students, if there is lots of information, you probably need to narrow your topic, and if there is very little, the topic may need to be broadened.

Bibliography Cards/Note Taking

Even if your search is the pursuit of a hobby or leisure activity, *from the start keep a file of bibliography cards* showing the exact citation for the information and, if the work is more academic, the source of the citation. There is more wasted time, more wheel spinning, on the part of students, housewives, reporters, authors, businessmen, bakers, and candlestick makers because they copied a citation incorrectly, can't find again something they found once before, or did not record an important part of a citation that is now needed for a bibliography. If you don't think you need such notation, make it anyway; the notes can be thrown out in the spring if that's true, and meanwhile, you have it if you need it.

A bibliography card should include:

1. The call number for the book or periodical and the name of the library if more than one library is being used.
2. Author, title, subtitle, edition, place of publication, publisher, date of publication.

    Or, if it's a periodical: Author, title of article, title of periodical, volume number, month, year, page numbers.
3. An annotation—a brief summary of the information. Writing an annotation forces one to begin thinking critically by identifying major themes and conclusions and making it easier to recall later. It also helps the reader notice how people write.
4. Source. Where was this title found?

If this information is on cards, one item to a card, they are more easily arranged or shuffled into appropriate groups or subdivisions if you are writing a paper, book, or article. They are also easily arranged alphabetically for a bibliography.

An annotation is not necessarily note taking. Extensive notes can be done on separate papers or on the back of the bibliography card and can flow onto several cards. Be sure to identify the source on separate note pages.

Try to take notes in your own words in order to begin the creative process and critical thinking. If you take down a direct quote, use quo-

```
Library &          Author.  Title: subtitle.  Edition
Call number             Place of publication:  Publisher,
                        Date of publication

        Library &              Author.  "Title of article."
        Call number              Title of Journal, volume #
                                 (month, year), page numbers


        Annotation:

        Summary of information.  Main points, conclusions,
        notes, quotes


        Source:  Name of reference book, book, or
                 bibliography in which a citation for
                 the above item was found
```

tation marks and make a note of the text page from which it came. If you use the quote in your work, you need the full citation and the page number. Always give credit to the author quoted, and take care to quote accurately word for word.

Take notes that suggest the substance of the material without simply copying long paragraphs or pages. Choose the main theme and minor points, arranging them to show relationships. Note enough information to give you a clue later to the whole work. A brief outline is effective, and often the table of contents is worth noting.

For assistance in mapping a search strategy, ask a reference librarian. People have been searching for information since the beginning of time. If you think of research as an ongoing process, it will be easier to persevere.

CHAPTER 2   *THE LIBRARY AND ITS CATALOG*

The giant step forward in any reference project is familiarity with the library and an understanding of its catalog or catalogs. The idealized view is that a reader can serenely browse through the library stacks and spot whatever is needed. However, work in the library is not serendipitous—well, not usually. The catalog is the key to finding things in the library; it carries the code to the location of books and other items. (Remember, though, that libraries own some materials that are not listed in catalogs. Some carry pamphlets, clipping files, and audiovisual works that are not cataloged. Frequently government documents are filed in separate locations and are not in the general catalog. Ask a librarian if any arrangement in a library is not apparent.)

Let's take a brief look at classification systems, call numbers, catalogs (both card catalogs and online catalogs), subject headings, and alphabetization and filing orders.

CLASSIFICATION SYSTEM

Books are arranged within the library according to a classification system. They are classified or sorted into groups so that books on the same subject are located together.

There are two main classification systems used by libraries: the Dewey decimal system (used in most libraries because it can be easily adapted to the needs of a small collection of books) and the system of the Library of Congress (used in very large collections because it allows for greater subdivisions without making lengthy class numbers). These two systems are divided into the main groups as illustrated on page 9.

Within each of these large groups there are further divisions indicated by numbers or letters.

DEWEY DECIMAL CLASSIFICATION	LIBRARY OF CONGRESS CLASSIFICATION	
	A	General works—polygraphy
000 General works	B	Philosophy—religion
	C	History—auxiliary sciences
100 Philosophy	D	History and topography (except America)
	E-F	America
200 Religion		Geography—anthropology
	H	Social sciences
300 Social sciences	J	Political science
	K	Law
400 Language	L	Education
	M	Music
	N	Fine arts
500 Pure science	P	Language and literature
	Q	Science
600 Technology	R	Medicine
	S	Agriculture—plant and animal industry
700 The arts	T	Technology
	U	Military science
800 Literature	V	Naval science
	Z	Bibliography and library
900 History		science

In the Dewey system, for example, the 900's are shown as the identification for history. But within that, 940 is the number for European history, and 973 begins American history. And within the 973's you will find still more divisions, such as:

973   American History
973.1   American Discovery and Exploration
973.2   American Colonial Period
973.3   American Revolution
973.4   American Constitutional Period
973.5   Early Nineteenth-Century America
973.6   Middle Nineteenth-Century America
973.7   American Civil War

and so on into the twentieth century. That's how it works. You don't need to remember it. Use the card catalog to get the number.

CALL NUMBER

The location of a book in the library is determined by the call number. The call number is a combination of the subject classification number and a letter or letter number indicating the author. The *Encyclopedia of the American Revolution* by Mark M. Boatner might have this call number:

973.3
B

or in larger libraries a more precise author identification:

973.3
B63

which will appear on the spine of the book and on the cards in the catalog that refer to that book. Books are arranged on the shelves first according to number and then alphabetically by the author's name.

LIBRARY CATALOGS

The library catalog shows what books and other materials are in the library's collection and where they may be found. People are most familiar with card catalogs, but some libraries today have online catalogs, on which, using a computer terminal, a patron brings up a citation on a screen. The visual citation contains the same information found on a card in the card catalog. Libraries may use *both* the card catalog, identifying older works, and the online catalog, identifying newly cataloged materials.

Depending on the classification system, the size of the collection, and perhaps the whim of the person assigning the numbers, a book may be given different numbers in different libraries, so always check the card catalog. Often fiction (though usually arranged alphabetically by author) and biographies (though usually set out alphabetically by biographee) are treated differently from library to library.

Card Catalog

Some libraries with card catalogs may have a *divided catalog*—a catalog for authors and titles and another catalog for subjects—while other libraries have a *dictionary catalog*—with authors, titles, and subjects all in one alphabetical arrangement.

A single book may have as many as five or six cards in the catalog to accommodate various approaches by the reader. The three most common cards are for author, title, and subject, but there may be cards for editors, joint authors, the name of a series, institutions, or "corporate authors." Here are simple examples of author, title, and subject cards:

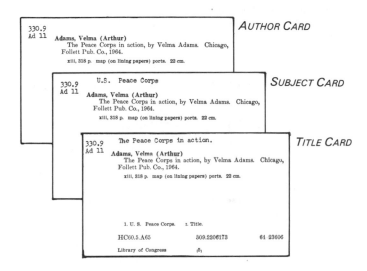

The most complete information is on the main entry card (that is usually the author card, but it could be an organization or corporate author card or, if there is no author, the title card). On the main entry card you will find:

The call number of the book
The author's name
Title and subtitle
The name of the publisher
Copyright date or date of publication

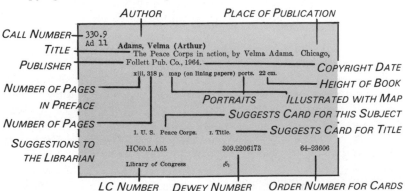

When person, place, subject, and title are the same, the arrangement (usually) is as follows:

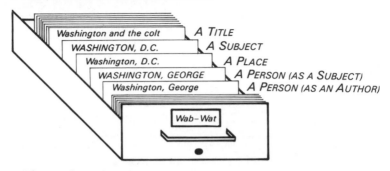

The card catalog also has "see" and "see also" references (discussed in the use of periodical and newspaper indexes, page 59). An example of a "see" reference—a direction from a heading not used to the heading used—is:

PEACE CORPS
see
U.S. Peace Corps

An example of a "see also" reference—a direction to related material—is:

GHOSTS
see also
Demonology
Spiritualism
Superstition

Online Catalog

Catalogs on computers contain the same information and have the same general approaches (author, title, subject, etc.) as card catalogs, and carry other features as well. Every effort is made to make computerized catalogs "user-friendly." They require simple commands for searching and usually explain, on the screen, the options or next steps as you go along.

Online systems are fast and have certain advantages not offered by card catalogs. The reader can combine searches. For example, a search could combine a search for an author and a key word in the title. Or a search could be made on just the key word in the title, if the reader can't remember the exact title of a book. Systems may be "browsed" and show lists of subject headings when the reader needs them. A list of all books by an author on a subject can be shown, and the reader can stop the list to display the full information and call number on one book.

Systems vary, but all are simple and have printed guides to their use. For example, an online catalog may require an easy command like "FIND NT" (standing for "name" and "title"), followed by an author's name and/or title or a key word in the title to request a book when the author and/or title are known. A command like "FIND SU" (standing for "subject"), followed by the subject heading, will bring up a list of books on a particular subject. So you might type into the computer:

"FIND NT STEINBECK"	(to see all books by that author)
"FIND NT STEINBECK GRAPES"	(to call up one book by that author)
"FIND SU WHALES"	(to see a list of books on the subject of whales)

By the way, don't confuse an online catalog, which uses a computer to find books in the library, with the computerized literature searches and databases discussed later in this book.

SUBJECT HEADINGS

A subject heading is a uniform word or phrase used to bring together in a catalog materials with a common topic. The Dewey classification usually uses the *Sears List of Subject Headings,* and the Library of Congress classification uses the *Library of Congress List of Subject Headings.* You may have to look under several headings to find related material on a subject. Usually there will be cross-references within the catalog, as shown above, but if you find nothing under your subject, check the appropriate list to see what the correct heading is. If you look up "Unidentified flying objects," for example, you are referred to the heading "Flying saucers" in the Library of Congress list, and if you look up "Shoes," you are referred to the heading "Boots and shoes." "Unicorns in literature" is a Library of Congress subject heading and an example of one that might not pop into your mind without your using the subject heading list.

On the analyzed catalog card shown on page 11, it is worth noting the place at the bottom of the card where subject headings are suggested and numbered. Suppose, through a bibliography, you found a perfect book for your topic; you could look it up in the catalog and, if your library owned the book, see what subject headings had been assigned to the book and use those same headings to find more information. (These catalog notes are called tracings because librarians can trace all the cards in the catalog on a particular book.)

ALPHABETIZATION

Knowing the alphabet does not mean you're home free. Alphabetization for indexes and filing cards has two major systems. One is a word-by-word system (as used in the *Encyclopedia Americana),* and the other is a letter-by-letter system (as used in the *Encyclopaedia Britannica),* in which each entry, no matter how many words, is treated as though it spelled one word.

Word by Word	Letter by Letter
West Point	Western Union
West York, Pa.	Westminster Abbey
Western Union	West Point
Westminster Abbey	Westward Ho!
Westward Ho!	West York, Pa.
Wheat	Wheat
Wheat germ	Wheatear (bird)
Wheatear (bird)	Wheat germ

Filing of names, especially foreign names, is complicated, but three common stumbling blocks are:

The "St.," in, for example, "St. Valentine's Day," is usually filed as though spelled out: Saint Valentine's Day.
Names beginning with *Mc* are sometimes filed ahead of all the *M*'s, sometimes filed as though spelled *Mac,* and sometimes filed as *Mc* in a letter-by-letter style.
Prefixes such as "Lord," "Mrs.," "Viscount" are usually ignored in filing:

Long, *Mrs.* Adam
Long, *Baron* Paul

If you can't find something you expect to find in a certain source or in the card catalog, check the instructions, try an alphabet variation, or ask for assistance.

Only the most common arrangements and catalogs are discussed here. There are many variations because each library has its unique character. Take the time to know your library, and if you can't find something or do not understand a card reference, ask a librarian.

Libraries offer many services in addition to housing and lending books. Many libraries offer courses, book discussions, and community services. Reference services will help you find information and learn how to use the library. Most libraries offer some kind of interlibrary loan service, which allows readers to request a book from another library if it is not in their library's collection. Libraries are a vital source not only of information but also of entertainment.

CHAPTER 3 TERMS USED IN REFERENCE MATERIALS

Abstract A brief summary of the content of an article or document.

Acronym A word made from the initial letter or letters of the major parts or names of an organization or phrase, such as NATO.

Annotation A brief statement evaluating the scope or content of a work or document. It is frequently used to describe an item in a bibliography.

Appendix (plural **Appendixes** or **Appendices**) Additional material following the main text of a book. The material is usually supplementary and not essential to the book. Appendixes often contain the complete texts of documents and statistical information.

Bibliography A list of books and articles by an author or about a particular subject (or a list of books published in a country, in certain languages, etc.). In a reference book the bibliography usually is a list of sources the author used in writing the book or article, and it also serves as a guide for the reader to additional information on the subject.

Citation A bibliographic note identifying the source of a quoted statement, book, document, or reference.

Collation The description of the physical structure of an item such as a book, including information on its format, illustrations, pages, etc.

Concordance An alphabetical index of the principal words of a book (such as the Bible) shown in context and with a reference to the passages in which they occur.

Copyright Usually the back of the title page contains the copyright date. Books published after September 15, 1955, have the symbol ©, which protects copyright holders. It is the exclusive right, granted by law for a certain number of years, to control copies of a literary, musical, or artistic work. Sometimes a frequently revised book will show a copyright date for each revision. Additional "printings" may be listed here, but the latest copyright date shown is the year the book was first printed in its present form. (The copyright date is not always the same as the publication date—see TITLE PAGE definition.)

Cross-References There are two kinds of cross-references: "see" references and "see also" references. A "see" reference directs the reader from a heading not used to the one used by the author. (For example: "Farming see Agriculture.") A "see also" reference is one that gives pages for the heading checked and then refers the reader to related topics. (For example: "Latin America see also Alliance for Progress.") Some indexes put the page references under all headings rather than use cross-references. And unfortunately some indexes have no cross-references and do not put the references under various possible headings so the reader must search his vocabulary for synonyms to determine the subject heading used.

Edition All the impressions of a work made from a single set of plates. A change in the text constitutes a new edition. The record of editions is usually found on the verso (back) of the title page.

Festschrift A collection of essays by several authors, usually representing original research, published in honor of a person or institution.

Gazetteer A geographical dictionary giving names and descriptions of places.

Glossary An explanation of the vocabulary used in the book—especially in books using foreign or scientific terms that need definition. (This list of terms that you are reading is a glossary.)

Imprint The information concerning the publication of a book: place, publisher, and date. It is usually found on the title page.

Incunabula Literally this means "things of the cradle," and it refers to books printed in movable type before 1501.

Index An alphabetical list of people, places, and topics mentioned in the text of a book or a set of books. After each entry the numbers of the pertinent page or pages are given (or the volume number and pages if the index is to a set of books).

Introduction, Preface, and Foreword Terms that are often used interchangeably. They refer to the sections in the front of the book which give a brief statement about the book by the author (or another person) and contain acknowledgment of the assistance of others and suggestions by the author to the reader about the material.

Leaf The basic unit of a book. Each leaf has two sides, or pages, the recto (front) and the verso (back).

Printing An impression made at one time for one setting of type. There may be several printings of an edition, but substantial change or revision of the type constitutes a new edition. The history of a printing is usually on the verso (back) of the title page.

Publication Date   The year in which a book was published, usually printed on the title page or its verso.

Recto   The front of a printed leaf; the right-hand page of an open book, usually an odd-numbered page.

Text   The main part or body of a book.

Title Page   The page at the front of the book with much important information. It gives the full title, the name of the author and sometimes his or her degrees, etc., the name of the publisher, and the place and date of publication. (Note: The publication date may be different from the copyright date, which usually appears on the back of the title page.)

Tracings   The record of other headings under which a book or an item can be found in a library's catalog. It is usually near the bottom of a catalog card.

Verso   The back of a printed leaf; the left-hand page of an open book, usually an even-numbered page.

Vertical File   Pamphlets, clippings, and other materials that are not suitable for classification and a place on the library shelf are often filed in an "information file" or "vertical file" (because the items are filed standing on edge). Such material is given a subject heading, placed in a folder with that same heading, and then filed in deep-drawer cabinets.

CHAPTER 4

ABBREVIATIONS USED IN REFERENCE MATERIALS

anon.	anonymous
c	copyright
cf.	confer; or compare
ch.	chapter
col., cols.	column, columns
comp.	compiler
cm.	centimeters (the size of the book as shown on the catalog card)
diagrs.	diagrams
ed.	editor, edition, edited
e.g.	*exempli gratia;* for example
enl. or enlar.	enlarged (material added)
et al.	and others
et seq.	*et sequens;* and following
f., ff.	page or pages following
fac.	facsimile
fig., figs.	figure, figures
ibid.	*ibidem;* the same reference as the one immediately preceding
id.	*idem;* in the same place
i.e.	*id est;* that is
illus.	illustrator, illustrated, illustration
incl.	including
loc. cit.	*loco citato;* the same passage as that just cited by the author whose name is given.
mounted pl.	mounted plates; full-page illustrations
ms., mss.	manuscript, manuscripts
op. cit.	*opere citato;* the same work as the one previously cited by the author whose name is given.
p., pp.	page, pages
passim	here and there

pseud.	pseudonym
q.v.	*quod vide;* which see
qq.v.	plural "which see" (a see reference to more than one other heading)
recto	right-hand page of a book
rev.	revised (the material has been changed and brought up-to-date)
sec., secs.	section, sections
[sic]	for "thus," bracketed and used to indicate that the preceding error is to be found in the original source
tr.	translator, translation
verso	left-hand page of a book
viz.	*videlicet;* namely
v. or vol., vols.	volume or volumes

CHAPTER 5   *SEARCHING BY COMPUTER*

The hum of computers can be heard throughout the land, and libraries are no exception. Fortunately modern technology has come to the aid of tired students and researchers by producing citations and information almost as magically as a rabbit is pulled out of a hat. Many of the indexing and abstracting services described in this book can be searched by computer. Computerized literature retrieval is used to create a bibliography from publications indexed by national and international abstracting and indexing services.

Large public libraries and college and university libraries offer computer searching (though, unlike most library services, there is usually a fee for this service). The same information found in printed indexes can be processed and stored in a computer as a DATABASE, a machine-searchable collection of information. VENDORS, the private suppliers of one or more databases, provide the necessary SOFTWARE (programs and related documentation of a computer system) and HARDWARE (physical equipment) to permit interactive searching by many individuals simultaneously.

A database can be searched by authors, titles, subjects, and other elements using a typewriterlike TERMINAL, which is connected by a telephone line to the computer. The results of a search can be obtained immediately in a PRINTOUT at the terminal if the search is done ONLINE. A long list of citations can be printed OFFLINE, and the results received at a later time, perhaps sent through the mail from another location. An offline search is cheaper than online. Sometimes the two methods are combined—a few citations are printed online to make sure the subject terms or descriptors used are producing the desired results, and the rest of the search is done offline.

Some fortunate libraries offer quick reference service on computers that may be used by the public, but in most situations involving extensive research, an appointment must be made with a computer searcher who will conduct the actual search and discuss topics to be investigated. A trained searcher can recommend appropriate databases and advise patrons on the feasibility of a computer search. Searching the literature by computer is most often used for current or complex topics in the sciences, education, or business, and though its use in the humanities and social sciences is increasing, some subjects are still best handled through printed indexes and bibliographies. If a patron is investigating a single subject heading, covering just a few years, a manual search may still be best. The computer is ideally suited to more complicated searches using two or three subject headings.

Each database has its own subject headings and usually issues a THESAURUS, a CONTROLLED VOCABULARY, or a list of DESCRIPTORS, which serves as its subject term guide.

When one uses a computer, many search elements can be combined according to BOOLEAN LOGIC. This system, invented by English mathematician George Boole (1815–1864), uses the connectors AND, OR, and AND NOT to link subject terms. "Grain AND spoilage AND Italy AND NOT wheat" would retrieve citations on nonwheat grain spoilage in Italy.

Boole's logic is different from the logic commonly assumed with these connecting words. For example, a searcher might assume that the AND connector equals "plus" and therefore that it adds terms together to make a greater sum (as in "I want cheese *and* crackers"). Also, it is usually assumed that the OR connector reduces the sum (as in "I want cheese *or* crackers but not both"). Actually, the opposite happens in Boolean Logic: AND reduces; OR expands.

This logic was graphically explained by English logician John Venn (1834–1923), in what are known as Venn diagrams. The result of each search on the terms "Opera" and "Verdi" is represented by the shaded area in these Venn diagrams.

AND yields the intersection of two sets.　　*OR yields the union of two sets.*

Search:　　　　　　　　　　　　　　*Search:*
FIND SUBJECT OPERA AND *VERDI*　FIND SUBJECT OPERA OR *VERDI*

AND NOT yields the exclusion of one set from another.

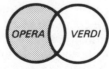

Search:
FIND SUBJECT OPERA AND NOT *VERDI*

Remember, a CITATION gives the author, title, and source of the information, and the researcher must then seek out those books and journal articles. If an ABSTRACT is requested (increasing the cost of the computer search), the reader receives a brief summary of the article or book or other item in addition to the citation. An abstract saves time by indicating whether or not an item is worth tracking down. Some databases will retrieve the full text of an article or document.

Ordinarily the cost of computerized literature searching depends on whether the information is obtained online or offline, whether citations, abstracts, or full texts are requested, how many databases are searched, and how much time is spent online.

Often arrangements can be made for a "standing order" for computer searches to be done automatically every one or two months for new material on a particular subject. This current awareness service is particularly useful in a field like medicine in which there are new and frequent developments.

A computer search can be very useful because:

- It is fast.
- It is more up-to-date than a printed index. Current publications are often included in the database long before they appear in printed indexes.
- Searching approaches can be combined, such as:

  Authors and subjects (e.g., Linus Pauling and vitamin C)
  Subject terms (e.g., television and violence and children)
  Specific exclusions (e.g., rockets since 1975)

- Different time periods are available—recent material only, everything on a topic regardless of date, current awareness services.
- More thorough searching is possible. Many databases can be commanded to search for words found in titles and abstracts as well as for the subject headings. And more subject headings are assigned to each item in the database than in the printed version.
- The computer can vary the printed formats such as author and title, title only, complete citation and abstract, and others.

SELECTED LIST OF AVAILABLE DATABASES

A look at the following selected list gives an idea of the variety of subjects now available for online searching.

ABI/INFORM (1971+) Business-related journal articles
ACCOUNTANTS INDEX (1974+)

AGLINE (1977+)
AGRICOLA (1970+)
    Bibliography of Agriculture,

National Agricultural Library
Catalog
AMERICA: HISTORY AND LIFE
(1964+)
AMERICAN STATISTICS INDEX
(1973+)
APTIC (1966–1978)
Air Pollution Abstracts
AQUALINE (1974+)
AQUATIC SCIENCES AND
FISHERIES ABSTRACTS (1978+)
AQUACULTURE (1970+)
ARTBIBLIOGRAPHIES MODERN
(1974+)
AVLINE
Health sciences audiovisuals
BHRA FLUID ENGINEERING
(1974+)
BILINGUAL EDUCATION (1978+)
BIOETHICSLINE (1973+)
Bibliography of Bioethics
BIOSIS (1969+)
Biological Abstracts, Biological
Abstracts/RRM
BOOKS INFORMATION
Current books in print
CAB ABSTRACTS (1973+)
22 abstracting journals from the
Commonwealth Agricultural
Bureaus
CANCERLIT (1962+)
CHEMICAL ABSTRACTS (1970+)
CHILD ABUSE AND NEGLECT
(1965+)
CLAIMS/PATENT FILES
COLD REGIONS (1962+)
Antarctic Bibliography (1962+),
Bibliography on Cold Regions
Science and Technology (1969+)
COMPENDEX (1970+)
Engineering Index
COMPREHENSIVE DISSERTATION
INDEX (1861+)
CONFERENCE PAPERS INDEX
(1973+)
CONGRESSIONAL INFORMATION
SERVICE INDEX (1970+)
CONGRESSIONAL RECORD (1976+)

DRUG INFO/ALCOHOL USE-ABUSE
ECONOMICS ABSTRACTS
INTERNATIONAL (1974+)
Economic Titles and Abstracts
EIS INDUSTRIAL PLANTS (current)
EIS NONMANUFACTURING
ESTABLISHMENTS (current)
ELECTRIC POWER (1975+)
ENCYCLOPEDIA OF ASSOCIATIONS
(latest edition of printed volume)
ENERGYLINE (1971+)
Energy Information Abstracts
ENVIROLINE (1971+)
Environment Abstracts
ENVIRONMENTAL PERIODICALS
BIBLIOGRAPHY (1974+)
ERIC (1966+)
Resources in Education (1966+)
Current Index to Journals in
Education (1969+)
EXCEPTIONAL CHILD EDUCATION
RESOURCES (1966+)
EXCERPTA MEDICA (1974+)
FAMILY RESOURCES (1970+)
FEDERAL INDEX (October 1976+)
FEDERAL REGISTER ABSTRACTS
(1977+)
FEDEX (1976+)
Compilation of Federal Register,
Congressional Record, Commerce
Business Daily, Washington Post,
and others
FEDEX (1977+)
Statistical tabulations of energy
information agencies
FOOD SCIENCE & TECHNOLOGY
ABSTRACTS (1969+)
FOREIGN TRADERS INDEX
(current five years)
FOUNDATION DIRECTORY (current)
FOUNDATION GRANTS INDEX
(1973+)
GEOARCHIVE (1974+)
GEOREF (1961+)
Bibliography and Index of Geology,
Geophysical Abstracts
GRANTS
Available current grants with
deadline dates

HEALTH PLANNING AND
ADMINISTRATION (1975+)
HISTLINE (1970+)
History of Medicine
HISTORICAL ABSTRACTS (1973+)
INSPEC (1969+)
Computer and Control Abstracts,
Electrical and Electronics
Abstracts, Physics Abstracts
INTERNATIONAL
PHARMACEUTICAL ABSTRACTS
(1970+)
IRL LIFE SCIENCES (1978+)
15 life sciences abstracting
journals
ISMEC (1973+)
Information Service in Mechanical
Engineering
LABORDOC (1965+)
International Labor
Documentation
LANGUAGE AND LANGUAGE
BEHAVIOR ABSTRACTS (1973+)
LEGAL RESOURCES INDEX (1980+)
MAGAZINE INDEX (1976+)
MANAGEMENT CONTENTS (1974+)
MEDLINE (1966+)
Index Medicus, International
Nursing Index, Index to Dental
Literature, Hospital Literature
Index Backfiles, 1966–1977
MEDOC (1976+)
Health-related U.S. government
documents
METADEX (1966+)
Review of Metal Literature
(1966–67), Metal Abstracts (1968+),
Alloys Index (1974+)
METEOROLOGICAL AND
GEOASTROPHYSICAL
ABSTRACTS (1972+)
MODERN LANGUAGE
ASSOCIATION BIBLIOGRAPHY
(1976+)
MONTHLY CATALOG OF U.S.
GOVERNMENT PUBLICATIONS
(July 1976+)
NATIONAL CRIMINAL JUSTICE
REFERENCE SERVICE (1972+)

NATIONAL FOUNDATIONS
(Current)
NATIONAL INSTITUTE OF MENTAL
HEALTH (1969+)
NATIONAL NEWSPAPER INDEX
(1979+)
NATIONAL TECHNICAL
INFORMATION SERVICE (1970+)
Government Reports
Announcements, Weekly
Government Abstracts
NEWSEARCH
NEWSPAPER INDEX (1976+)
NEW YORK TIMES INFORMATION
BANK (1977+)
NICEM (1964+)
National Information Center for
Educational Media
NIMIS (Early 1800's–1977) National
Instructional Materials
Information System
OCEANIC ABSTRACTS (1964+)
PACIFIC ISLANDS ECOSYSTEMS
(1927+)
PHARMACEUTICAL NEWS INDEX
PHILOSOPHERS INDEX (1940+)
PREDICASTS F & S INDEX (1972+)
PREDICASTS INTERNATIONAL
FORECASTS (1972+)
PREDICASTS INTERNATIONAL
TIME SERIES (1972+)
PREDICASTS PROMT (1972+)
PREDICASTS U.S. FORECASTS
(1972+)
PREDICASTS U.S. TIME SERIES
(1972+)
PREMED (current 3–4 months)
clinical medical journals
POLLUTION ABSTRACTS (1970+)
POPULATION BIBLIOGRAPHY
(1966+)
PSYCHOLOGICAL ABSTRACTS
(1967+)
PUBLIC AFFAIRS INFORMATION
SERVICE (1972+)
PAIS Bulletin (1976+), PAIS
Foreign Language Index (1972+)
RAPRA ABSTRACTS (1972+)
Rubber and Plastics Association of
Great Britain

RILM (1972+) Répertoire International de Littérature Musicale
SAFETY SCIENCE ABSTRACTS (1975+)
SCHOOL PRACTICES (current)
SCISEARCH (1970+)
Science Citation Index, Current Contents
SOCIAL SCISEARCH (1972+)
Social Sciences Citation Index Current Contents
SOCIETY OF AUTOMOTIVE ENGINEERS (1965+)
SOCIOLOGICAL ABSTRACTS (1963+)
SPECIAL EDUCATION MATERIALS (NICSEM) (1977+)
SPIN (1975+)
Searchable Physics Information Notices
SPORT AND RECREATION INDEX (1975+ for journals, 1949+ for monographs)
SSIE: Smithsonian Science Information Exchange (latest 2 years)

STANDARD & POORS (1979+)
STATE PUBLICATIONS (1976+)
SURFACE COATINGS ABSTRACTS (1976+)
TOXLINE (1965+)
TRADE OPPORTUNITIES (1976+)
TRIS (1964+)
Transportation Research Information Service (formerly Maritime Research Information Service)
TROPAG (1975+) Abstracts on Tropical Agriculture
TSCA INVENTORY
Toxic Substances Control Act Chemical Substance Inventory
U.S. POLITICAL SCIENCE DOCUMENTS (1975+)
U.S. PUBLIC SCHOOL DIRECTORY (current)
VOTES (1979+)
Roll call voting by U.S. Congress
WELDASEARCH (1967+)
Welding of metals and plastics
WORLD ALUMINUM ABSTRACTS (1968+)

More information on available online databases can be found in such directories as:

Cuadra, Ruth N.; Abels, David M.; and Wanger, Judith, eds. *Directory of Online Databases*. Santa Monica, Calif.: Cuadra Associates, Inc., 1982.

Williams, Martha E.; Lannom, Laurence; and Robbins, Carolyn G., eds. *Computer-Readable Databases—A Directory and Data Sourcebook*. White Plains, N.Y.: Knowledge Industry Publications, 1982.

Related sources of importance to those interested generally in computerized information and online searching are:

Derfler, Frank J., and Stallings, William. *A Manager's Guide to Local Networks*. Englewood Cliffs, N.J.: Prentice-Hall, 1983.

Katz, Bill, and Farley, Ruth A., eds. *Video to Online Reference Services and the New Technology*. New York: Haworth Press, 1983.

Zorkocsy, Peter. *Information Technology: An Introductory*. White Plains, N.Y.: Knowledge Industry Publications, 1983.

PART II

REFERENCE BOOKS BY TYPE

CHAPTER 6   ALMANACS AND ATLASES

Almanacs are an old information source. The early ones were often produced by astrologers because a belief in the influence of the stars on human behavior, a desire to know the future, and superstition created a popular demand for prophecy.

In the beginning almanacs predicted, in addition to the daily weather, such catastrophes as fires, famine, and plague. The editors faced the occupational hazards of being burned at the stake as sorcerers if they were right too often or of losing their reputations if they were too often wrong. So they resorted to ambiguous language. An almanac in 1580 predicted: "The Sommer and Autumne shall sometyme encline unto driness, sometyme unto moysture: so the winter shall be partlye rough and partlye milde." In other words, a nice day unless it isn't.

The first printed American almanac was *An Almanack for New England for the Year 1639*, compiled by William Pierce. In 1733, Benjamin Franklin launched *Poor Richard's Almanack,* which became famous for the proverbs used to fill little spaces that occurred between the calendar days. Famous Franklin adages which appeared in his almanack are:

Make haste slowly.
Three may keep a secret if two of them are dead.
Early to bed and early to rise,
   Makes a man healthy, wealthy, and wise.

Governments and newspapers began issuing almanacs in the 1800's. They included recipes and first-aid advice for injuries and snakebite. Gradually the weather predictions were abandoned except in the *Old Farmer's Almanac.* This almanac, founded in 1793, continues today with little reference value but an entertaining old-time flavor, still (some say accurately) predicting the weather and giving the rising and setting of the moon and sun.

Today's almanacs rarely preach, and they deal with much more than just the calendar. Almanacs now have a great many facts and much miscellaneous information in table form. Since they are published annually, a great deal of the information is associated with a single year, but modern almanacs have much more historical information than they once had.

The major almanacs are the *Information Please Almanac, Atlas and Yearbook*, the *Reader's Digest Almanac and Yearbook*, and the *World Almanac and Book of Facts.*

These give, to mention but a few items, chronologies of events of the previous year, facts about countries and their governments, lots of statistics on populations, elections, etc., and lists of colleges, of societies and associations, and of famous people.

Some of the special facts now appearing in almanacs are illustrated in this sampling. The reader can find:

The distances between major cities
A list of famous waterfalls with location and height
A brief description of major art museum collections
Postal information
The length of the Great Lakes
The state mottos (California's is "Eureka [I have found it]")
Pictures of the flags of the world

There are also almanacs covering special subjects. For example, the *Negro Almanac*, a reference work on the Afro-American, has sections on black history, civil rights, black population, education, religion, and black personalities, and a bibliography.

Other countries also publish almanacs with their own emphases. A well-known one is Whitaker's *Almanack*, published in Great Britain.

Atlases, in many ways, are graphic illustrations of the facts found in almanacs. An atlas is a collection of maps and a map is a representation of the earth's surface or part of it (there are also maps of the sky). The map is an ancient form and has been found on a Babylonian clay tablet dating from as early as 2300 B.C. "Atlas" has come to mean a book of maps because the figure of Atlas (from Greek mythology) was used by famous geographer Mercator on the title page of his map collections in the sixteenth century.

Today maps are valuable not only because they describe places through lines indicating boundaries and roads but also because they can illustrate information such as the elevation of land, crops, rainfall, population, and temperature through the use of symbols (dots, circles, triangles, etc.) and colors. Each map has a key that defines what the symbols and colors stand for.

Maps may give the general features of a place and also show that place in relation to the surrounding area or the world. An accurate map is drawn to scale—for example, a certain number of miles per inch. Then the reader can measure the distance on the map and figure the real distance on the earth's surface.

The introduction to *Goode's World Atlas* (listed below) has a good explanation of how to read maps, as does the *World Book Encyclopedia*. Most atlases and encyclopedias also explain the subject, and if you use maps, it is best to read some of this "get acquainted" material.

Over the years many fine atlases have been produced by *The Times* of London. The works are outstanding for their coverage, accuracy, and handsome format. The current one-volume *The Times Atlas of the World*, Comprehensive Edition, has a useful section on the resources of the world in relation to human needs, a glossary of geographical terms, and a table of geographical comparisons so you can see at a glance that our Mount McKinley is not as high as Asia's Everest but is higher than Tanzania's Kilimanjaro. Both editions of *The Times Atlas of the World* provide many inset maps of cities (Shanghai, Chicago, Brussels, New Orleans, etc.). The Comprehensive Edition combines the index-gazetteers of the Midcentury Edition in one alphabet and includes the English as well as the vernacular forms of place-names (Florence as well as Firenze).

The Times Atlas comes in a shorter version: *The New York Times Atlas of the World*. This is revised frequently and has many of the same features and the same maps as the larger work.

Goode's World Atlas is a student atlas, containing many world maps showing climate, rainfall, population, products, etc. It has maps of areas—polar regions, North America, South America, Europe, Asia, and Africa—and also shows the United States in section maps, not state by state. *Goode's* has a name pronouncing index.

The *Rand McNally New Cosmopolitan World Atlas* has maps covering the physical and political world, the solar system, world history, and American history. This atlas has individual maps of each American state.

Two other valuable world atlases are the *National Geographic Atlas of the World* and the *Hammond Medallion World Atlas*.

If you wanted to know the student population of Minot, North Dakota, the time difference between Alaska and Arabia, and the number of post offices in Boulder, Colorado, you'd find these facts in an atlas—the *Rand McNally Commercial Atlas and Marketing Guide*. Issued annually, this atlas has maps of general U.S. information and detailed commercial information in individual state maps. It includes transportation maps showing mileage and driving times, railroad and airline information, etc. Emphasis is on the United States, but there are also sections on Canada and other parts of the world.

History can be represented in maps, too, and sometimes the reader can get a better understanding of certain alliances between countries or wars over boundaries by seeing them on a map. The term "historical atlas" is applied to an atlas that is made up of maps illustrating past events or periods of history. It is not simply a collection of old maps. For example, the location and extent of the Navaho or Chickasaw Indian tribes in 1650 are shown in Paullin's *Atlas of the Historical Geography of the United States*. This atlas has many fascinating maps on explorations, elections, religious denominations, cities from 1775 to 1803, and the foreign-born populations of the United States.

Two historical atlases covering the world are *Muir's Historical Atlas, Medieval and Modern* and Shepherd's *Historical Atlas*. Shepherd's covers the world from 1450 B.C. to modern times and has maps that are stuffed with information. A single map, for example, on the westward development of the United States shows all of the following and more:

Routes of the forty-niners
Santa Fe Trail
Route of Lewis and Clark
Forts and trading posts
Routes of the Pony Express
Principal land grants
Population centers
Agricultural centers

There are historical atlases covering certain countries (Jackson's *Atlas of American History)* or certain periods of time (Heyden's *Atlas of the Classical World)*, and some atlases deal with certain subjects such as Bible or literary history. The history of war is examined in the *West Point Atlas of the American Wars*, which includes maps of campaigns, battles, etc., from colonial wars to the Korean War. The list is endless.

So an atlas can be an excellent way to visualize the past, and of course, the use of a map is a better way to get from place to place than the Hansel and Gretel breadcrumb method.

Gazetteers (geographical name dictionaries or indexes, which usually include brief factual information about each place) are discussed in the Geography section of this guide (page 107). They are often used in tandem with atlases.

BIBLIOGRAPHY: ALMANACS AND ATLASES

Almanacs

Information Please Almanac, Atlas and Yearbook. New York: A & W Publishers, 1947 to date. Annual.

Ploski, Harry A., and Williams, James, eds. *Negro Almanac: A Reference Work on the Afro-American.* New York: Wiley, 1983.

Reader's Digest Almanac and Yearbook. Pleasantville, N.Y.: Reader's Digest Assocation, 1966 to date. Annual.

Whitaker's Almanack. London: J. Whitaker & Sons, 1869 to date. Annual.

World Almanac and Book of Facts. New York: Newspaper Enterprise Association, Inc., 1868 to date. Annual.

Atlases

Espenshade, Edward B., Jr., and Morrison, Joel, eds. *Goode's World Atlas.* 16th ed. Chicago: Rand McNally, 1978.

Hammond Medallion World Atlas. Maplewood, N.J.: C. S. Hammond & Co., 1978.

Heyden, A. A. M. van der, and Scullard, Howard Hayes. *Atlas of the Classical World.* London: Nelson, 1960.

Jackson, Kenneth T., ed. *Atlas of American History.* Rev. ed. New York: Scribner, 1978.

National Geographic Atlas of the World. 5th ed. Washington, D.C.: National Geographic Society, 1981.

The New York Times Atlas of the World. New York: Times Books, 1981.

Paullin, Charles Oscar. *Atlas of the Historical Geography of the United States,* ed. by John K. Wright. Westport, Conn.: Greenwood, 1975. Reprint of the 1932 ed.

Rand McNally Commercial Atlas and Marketing Guide. Chicago: Rand McNally, 1876 to date. Annual.

Rand McNally New Cosmopolitan World Atlas. New census edition. Chicago: Rand McNally, 1984.

Shepherd, William Robert. *Historical Atlas.* 9th ed. New York: Barnes & Noble, 1964.

The Times Atlas of the World. Comprehensive edition. Maps prepared by John Bartholomew & Son, Edinburgh. A publication of *The Times,* London. New York: Times Books, 1980.

Treharne, R.F., and Fullard, Harold, eds. *Muir's Historical Atlas, Medieval and Modern.* 10th ed. New York: Barnes & Noble, 1964.

U.S. Military Academy, West Point, Department of Military Art and Engineering. *The West Point Atlas of the American Wars,* chief editor, Vincent J. Esposito. New York: Holt, Rinehart & Winston, 1978.

CHAPTER 7   BIBLIOGRAPHY

A bibliography is simply a list of books and/or articles by an author or about a particular subject. Or it can be a list of books in a library's collection or a list of books published in a country, in certain languages, etc.

Finding a good bibliography is like striking gold when you are doing a research project. It means that someone has begun your work for you by giving you a guide to the important sources on a subject. Bibliographies may appear in books and articles under such titles as "References," "Suggested Readings," and "Sources" and many show up at the end of chapters, in footnotes, or at the end of books. In a reference book the bibliography is usually a list of sources the author used. Bibliographies for current awareness are found in the annual reviews of a subject area. The *Annual Review of Sociology* and the *Annual Review of Anthropology* are examples.

There are some wonderful sources for finding bibliographies:

Bibliographic Index, a cumulative bibliography of bibliographies, is a sort of *Readers' Guide* to bibliographies. It has an alphabetical subject arrangement of separately published bibliographies as well as bibliographies published in books and periodicals, many in foreign languages.

Theodore Besterman's *A World Bibliography of Bibliographies* is a classified list of separately published bibliographies in books and manuscripts. It is international in scope. This monumental five-volume work is updated by Alice Toomey's two-volume decennial supplement.

The *Subject Guide to Books in Print* (see description under Books and Literature) can be used to form a bibliography of current materials.

Countries have national libraries that publish catalogs of their book collections. An example is the Library of Congress's *National Union Catalog*. There are published lists of other major library collections, many of which have a subject approach. Some useful library catalogs are:

CHILE—*Continued*

History

Sater, W. F. History of Chile; from the Conquest to Arturo Alessandri. Hist Teach 14: 327-39 My '81

War of Independence, 1810-1824

Valencia Avaria, Luis. Bernardo O'Higgins; el buen genio de América. Editorial universitaria '80 p481-7

1920-

Drake, P. W. History of Chile, 1920-1980. Hist Teach 14:341-7 My '81

Politics and government

Smith, Brian H. Church and politics in Chile; challenges to modern Catholicism. Princeton univ. press '82 p357-75

Wright, Thomas C. Landowners and reform in Chile; the Sociedad nacional de agricultura, 1919-40. Univ. of Ill. press '82 p224-33

1565-1810

Barbier, Jacques A. Reform and politics in Bourbon Chile, 1755-1796. (Cahiers d'hist. no 10) Univ. of Ottawa press '80 p215-18

1970-

Entessar, Nader. Political development in Chile; from democratic socialism to dictatorship. Bagchi & co. '80 p 193-203

CHILOPODA. See Centipedes

CHIMNEY plumes. See Smoke plumes

CHIMPANZEES

McHenry, H. M, and Corruccini, R. S. Pan paniscus and human evolution. Am J Phys Anthropol 54:365-7 Mr '81

Psychology

Speaking of apes; a critical anthology of two-way communication with man; ed. by Thomas A. Sebeok and Jean Umiker-Sebeok. Plenum '80 p449-69

CHINA

See also
Taiwan

China; Natur, Geschichte, Gesellschaft, Politik, Staat, Wirtschaft, Kultur; hrsg. von Brunhild Staiger; im Auftrag des Insts. für Asienkunde Hamburg. (Buchreihe Ländermonog. v 12) Erdmann '80 p48'-99

Lee, Don Y. Annotated bibliography of selected works on China. Eastern press '81 270p

Murdoch university. Library. Library guide for students of Chinese studies. (Murdoch bibliogs. 4) The library '80 63p

Wolff, Ernst. Chinese studies; a bibliog. manual; with the assistance of Maureen Corcoran. (Bibliog. ser, 1) Chinese materials center '81 152p annot

Antiquities

Chang, Kwang-Chih. Shang civilization. Yale univ. press '80 p373-406

Biography

Curtis, Emily Byrne. Reflected glory in a bottle; Chinese snuff bottle portraits. Pi yen hu hua hsiang; pref. by L. Carrington Goodrich. Soho Bodhi '80 p 107-11

Civilization

Chinese civilization and society; a sourcebk; ed. by Patricia Buckley Ebrey. Free press '81 p418-26

Hsu, Francis L. K. Americans and Chinese; passage to differences. 3rd ed Univ. press of Hawaii '81 p505-21

Hsün, Yüeh. Hsün Yüeh and the mind of late Han China; a tr. of the Shen-Chien with introd. and annots [by] Ch'i-yün Ch'en. Princeton univ. press '80 p 199-207

Sources

Chinese civilization and society; a sourcebk; ed. by Patricia Buckley Ebrey. Free press '81 p418-26

Constitutional history

Meienberger, Norbert. Emergence of constitutional government in China (1905-1908) the concept sanctioned by The Empress Dowager Tz'u-hi. (Schweizer asiatische Studien. Monog. v 1) Lang, P. '80 p 101-6

Economic conditions

Ashley, Richard K. Political economy of war and peace; the Sino-Soviet-Am. triangle and the modern security problematique. Nichols '80 p353-6

De Chinese economie; een aantal verkenningen; onder red. van Michael Ellman. Stenfert Kroese '80 p207-11

Eckstein, Alexander, ed. Quantitative measures of China's economic output; sponsored by the Social science res. council. Univ. of Mich. press '80 p435-40

Leung, Chi-Keung. China; railway patterns and natl. goals. Dept. of geography. Chicago. Univ. '80 p215-43

Organizational behavior in Chinese society; ed. by Sidney L. Greenblatt [et al; bibliog. by Gordon Bennett] Holt. Rinehart & Winston '81 p256-69

Wilkinson, Endymion. Studies in Chinese price history. Garland '80 p266-81

Economic policy

Paine, S. Spatial aspects of Chinese development; issues, outcomes and policies 1949-79. J Devel Stud 17:188-90 Ja '81

Famines

Will, Pierre Étienne. Bureaucratie et famine en Chine au 18e siècle. (Civilisations et socs (Paris) 66) École des hautes études en sciences sociales '80 p277-88

Foreign relations

Camilleri, Joseph. Chinese foreign policy; the Maoist era and its aftermath. Univ. of Wash. press '80 p287-300

Joyaux, Francois. La Chine et le règlement du premier conflit d'Indochine; Geneve 1954. (Pubs. de la Corbonne. Sér. int, 9) Inst. d'hist. des relations int. contemporaines. Univ. de Paris I Panthéon-Sorbonne '79 p413-31 annot

Kang, Chong-Sook. China in Waffen; die Rüstungs- und Abrüstungspolitik der Volksrepublik China von 1969 bis zum Tod Mao-Tse-Tungs. (Int. Beziehungen. v2) Haag & Herchen '79 p 125-43

Pfennig, Werner. Chinas aussenpolitischer Sprung nach vorn; die Aussen- und Sicherheitspolitik der Volksrepublic China vom Ende der Kulturrevolution bis zum Vorabend der Chinareise Nixons (1969-1971) Schöningh '80 p203-9

Soviet Union

Ewing, Thomas E. Between the hammer and the anvil? Chinese and Russian policies in outer Mongolia, 1911-1921. (Uralic and Altaic ser. v 138) Res. inst. for inner Asian studies, Ind. univ. '80 p278-300

Jacobs, Daniel Norman. Borodin; Stalin's man in China. Harvard univ. press '81 p331-46

United States

Chern, Kenneth S. Dilemma in China; America's policy debate, 1945. Shoe String press '80 p251-65

Henson, Curtis T. Commissioners and commodores; the East India squadron and Am. diplomacy in China. Univ. of Ala. press. '82 p213-21

Lorence, J. J. Organized business and the myth of the China market; the Am. Asiatic assn, 1898-1937. Am Philos Soc Trans 71 pt4:103-10 '81

Stueck, William Whitney. Road to confrontation; Am. policy toward China and Korea, 1947-1950. Univ. of N.C. press '81 p299-311

History

Chinese civilization and society; a sourcebk; ed. by Patricia Buckley Ebrey. Free press '81 p418-26

Hoffmann, Rainer. Der Untergang des konfuzianischen China; vom Mandschureich zur Volksrepublik. Harrassowitz '80 p 173-84

Morton, William Scott. China; its hist. and culture. Lippincott & Crowell '80 p261-4

Rodzinski, Witold. History of China. Pergamon press '79 p443-51

Sources

Chinese civilization and society; a sourcebk; ed. by Patricia Buckley Ebrey. Free press '81 p418-26

Shang dynasty, 1766-1122 B.C.

Chang, Kwang-Chih. Shang civilization. Yale univ. press '80 p373-406

Han dynasty, 202 B.C.-220 A.D.

Hsu, Cho-yun. Han agriculture; the formation of early Chinese agrarian economy, 206 B.C.-A.D. 220; ed. by Jack L. Dull. (Han Dynasty. China, v2) Univ. of Wash. press '80 p337-57

Ming dynasty, 1368-1644

Huang, Ray. 1587, a year of no significance; the Ming dynasty in decline. Yale univ. press '81 p261-5

Mixius, W. Andreas. Nu-pien und die no-p'u von Kinagnan; Aufstände Abhängiger und Unfreier in Südchina 1644/45. (Mitteilungen. 80) Deutsche Gesellschaft für Natur- & Völkerkunde Ostasiens '80 p 165-72

Ch'ing dynasty, 1644-1912

Naquin, Susan. Shantung rebellion; the Wang Lun uprising of 1774. Yale univ. press '81 p211-19

Dictionary Catalog of the Schomberg Collection of Negro Literature and History, New York Public Library
Catalog of the Tozzer Library of the Peabody Museum of Archaeology and Ethnology, Harvard University
Library Catalog for the School of Oriental and African Studies, London University
Catalogs of the Sophia Smith Collection: Women's History Archive, Smith College

These four examples are published by G. K. Hall and are multivolume sets. If these seem like new research sources, think about the fact that a reference tool in antiquity was a catalog of the Library of Alexandria in the middle of the third century B.C.

Remember that "Bibliography" is a subdivision under many subject headings in a library catalog:

Art—Bibliography
China—Bibliography

Bibliographical Guides

These are guides to the literature in a subject field. They include an overview of the field, subject headings, and major reference tools (bibliographies, indexes, abstracting services, dictionaries, encyclopedias), and usually list societies, museums, and libraries important to the field. Examples are listed under the subject area in Part II of this book.

BIBLIOGRAPHY: BIBLIOGRAPHY

Besterman, Theodore. *A World Bibliography of Bibliographies and of Bibliographical Catalogues, Calendars, Abstracts, Digests, Indexes, and the Like.* 4th ed. Lausanne: Societas Bibliographica, 1965–66. 5 vols.

Bibliographic Index: A Cumulative Bibliography of Bibliographies. New York: H. W. Wilson, 1938 to date.

Toomey, Alice F. *World Bibliography of Bibliographies, 1964–1974.* Totowa, N.J.: Rowman & Littlefield, 1977. 2 vols.

CHAPTER 8   *BIOGRAPHY*

It has been suggested that biography should be written by an enemy. The implication is, of course, that truth would then have a better chance of emerging. But the cynic who made the claim probably was not acquainted with some of the excellent sources of biographical information not, ostensibly at least, written by enemies.

INFORMATION ABOUT PEOPLE PAST . . .

The *Dictionary of American Biography* is known for its scholarly articles and its objectivity. Note the following candid account of Andrew Johnson when he took the oath of office as Vice President at Lincoln's second inauguration:

> . . . His health was impaired, and only Lincoln's urgent request hurried him to Washington in time for the inaugural ceremonies. The result was most unfortunate, for Johnson, when he took the oath of office, was under the influence of liquor . . . . No doubt the faux pas was due to illness and exhaustion, but it gave malice something to feed upon.

The *DAB*, as this multivolume set is nicknamed, does not include the living. It covers only famous Americans of the past, and it is exact about some legends, too. If you look up Molly Pitcher, for example, you will be referred to an interesting biography under her real name, Mary Ludwig Hays McCauley.

The *Dictionary of National Biography*, or the *DNB*, includes men and women in British history, and this set was the model for the American series. It was edited by two scholars, one of whom, Leslie Stephen, was the father of author Virginia Woolf. In both these sets the articles are signed and followed by bibliographies. Those are indications of reliable and thorough reference materials. Some early American colonists appear in both sets since they were first British and then American.

The articles in both the *DAB* and the *DNB* vary in length. Some run less than a page, and some, dealing with important figures like George Washington, are several pages long.

Other works dealing with historical people but with only brief articles are: *Who Was Who in America: Historical Volume 1607–1896* and *Who Was Who in America* (seven volumes and an index volume covering 1607–1981). (For a typical *Who's Who* entry, see sample under *Who's Who in America,* page 40.)

Two one-volume dictionaries that have brief identifications of people both living and dead and of all nations are *Webster's Biographical Dictionary* and *Chambers's Biographical Dictionary.*

If you have a name you can't identify, the best place to look first is the *New Century Cyclopedia of Names.* This three-volume work includes persons, places, literary characters, works of art, plays, and operas as well as real people. Mythological and legendary persons are listed. Under "Baker" the cyclopedia identifies by that name:

A city
A mountain
A lake
An island
The Battle of Baker
Twenty-nine people
One pseudonym

INFORMATION ABOUT PEOPLE TODAY . . .

Current Biography has interesting articles about people in the news here and abroad. It is issued monthly and then as an annual cumulated volume. The biographies generally are one or two pages long. A perusal of a few recent volumes reveals the following variety of facts:

Bob Dylan was born Robert Zimmerman but officially changed his name in 1962 in honor of the poet Dylan Thomas, whom he admired.

As a child, Coretta King, widow of Dr. Martin Luther King, Jr., walked five miles each day to a one-room schoolhouse.

Cesar Chavez, Mexican-American organizer of migratory farm workers, grew up in a series of labor camps where home was a tarpaper shack, and he attended more than thirty elementary schools scattered along the family's itinerary.

Julia Child, the TV cook, majored in history while in college and wanted to be a spy during World War II. She didn't take up cooking until she was over thirty.

Popular Yiddish writer Isaac Bashevis Singer says of his early life: "I was born with the feeling that I am part of an unlikely adventure, something that couldn't have happened, but happened just the same. The atmosphere of adventure permeated my home. . . ."

When a child, actor Dudley Moore suffered from a clubfoot and took refuge in music, studying the piano and violin.

Fernando Valenzuela, the baseball player, was born in Sonora, Mexico, the seventh son and youngest of twelve children in his family.

For brief biographical data about the living the books in the *Who's Who* series are useful. Some of these are: *Who's Who* (British and a few other people of international reputation), *Who's Who in America,* and *Who's Who in (various countries).* The Europa *International Who's Who* covers a wide range from Zubin Mehta to Willy Brandt. Here is a sample from *Who's Who in America* of the typical, brief entry:

KOPIT, ARTHUR, playwright; b. N.Y.C., May 10, 1937; s. George and Maxine (Dubin) K.; A.B. cum laude, Harvard U., 1959; m. Leslie Ann Garis; 1 son. Author plays produced at Harvard: Questioning of Nick, 1957, Gemini, 1957, On the Runway of Life You Never Know What's Coming Off Next, 1958, Across the River and into the Jungle, 1958, Sing to Me Through Open Windows, 1959, Aubade, 1959, Oh Dad, Poor Dad, Mamma's Hung You in the Closet and I'm Feelin' So Sad, 1960 (also prod. in London, Eng., 1961, off Broadway, 1962, on Broadway, 1963) released as a motion picture in 1967, What's Happened to the Thorne's House, 1972, Louisiana Territory, 1975, others; fellow Center for Humanities, Wesleyan U., 1974-75, playwright-in-residence, 1975-76; CBS fellow Yale U., 1976-77. Recipient of the Vernon Rice award, 1962, Outer Circle award, 1962. Shaw Travelling fellow Harvard, 1959, Guggenheim fellow, 1967, Rockefeller grantee, 1968, Nat. Endowment Humanities grantee, 1974. Mem. Writers Guild Am., Hasty Pudding Soc., Signet Soc., Phi Beta Kappa. Club: Harvard (N.Y.C.). Author: (6 one-act plays) The Day the Whores Came Out to Play Tennis, and Other Plays, 1965; Indians, 1969; Wings, 1977. Address: care Audrey Wood Internat Creative Mgmt 40 W 57th St New York NY 10019*

INFORMATION ABOUT PEOPLE IN SPECIAL FIELDS . . .

There are biographical dictionaries in almost all fields, but some on authors, scientists, and scholars are of particular interest and are good examples of specialized biographies.

Twentieth Century Authors (1942), edited by S. J. Kunitz and H. Haycraft, and its *First Supplement* (1955), edited by S. J. Kunitz and V. Colby, are outstanding sources. The articles contain lists of works by and about the authors, and the sketches are very readable. Here J. D. Salinger is quoted:

> I'm aware that a number of my friends will be saddened, or shocked, or shocked-saddened, over some of my chapters of *The Catcher in the Rye.* Some of my best friends are children. In fact, all of my best friends are children. It's almost unbearable to me to realize that my book will be kept on a shelf out of their reach.

Kunitz and Haycraft have done other books on authors: *American Authors 1600–1900, British Authors Before 1800, British Authors of the Nineteenth Century,* and *Junior Book of Authors.* Another book about authors of books for young people is *More Junior Authors,* edited by Muriel Fuller.

Contemporary Authors: A Bio-bibliographical Guide to Current Authors and Their Works is an up-to-date source and includes many little-known authors. Each brief article is followed by a list of all the author's published works.

Another work dealing with authors is the *Cyclopedia of World Authors,* which covers the authors whose works are included in *Masterplots* (see Books and Literature, page 84). Each entry gives biographical details, critical evaluations, and a list of the writer's principal works.

Two other highly regarded works are the eight-volume *American Men and Women of Science* (with biographies in the physical and biological sciences and in the social and behavioral sciences) and the *Directory of American Scholars,* a four-volume set (with biographies of U.S. and Canadian scholars in English, speech, drama, foreign languages, linguistics, philology, philosophy, religion, and law).

INDEXES TO BIOGRAPHY . . .

Biography Index is a quarterly, cumulative index to biographical material in both books and magazines. Each issue contains a useful index by professions and occupations.

Biographical Dictionaries Master Index is a guide to more than fifty current *Who's Whos* and other works of collective biography. The new edition of this index is called *Biography and Genealogy Master Index.* There is also an *Author Biographies Master Index,* a consolidated guide to information on authors living and dead as they appear in major biographical dictionaries.

The New York Times Biographical Edition compiles general-interest biographies from the newspaper, and *The New York Times Obituaries Index* (1858-1968, 1969–1978) gathers index biographies that appeared under "deaths."

GENEALOGY. . .

Finding out who we are can be a complicated search indeed. There are many guides to such research, like G.H. Doane and J.B. Bell's *Searching for Your Ancestors: the How and Why of Genealogy*, and an investigation of the catalog of a large library will reveal guides to the genealogies of particular groups and countries as well as other general guides.

BIBLIOGRAPHY: BIOGRAPHY

Author Biographies Master Index. Detroit: Gale Research, 1978. Supplements, 1979.

Barnhart, C. L., ed. *New Century Cyclopedia of Names*. Norwalk, Conn.: Appleton-Century-Crofts, 1954. 3 vols.

Biographical Dictionaries Master Index. 1975/76. Detroit: Gale Research, 1975. Supplements. The 2d edition of this title is a multivolume set under a new title: Herbert, Miranda C., and McNeil, Barbara, eds. *Biography and Genealogy Master Index*. Detroit: Gale Research, 1980.

Biography Index: A Cumulative Index to Biographical Material in Books and Magazines. New York: H. W. Wilson, September 1946 to date.

Current Biography. New York: H. W. Wilson, 1940 to date. Monthly except December, with annual cumulations.

Dictionary of American Biography. New York: Scribner's, 1926 to date. 17 vols. plus supplements.

Doane, Gilbert Harry, and Bell, James B. *Searching for Your Ancestors: The How and Why of Genealogy*. 5th ed. Minneapolis: University of Minnesota Press, 1980.

Ethridge, James N., ed. *Contemporary Authors: A Bio-bibliographical Guide to Current Authors and Their Works*. Detroit: Gale Research, 1962 to date. Annual. Also, *Contemporary Authors: Permanent Series*, 1975 to date, and *Contemporary Authors: New Revision Series*, 1981 to date.

Fuller, Muriel, ed. *More Junior Authors.* New York: H. W. Wilson, 1963.
International Who's Who. London: Europa, 1935 to date. Annual.
Jaques Cattell Press, ed. *American Men and Women of Science.* 15th ed. New York: R. R. Bowker, 1982. 7 vols. *Social and Behavioral Sciences* vol., 1978.
————. *Directory of American Scholars.* New York: R. R. Bowker, 1982. 4 vols.
Kunitz, S. J., and Haycraft, H. *American Authors: 1600–1900.* 8th ed. New York: H. W. Wilson, 1977. Reprint of 1969 edition.
————. *British Authors Before 1800.* New York: H. W. Wilson, 1952.
————. *British Authors of the Nineteenth Century.* New York: H. W. Wilson, 1936.
————. *Junior Book of Authors.* 2d ed. rev. New York: H. W. Wilson, 1951.
————.*Twentieth Century Authors.* New York: H. W. Wilson, 1942.
————and Colby, V. *Twentieth Century Authors. First Supplement.* New York: H. W. Wilson, 1955.
Magill, Frank N., ed. *Cyclopedia of World Authors.* Englewood Cliffs, N.J.: Salem Press, 1974. 3 vols.
The New York Times Biographical Edition. New York: The New York Times, 1970–1974. Continued by The New York Times Biographical Service, 1975 to date.
The New York Times Obituaries Index 1958–1968. Sanford, N.C.: Microfilming Corporation of America, 1970.
The New York Times Obituaries Index 1969–1978. New York: The New York Times Co., 1980.
Smith, George, Stephen, Leslie, and Lee, Sidney, eds. *Dictionary of National Biography.* London: Oxford University Press, 1922. 22 vols. and supplements through 1981.
Thorne, J. O., and Collocott, T. C., eds. *Chamber's Biographical Dictionary.* New York: Hippocrene Books, 1974.
Webster's Biographical Dictionary. Springfield, Mass.: G. & C. Merriam, 1980.
Who's Who. London: Black, 1949 to date. Annual.
Who's Who in America. Chicago: Marquis, 1899 to date. Biennial.
Who Was Who in America 1607–1981. Chicago: Marquis, 1942–1981. 7 vols. and index.
Who Was Who in America: Historical Volume, 1607–1896. A component volume of *Who's Who in American History.* Chicago: Marquis, 1963.

CHAPTER 9   *DICTIONARIES*

What's the difference between "abjure" and "adjure," or "anecdote" and "antidote," or even "ant" and "aunt"? How about "allusion," "elusion," "illusion," and "delusion"? What do the initials *LSD* really stand for, and how do you pronounce *faux pas?*

If you can get through life without using a dictionary, then you're practicing thaumaturgy.

Dictionaries have been around for a long time, and they're getting better all the time. The first English dictionary was compiled in 1604 by a schoolmaster, Robert Cawdrey, and it carried the straightforward title *A Table Alphabeticall Conteyning and Teaching the True Writing and Understanding of Hard Usuall English Wordes.* Cawdrey had so little faith in the intelligence of the reader that he instructed in the preface: "If thou be desirous (gentle reader) rightly and readily to understand and profit by this Table, and such like, then thou must learn the alphabet. . . ."

Certainly it helps to know the alphabet because a dictionary, of course, is an alphabetical arrangement of words with their meanings, derivations, and pronunciations.

Two famous works in the history of the dictionary are Samuel Johnson's *A Dictionary of the English Language,* which appeared in 1755, and Noah Webster's *American Dictionary of the English Language,* which first appeared in 1828.

Cawdrey's dictionary contained about 3,000 words. Today's unabridged dictionaries contain hundreds of thousands of words. An "unabridged" dictionary is very large and has the most complete list of words. An "abridged" dictionary is a smaller version with fewer words and shorter definitions but which retains the features of the unabridged work. Strictly speaking, a "desk dictionary" is still smaller, being a general-purpose work with only a selection of the words of a language. However, the term "desk dictionary" is sometimes loosely used to apply to any abridged dictionary.

UNABRIDGED DICTIONARIES

Funk & Wagnalls New Standard Dictionary (1963) is one of the standard unabridged dictionaries and is available for use in libraries, but it is now outdated. The last thorough revision was in 1913, though it has been updated by insertions of new words and shortening or deletion of older material. It contains about 458,000 words, including about 70,000 proper names. It gives current meanings first and provides pronunciation, etymology (the history of a word), and geographical entries (population figures may be out of date). The appendix has a list of foreign words and phrases, rules for simplified spelling, and disputed pronunciations.

Random House Dictionary of the English Language (1966) is now considered an unabridged dictionary, but it has fewer words than the others listed. It contains more than 260,000 words and emphasizes words and phrases recently in use in the language. It also carries personal and place-names and encyclopedic information, such as a list of colleges, an atlas, a list of reference books, etc. The most common meaning of each word is given first.

Webster's Third New International Dictionary (1961) is frequently revised, contains about 450,000 words, and does *not* include personal and place-names (as did its predecessor, the excellent *Webster's New International Dictionary of the English Language,* 2d edition). Current meaning is given last and, except for some abbreviations and symbols, the main entries are set in lower case and capitalization is indicated within the definition in italics as "cap," "usu cap," "often cap," or "sometimes cap." This work was considered unconventional and "permissive" when it first appeared because it presents the language as it is now *used* and therefore includes many words regarded as colloquial and even incorrect. Regardless of the varying opinions, it is an extremely complete and careful work.

All unabridged dictionaries define words and give examples of usage (and changes in meaning) in sentences and quotations. A note on the parts of speech gives the word's grammatical use ("n." for noun, "adv." for adverb, etc.). Popular phrases that include the key word are also given and defined (under "limb" the phrase "out on a limb" is defined). Derivations or the origins of words are indicated by giving the language a word comes from and its meaning in that language. > is the symbol that means "comes from."

The pronunciation key is given on each page in *Funk & Wagnalls* and *Random House.* The front of the book carries the key in *Webster's Third.*

There are full-page illustrations in the unabridged dictionaries (showing birds, flowers, flags of the world, etc.) as well as small illustrations that accompany and clarify definitions.

A, First position; B, Second position; C, Third position; D, Fourth position; E, Fifth position

first/ posi/tion, *Ballet.* a position of the feet in which the heels are back to back and the toes point out to the sides.

fish·hook \'fish,hůk, 'fi,shůk\ *n* [ME *fishhok,* fr. *fish* + *hok*

fishhooks 1: *1* Limerick, *2* kirby, *3* Carlisle, *4* Kendal sneck bent, *5* sproat, *6* Aberdeen, *7* barbless

hook — more at HOOK] **1 :** a hook for catching fish **2 :** a large hook with a pendant to the end of which the fish tackle is hooked in fishing an anchor

gui-tar', 1 gɪ-tär'; 2 ĕi-tär', *n.* A musical instrument with a body and neck somewhat like a violin, and usually six strings, three of gut and three of silk spun over with silver wire, played by the fingers of one hand, while the notes are stopped by the fingers of the other on the frets of the neck. It is tuned as shown below, according to its written nota- tion, but sounds an octave lower. [< F. *gui- tare,* < L. *cithara,* < Gr. *kithara,* kind of lyre.] — **gui-tar'·fid"dle,** *n.* *Mus.* A five-stringed viol, predecessor of the violin, flat-bodied like the guitar.—

Manner of Tuning Guitar.

An example of the comprehensiveness of the unabridged dictionaries is seen in the treatment of the word "the" in *Webster's Third.* It's given almost two columns.

ABRIDGED AND DESK TYPES OF DICTIONARY

The American Heritage Dictionary of the English Language is a fine work, first published in 1969. It contains more than 155,000 entries, including biographical and geographical names. It has good coverage of modern words and interpretations (for example, under "grass" the dictionary notes that a secondary use of the word is slang for "marijuana"). It is up-to-date and based on a high standard of good English.

Webster's New World Dictionary of the American Language has more than 150,000 entries and includes proper names. Idiomatic and slang terms are represented, and there are articles on Americanisms and etymology, forms of address, lists of colleges and universities, and signs and symbols.

Webster's Ninth New Collegiate Dictionary is the latest edition of a longtime best seller. With more than 152,000 words, this is a very good all-purpose dictionary for students and general readers. It has a style manual and other appended useful material and is continuously revised.

World Book Dictionary has about 225,000 entries which the editors believe are the most important and frequently used words in the English language. It complements *The World Book Encyclopedia,* so it omits geographical, biographical, and other encyclopedic information. It contains sections on the use of language and on how to write effectively.

For a feeling of how dictionaries vary, the example on page 48 shows how the same word ("peace") is treated in the unabridged *Webster's Third* and in the abridged *American Heritage Dictionary of the English Language.*

Webster's Third has more details, more illustrations showing an appropriate use of the word in context (the matter in angle brackets < > with the slung dash ~ standing for the word "peace"), many more words between "peace" and "peach," and no capitalization except for an indication of it within the definition of "peace of god." The *American Heritage Dictionary* shows proper names and geographical entries, so it has "Peace Corps" and "Peace River," which are not given in *Webster's* since the latter does not include names. The *American Heritage* also shows capitalization in the names.

For complete, detailed information on the many fine dictionaries that are available, see *Dictionary Buying Guide* by Kenneth F. Kister. It offers valuable information on the best dictionary to use or purchase for your needs.

WEBSTER'S THIRD NEW INTERNATIONAL DICTIONARY *Unabridged*

¹peace \'pēs\ n -s often attrib [ME pes, pees, pais, fr. OF pes, pais, fr. L pac-, pax peace; akin to L pacisci to agree, contract — more at PACT] 1 a : freedom from civil clamor and confusion : a state of public quiet (~ and order were finally restored in the town) b : a state of security or order within a community provided for by law, custom, or public opinion — often used with the (a breach of the ~) 2 : a mental or spiritual condition marked by freedom from disquieting or oppressive thoughts or emotions : calmness of mind and heart : serenity of spirit (the bitter, restless struggling of the last months gave way to ~ —Rose Macaulay) (I have been in perfect ~ and contentment; I never have had one doubt —J.H.Newman) (a ~ of mind because you could no longer be surprised —Stuart Cloete) (farewell ~ be with you) — compare PEACE OF GOD 3 a : a tranquil state of freedom from outside disturbance and harassment (decided to accept a year-round post . . . and have ~ to write —Newsweek) (now remembered sharply the ~ and quiet of the place —Sherwood Anderson) b : eternal repose (may he rest in ~) 4 : harmony in human or personal relations : mutual concord and esteem (he knew that there would never be ~ again while they lived —Graham Greene) 5 a (1) : a state of mutual concord between governments : absence of hostilities or war (he had given the world ~, and the world now turned to him for security —John Buchan) (2) : the period of such freedom from war (a ~ of 50 years) b : a pact or agreement to end hostilities or to come together in amity between those who have been at war or in a state of enmity or dissension : a formal reconciliation between contending parties; esp : a peace treaty (signed ~ in the spring of 1918 —C.E.Black & E.C.Helmreich) (offered the possibility of a negotiated ~ —N.Y.Times) 6 : absence of activity and noise : deep stillness : QUIETNESS (the ~ of the woods) (the ~ of sky and mountain) 7 : one that makes, gives, or maintains tranquillity (God is our only ~) — at peace adv : in a state of concord or tranquillity (a world once more at peace) (the problem was settled and his mind was at peace) (help man live at peace with his unconscious —Time)
²peace \"\ vi -ED/-ING/-S [ME peesen, fr. pes, pees, pais peace (n.)] : to become quiet or still : be, become, or keep silent (when the thunder would not ~ at my bidding —Shak.) — often used interjectionally
peace·abil·i·ty \,pēsə'bilad-ē, -lətē, -i\ n : PEACEABLENESS (snore himself to ~ —P.A.Rollins)
peace·able \'pēsəbəl\ adj [ME pesible, pesable, paisible, fr. MF pesible, paisible, fr. pes, pais peace + -ible — more at PEACE] 1 a : disposed to peace : having an amicable disposition disinclined to strife : not contentious or quarrelsome (the quiet, humble, modest and ~ person —William Cowper) (his tongue was not always ~ —W.R.Inge) b : lacking noisiness or restlessness : quietly behaved : CALM (was pleased to see how ~ the horse had become) 2 : marked by freedom from war, strife, hostilities, or disorder (in the most ~ and orderly manner, without the smallest sign of tumult or sedition in the city —J.G.Frazer) (the company . . . in ~ times makes chiefly freight cars —E.D.Kennedy) syn see PACIFIC
peace·able·ness n -ES [ME pesiblenesse, fr. pesible, pesable, paisible + -nesse -ness] : the quality or state of being peaceable
peace·ably \-blē,-bli\ adv [ME pesibly, paisibly, fr. pesible, paisible + -y] 1 : in a peaceable and friendly manner : without contention or strife (possible for more than one religion to survive comparatively ~ in the same state —Alfred Cobban) 2 : without subjection to annoyance or confusion : in peace : QUIETLY (disturb him not; let him pass ~ —Shak.)
peace belt n : a wampum belt used to symbolize peace among No. American Indians

peacebreaker \'·,··\ n : a violator of peace or of the peace : a perpetrator of strife
peacebreaking \'·,··\ n : the action of violating peace : the commission of a breach of the peace
peace democrat n, usu cap P&D : a Democrat in the northern states advocating peaceful measures as opposed to prosecution of the Civil War
peace dollar n : a silver dollar of the U.S. struck from 1921 to 1928 and in 1934 and 1935 to commemorate the peace at the end of World War I
peace·ful \'pēsfəl\ adj, sometimes peacefuller; sometimes peacefullest [ME paisful, pesful, fr. pais, pes, pees peace + -ful — more at PEACE] 1 a : PEACEABLE 1 (the ~ comportment of the seals had quieted my alarm —Jack London) (the modest man becomes bold . . . or the impetuous prudent and ~ —W.M.Thackeray) 2 : marked by, conducive to, or enjoying peace, quiet, or calm : untroubled by conflict, agitation, or commotion (the feeling . . . that we as neighbors could settle any disputes in ~ fashion —F.D.Roosevelt) (rocky promontories shelter ~ bays —Samuel Van Valkenburg & Ellsworth Huntington) 3 : of or relating to a state or time of peace (a bomb material as well as a ~ fuel —Oliver Townsend) 4 : devoid of violence or force : without recourse to warlike methods (all the political groups . . . employed ~ tactics —Collier's Yr. Bk.) (~ procedures . . . mediation, investigation and conciliation —Current History) syn see CALM, PACIFIC
peace·ful·ly \-fəlē, -li\ adv : in a peaceful manner (cattle which ~ browse —Tom Marvel) (a ~ inclined and responsible government —Vera M. Dean)
peace·ful·ness \-fəlnəs\ n -ES : the quality or state of being peaceful (the ~ and neighborliness of the parish is proverbial —Amer. Guide Series: La.)
peace·keeper \'·,··\ n : a maintainer of peace or of the peace : a pacific country or person
peace·less \'pēsləs\ adj : having no peace — peace·less·ness n -ES
peacemaker \'·,··\ n [ME peace maker, fr. pease, pes, pees, pais peace + maker] : one that makes or seeks to make peace esp. by reconciling parties or persons at variance
¹peacemaking \'·,··\ n : the action of bringing about peace
²peacemaking \"\ adj : bringing about peace or done in an effort to bring about peace
peacemonger \'·,··\ n 1 : PEACEMAKER; esp : one making or seeking peace unrealistically or at the expense of honor — usu. used disparagingly
peacemongering \'·,·(·)·\ adj : PEACEMAKING — usu. used disparagingly
peace offensive n : a campaign designed to serve the interests of a nation by the expression of wishes to end a war or of intentions to resolve conflicts peacefully and thus cause hostile or unfriendly nations to relax their efforts or become less vigilant
peace offering n 1 : an ancient Hebrew votive, freewill, or thank offering 2 : a gift or service to procure peace or reconciliation
peace officer n : a civil officer (as a sheriff, constable, policeman) whose duty it is to preserve the public peace
peace of god 1 cap G : the peace of heart which is the gift of God 2 usu cap P & cap G : an exemption from attack in feudal warfare urged by the church beginning in the latter part of the 9th century for all consecrated persons and places and later for all who claimed the protection of the church (as pilgrims, the poor) — compare TRUCE OF GOD
peace pipe n 1 : CALUMET
peaces pl of PEACE, pres 3d sing of PEACE
peacetime \'·,··\ n : a time when a nation is not at war (as anxious to save lives in ~ as . . . in wartime —Tomorrow)

AMERICAN HERITAGE DICTIONARY OF THE ENGLISH LANGUAGE *Abridged*

peace (pēs) n. 1. The absence of war or other hostilities. 2. An agreement or treaty to end hostilities: the Peace of Westphalia. 3. Freedom from quarrels and disagreement; harmonious relations: They made peace with each other. 4. Public security; law and order: disturbing the peace. 5. Inner contentment; calm; serenity: peace of mind. —at peace. 1. In a state of tranquillity; serene. 2. Free from strife. —hold (or keep) one's peace. To be silent. —keep the peace. To maintain or observe law and order. [Middle English pes, pais, from Old French, from Latin pāx (stem pāc-). See pag- in Appendix.*]
peace·a·ble (pē'sə-bəl) adj. 1. Inclined or disposed to peace; promoting calm: They met in a peaceable spirit. 2. Peaceful; undisturbed. —peace'a·ble·ness n. —peace'a·bly adv.
Peace Corps. A Federal government organization, set up in 1961, that trains and sends American volunteers abroad to work with people of developing countries on projects for technological, agricultural, and educational improvement.
peace·ful (pēs'fəl) adj. 1. Undisturbed by strife, turmoil, or disagreement; tranquil. 2. Opposed to strife; peaceable. 3. Of

or characteristic of a condition of peace. —See Synonyms at calm. —peace'ful·ly adv. —peace'ful·ness n.
peace·mak·er (pēs'mā'kər) n. 1. One who makes peace, especially by settling the disputes of others. 2. A revolver, especially the 1873 Colt model, used by law officers on the U.S. frontier. —peace'mak'ing n. & adj.
peace offering. 1. Any offering made to an adversary in the interests of peace or reconciliation. 2. An offering made to God in thanksgiving, especially a sacrificial offering as prescribed by Levitical law. Leviticus 3:2-6.
peace officer. A law officer, such as a sheriff, responsible for maintaining civil peace.
peace pipe. The calumet (see).
Peace River. A river rising in east-central British Columbia, Canada, and flowing 1,065 miles east and northeast to join the Slave River in northeastern Alberta.
peace·time (pēs'tim') n. A time of absence of war. —peace'·time' adj.

THE OXFORD ENGLISH DICTIONARY

This thirteen-volume dictionary must be singled out for special attention. It is the most authoritative dictionary of the English language, and its purpose is to give the etymology, or history, of all the words in the language from the year 1150 to its publication (1888–1933). It shows how each word came into the language and the changes in spelling and meaning that have occurred. Quotations from the first-known use of the word to the latest are given. Some of the words in it have a very different meaning today:

> **Hippy,** a. *colloq.* [f. HIP *sb.*3] = HIPPISH.
> **1891** *Temple Bar Mag.* Aug. 478 [She] led him such an awful life, No wonder he was hippy.

and "hippish" is defined as "somewhat hypochondriacal; low-spirited."

Here's another:

> **Groovy** (grū·vi), a. [f. GROOVE *sb.* + -Y 1.]
> **1.** Of or pertaining to a groove; resembling a groove.
> **1853** O. BYRNE *Artisan's Hand-bk.* 383 Its main purpose is to keep the surface of the ivory slightly lubricated, so that the rag may not hang to it and wear it into rings or groovy marks.
> **2.** *fig.* Having a tendency to run in 'grooves' (cf. GROOVE *sb.* 4). *colloq.*
> **1882** *Railway News* 12 Aug. 245/1 Railway managers are apt..to get a little 'groovy'. **1893** FARMER *Slang, Groovy,* settled in habit; limited in mind. **1896** *Blackw. Mag.* July 96 Schoolmasters as a class are extremely groovy.

Schoolmasters today would probably be pleased to be thought of as groovy. These are rather short samples; many entries are longer. The *OED* goes on for four pages with the unhappy word "war".

There is often confusion over its title. It was first published as the *New English Dictionary on Historical Principles,* then later reissued as the *Oxford English Dictionary,* and both of these are often abbreviated, the first as the *NED,* the second as the *OED.* And there's still another. It is also called *Murray's Dictionary* because the main editor was Sir James Augustus Henry Murray. Whatever the name used, call it interesting.

There is an abridged edition of the *OED,* the *Shorter Oxford English Dictionary on Historical Principles,* in two volumes, which also serves as a supplement to the *OED* because it has additional words.

SPECIAL DICTIONARIES AND LANGUAGE HANDBOOKS

There is no such thing as a last word on the subject of grammar and usage, but Fowler's *A Dictionary of Modern English Usage* is thought to come closest to it. It is not always easy to use, however, since some of the headings of this British work are not familiar to Americans. But the second edition (revised by Sir Ernest Gowers in 1965) has a classified guide in the front that helps readers find the items they need. This is an alphabetical arrangement of explanations of such things as fused participles, verbless sentences, and the proper use of such words as "forwards" and "forward."

Two American books on the subject of usage are especially lucid and witty. *The Careful Writer* by Theodore M. Bernstein deals with split infinitives, punctuation, and "got" versus "gotten," and though he doesn't completely condemn clichés, he cautions against "curdled clichés" ("It's in the lap of the cards." "That hits it right on the nutshell." "He needs some money to tidy him over." "I was smoking like a chain"). Here is Bernstein's example of a grammatical exception:

FLIED

You won't find it in most dictionaries, but *flied* is the past tense of *fly* in one specialized field: baseball. You could not say of the batter who hoisted a can of corn to the center fielder that he "flew out"; you must say he *flied out*.

A *Dictionary of Contemporary American Usage* by Bergen and Cornelia Evans is a scholarly and informal book on modern usage. It covers the basics and includes witty dividends like the one on the facing page.

Two important books tell you about related words and help you find another word for one you may have already repeated too many times. *Webster's New Dictionary of Synonyms* gives words with like meanings and includes antonyms, words with opposite meanings. *Roget's International Thesaurus* groups synonyms and antonyms according to the ideas to which they relate. There are various editions of *Roget's Thesaurus;* some require use of the pinpoint index, and one is alphabetized.

> **kith and kin** is a cliché, one of those meaningless phrases kept current by alliteration. A fitting punishment for anyone who uses it would be to require him to use the word *kith* at once in some other context. The chances are overwhelming that he couldn't do it. The word meant originally those who are known to us, friends, fellow-countrymen, neighbors, acquaintances. It is related to the old word *couth*, known. In the stable societies of older times all of one's kin were probably kith, though not all who were kith were kin. When Middleton wrote, in 1620, *A maid that's neither kith nor kin to me*, he seems to have the proper distinction in mind. But for well over a century the two words have been assumed to be synonymous. Burns wrote *My lady's white, my lady's red,/ And kith and kin o' Cassillis' blude*, though one cannot be kith of blood.

SLANG DICTIONARIES

Mitford Mathews's *Americanisms: A Dictionary of Selected Americanisms* and William Craigie's *A Dictionary of American English on Historical Principles* give you, without a trace of a smile, very serious discussions of words like "hot dog," "hamburger," and "meathead." Harold Wentworth and Stuart Flexner's *Dictionary of American Slang* includes rhyming terms, black slang, pig Latin, and lists of suffixes like *-nik* (beatnik, folknik, neatnik) and prefix words like *soul-* (soul brother, soul food, soul music), etc.

Another standard work on slang is Eric Partridge's *Dictionary of Slang and Unconventional English*, which uses the historical approach.

There's a "dictionary of" just about every subject, and many are included in this guide under specific subject headings. There are rhyming dictionaries, abbreviation dictionaries, and many on music, literature, and sports. There is plenty of printed proof that there will never be a last word on any subject.

BIBLIOGRAPHY: DICTIONARIES

Barnhart, Clarence L., and Barnhart, Robert K., eds. *World Book Dictionary*. A Thorndike-Barnhart Dictionary. Chicago: World Book-Childcraft, 1979.

Bernstein, Theodore M. *The Careful Writer.* New York: Atheneum, 1965.

Craigie, Sir William, and Hulbert, James R. *A Dictionary of American English on Historical Principles.* Chicago: University of Chicago Press, 1936–1944. 4 vols.

Evans, Bergen and Cornelia. *A Dictionary of Contemporary American Usage.* New York: Random House, 1957.

Fowler, Henry Watson. *Dictionary of Modern English Usage.* 2d ed., rev. by Sir Ernest Gowers. New York: Oxford University Press, 1965.

Funk & Wagnalls New Standard Dictionary of the English Language. New York: Funk & Wagnalls, 1963.

Guralnik, David B., ed. *Webster's New World Dictionary of the American Language.* New York: Popular Library, 1982.

Kister, Kenneth F. *Dictionary Buying Guide.* New York: R. R. Bowker, 1977.

Mathews, Mitford M. *Americanisms: A Dictionary of Selected Americanisms on Historical Principles.* Chicago: University of Chicago Press, 1966.

Morris, William, ed. *American Heritage Dictionary of the English Language.* Boston: American Heritage and Houghton Mifflin, 1981.

Murray, Sir James A. H. *New English Dictionary on Historical Principles.* Oxford: Clarendon Press, 1888–1933. 10 vols. and supplement. Reissued 1933 in 13 vols. under the title *Oxford English Dictionary.* Supplements to the *OED*, 1972, 1982, and in progress. *Shorter Oxford English Dictionary on Historical Principles* prepared by William Little, H. W. Fowler, J. Coulson. Rev. and ed. by C. T. Onions, 3d ed. with addenda. Oxford: Clarendon Press, 1962. 2 vols.

Partridge, Eric. *Dictionary of Slang and Unconventional English.* 7th ed. New York: Macmillan, 1970.

Roget's International Thesaurus. 4th ed. New York: Crowell, 1977.

Stein, J. M., ed. *Random House Dictionary of the English Language.* New York: Random House, 1966.

Webster's New Dictionary of Synonyms. Springfield, Mass.: G. & C. Merriam, 1978.

Webster's Ninth New Collegiate Dictionary. Springfield, Mass.: G. & C. Merriam, 1983.

Webster's Third New International Dictionary. Springfield, Mass.: G. & C. Merriam, 1981.

Wentworth, Harold, and Flexner, Stuart Berg. *Dictionary of American Slang.* 2d ed. New York: Crowell, 1975.

CHAPTER 10 *ENCYCLOPEDIAS*

"Encyclopedia" is a word of Greek origin that means the "circle of knowledge" of the ancients. It is indeed an ancient form of reference book.

Aristotle did something like an encyclopedia, and the oldest is said to have been one dating from A.D. 77 by Pliny the Elder, a friendly but unlikely name that sounds as if it belongs to a rock group.

So people have apparently always been eager to put together all they know, in some kind of order, of course. That's what an encyclopedia is: "all" knowledge usually arranged alphabetically or by subject.

In recent years a certain disdain for encyclopedias has become fashionable, probably because they are so easy to use (when did the difficult become equated with the best?) and because a teacher's requirement that students use other materials in addition to encyclopedias is misinterpreted as meaning to avoid altogether the use of encyclopedias.

In fact, encyclopedias are the best place to start to search a subject. An important beginning can be made in understanding a topic by reading the systematic summary in an encyclopedia. For here you can get the basic background information on a subject, the overview by an expert.

The *Americana*, the *Britannica*, and *Collier's* all are "adult" encyclopedias. The *World Book* ranges from "young people's" to "general adult" encyclopedia, and *Compton's* is a "school" or "young people's" set. But don't quite believe those labels and what they imply. In some ways and on some subjects the *World Book* is of better service to an adult and the *Britannica* might be of more use to a young student.

Encyclopedias are usually kept up-to-date by annual yearbooks that have the latest information on various subjects and personalities. Also, the major encyclopedias (all those mentioned above) are produced through a program of "continuous revision." That means that editors are always revising and adding material, and each year's issue of the set contains articles changed or added.

Academic American Encyclopedia is a new set intended "for students in junior high school, high school, or college and for the inquisitive adult." *Academic* is a general-information, multivolume encyclopedia presenting a broad spectrum of up-to-date information usually in short-entry style. It has made an effort to be objective and free of bias and presents material accurately and concisely.

Collier's Encyclopedia, first published in 1949, has a popular, though still comprehensive, approach and is geared to modern interests. The index volume has a valuable study guide to many subjects and contains an excellent bibliography. Its style is popular and readable, and its appearance is attractive.

Compton's Encyclopedia and Fact Index is geared to meet the requirements of the school curricula and so is aimed at children and young people. It is easy to use and comprehend and is still abundantly illustrated, though the "pictured encyclopedia" has been dropped from the title. There is a fact index at the end of each volume so the reader can quickly locate a single fact and find the information gathered from all volumes relating to the subject.

The Encyclopaedia Britannica has a long and noble history. It was first printed in Scotland in 1771 by a "Society of Gentlemen" and has been American-owned and -published since 1902. It is a fine work with detailed and scholarly—and sometimes ponderous—treatment of subjects. It is probably the most comprehensive of encyclopedias and is international in scope. *The New Encyclopaedia Britannica,* the fifteenth edition, is referred to as *Britannica Three* because of its radically new arrangement and division into three interrelated parts: *Propaedia* (Outline of Knowledge), *Micropaedia* (Ready Reference and Index), and *Macropaedia* (Knowledge in Depth). Unfortunately the *Micropaedia* does not literally index the set, and, though a *Library Guide to the Encyclopaedia Britannica* lists main entries and citations in the set, without a serviceable index, the new edition lacks the usefulness of earlier editions. However, a two-volume index is in preparation and will be issued sometime in 1985.

The Encyclopedia Americana first appeared in 1829. It has a reputation for being especially strong in science and technology probably because it was edited at one time by Frederick Converse Beach, who was also an editor of *Scientific American* magazine. It is of particular use for summaries of famous books, biography, and histories. Treatment is scholarly, and this encyclopedia carries short articles on small subjects as well as long, detailed articles.

The World Book Encyclopedia has a distinct, colorful personality. The format is perfect for quickly finding a fact or understanding the main points of a subject because the highlights of articles are brought forward in illustrations, chronological lists of important events, lists of people associated with the subject, etc. The last volume has a comprehensive index, reading and study guides, and an instructional section—"How to Do Research."

ONE-VOLUME ENCYCLOPEDIAS

The New Columbia Encyclopedia is an excellent one-volume encyclopedia containing more than 50,000 articles and many illustrations. It has short, concise, accurate articles on an astonishing number of subjects.

The New Lincoln Library Encyclopedia, formerly called the *Lincoln Library of Essential Information*, comes now in three volumes and is arranged in twelve broad topical sections called departments. Each department, such as biography or mathematics, is made up of essays presented in A to Z dictionary form.

The Random House Encyclopedia is an attractive reference work, enthusiastic about knowledge. The Colorpedia has heavily illustrated two-page articles on broad topics. The Alphapedia offers short, factual A to Z entries.

SPECIAL-SUBJECT ENCYCLOPEDIAS

There are many outstanding encyclopedias for special topics. Some of these will be discussed under their proper subject areas later in this guide; a few are mentioned here.

The International Encyclopedia of the Social Sciences has topical articles addressed to concepts, theories, and methods in fields such as anthropology, history, political science, and sociology. For example, there is in this work a discussion of the concept of a just war, an article on evolution, and another on Sigmund Freud. These are scholarly articles with bibliographies.

There are encyclopedias of art, education, religion, philosophy, American history, sports. One that does not exactly fit the conventional idea of an encyclopedia is the *Encyclopedia of Associations*. This extremely useful and interesting work lists American organizations in all fields, including business, government, science, medicine, education, religion, and so on. The entry for each association gives the name of the executive director, the founding date, address, and purpose. A look at this work usually surprises readers because of the variety and number of groups. Have you heard of the American Medical Association? Probably. But have you heard of the International Wizard of Oz

Club and the Society of the Whiskey Rebellion of 1794? Volume I of the work is in two parts, listing associations, and there is another volume of Geographic and Executive Indexes and still another of New Associations and Projects.

ABOUT ENCYCLOPEDIAS

If you're interested in some encyclopedic information about encyclopedias and especially if you're going to buy one, take a look at *The Encyclopedia Buying Guide: A Consumer Guide to General Encyclopedias in Print.* The author discusses all aspects of encyclopedias—arrangement, scope, history, format, reliability, objectivity, clarity, bibliographies, special features, and graphics—and refers readers to other critical opinions and reviews.

The best way to get the feeling of the different personalities of encyclopedias is to pick any subject you're familiar with and see how it is treated in each work. Even a quick glance will tell you a lot. You'll find a tremendous amount of information packed into a small space, and that's why an encyclopedia has been called an intellectual bazaar.

BIBLIOGRAPHY: ENCYCLOPEDIAS

Academic American Encyclopedia. 1st ed. Princeton, N.J.: Arete Publishing, 1980. 20 vols.

Collier's Encyclopedia. New York: Macmillan Educational Corp., 1980. 24 vols.

Compton's Encyclopedia and Fact Index. Chicago, F. E. Compton Company, 1982. 26 vols.

The Encyclopedia Americana. New York: Grolier Educational Corp., 1982. 30 vols.

Encyclopedia of Associations. 17th ed. Detroit: Gale Research, 1982. 3 vols.

Harris, William H. and Levey, Judith S., eds. *The New Columbia Encyclopedia.* 4th ed. New York: Columbia University Press, 1975.

Kister, Kenneth F. *Encyclopedia Buying Guide.* 3d ed. New York: R. R. Bowker, 1981.

The New Encyclopaedia Britannica. 15th ed. Chicago: Encyclopaedia Britannica, 1983. 30 vols.

The New Lincoln Library Encyclopedia. 40th ed. Columbus, Ohio: Frontier Press, 1981. 3 vols.

The Random House Encyclopedia. New York: Random House, 1983.

Sills, David L., ed. *The International Encyclopedia of the Social Sciences.* New York: Free Press, 1977. 18 vols.

The World Book Encyclopedia. Chicago: World Book-Childcraft, 1982. 22 vols.

CHAPTER 11   *NEWSPAPERS AND MAGAZINES*

One of the freedoms Americans enjoy is freedom of information, a citizen's right to know. Citizens have a right to know serious things like what happens to their taxes, how their representatives in Congress are voting, and when and where important meetings are being held. And they have the right to know what new books are published, what plays and movies are opening, and what the ball scores are.

Governments sometimes withhold information and sometimes lie to the people, but in a free society the hope is to keep this to a minimum. The difference between what is withheld or false and what is released and true is sometimes referred to as the credibility gap. The idea is to keep the gap from widening.

Newspapers and magazines help inform the public and narrow the credibility gap. Freedom of the press is the Siamese twin of freedom of information. As citizens have a right to know, the press has a right to tell them.

Newspapers and magazines are especially important sources because they give the most recent information on a subject and give material on subjects too new or perhaps too temporary to be covered in books.

Newspapers and some magazine articles are considered primary sources. A primary source is distinguished from a secondary source by the fact that it is an eyewitness account given by someone who participates in events or is present as an observer. A student or researcher, using a number of such primary sources, then produces a paper, which is a secondary source. The more removed a researcher gets from primary sources, the more likely it is that the information may be distorted. (See also the discussion of primary sources under "Critical Thinking" on page 185.)

Newspapers and magazines supply you with information today and, through indexes and preservation in such forms as microfilm, will supply that information in exactly the same way to your great-grandchildren at a later day. Future generations will be provided with undiluted history. The interpretation or significance of events may change in the light of history and new knowledge, but the basic facts and contemporary reactions are preserved.

MAGAZINE AND JOURNAL INDEXES

Magazines and scholarly journals are a way of keeping up-to-date and a way of finding various viewpoints on a subject. They're also called periodicals because they are issued at regular intervals—every week, every month, four times a year (quarterly), etc. Several issues of a journal or magazine make up a volume. Usually, but not always, a volume number covers a year's issues. Indexes refer to the name of the magazine or journal, the volume number, page number, and date of issue.

Readers' Guide to Periodical Literature

A popular index, the *Readers' Guide to Periodical Literature,* will be dealt with in detail here as an example of how most indexes may be used, but indexes vary, so as usual, it is a good idea to glance at the introductory information in any tool. Citation indexes and the *Magazine Index* will also be briefly discussed.

The *Readers' Guide* is an index to the articles in about 200 familiar and commonly used magazines. The magazine articles are indexed by subject and by author in one alphabetical list.

Actually the *Readers' Guide* is itself a periodical because it is issued in paperback form twice a month. These are eventually cumulated or interfiled into one alphabetical list covering longer periods of time and then bound into hardcover books. The covers of the issues and of the bound volumes indicate the time period encompassed (see illustration).

ABBREVIATIONS

The entries give the names of the magazines in abbreviated form. The front of the guide has a list of abbreviations used for the periodicals and another list with full bibliographic information for the periodicals indexed in the *Readers' Guide.* (See illustrations.)

Other abbreviations used are also given in a key at the front of each issue or volume. Those abbreviations used for the months are shown, "il" for illustration, "por" for portrait, etc.

APRIL 25, 1984

Vol. 84   No. 4

Includes indexing from March 13—March 26, 1984

READERS' GUIDE
to periodical literature
(UNABRIDGED)

An author subject index to

selected general interest periodicals

of reference value in libraries.

THE H. W. WILSON COMPANY

ISSN 0034-0464

◄ *Date index was issued.*

◄ *Period covered by the magazines indexed in Readers' Guide.*

◄ *SAMPLE COVER OF PAPERBACK ISSUE OF READERS' GUIDE*

SAMPLE SPINE OF BOUND VOLUME ►

READERS' GUIDE TO PERIODICAL LITERATURE

Period covered by magazines indexed. ►   **MARCH 1982– FEBRUARY 1983**

Readers' Guide volume number. ►   **42**

ABBREVIATIONS OF PERIODICALS INDEXED

For full information consult the list of Periodicals Indexed

*50 Plus — 50 Plus

A

Aging — Aging
Am Artist — American Artist
Am Craft — American Craft
Am Educ — American Education
*Am Herit — American Heritage
Am Hist Illus — American History Illustrated
Am Sch — The American Scholar
*America — America
Americana — Americana
Américas — Américas
Antiques — Antiques
Archit Dig — Architectural Digest
Archit Rec — Architectural Record
Art Am — Art in America
Art News — Art News
Astronomy — Astronomy
*Atlantic — The Atlantic
Audubon — Audubon
Aviat Week Space Technol — Aviation Week & Space Technology

B

*Better Homes Gard — Better Homes and Gardens
BioScience — BioScience
Black Enterp — Black Enterprise
Blair Ketchums Ctry J — Blair & Ketchum's Country Journal
Bull At Sci — The Bulletin of the Atomic Scientists
Bus Week — Business Week
Byte — Byte

C

Car Driv — Car and Driver
Cent Mag — The Center Magazine
Change — Change
*Changing Times — Changing Times
Channels Commun — Channels of Communications
Child Today — Children Today
Christ Century — The Christian Century
Christ Today — Christianity Today
Commentary — Commentary
Commonweal — Commonweal
Comput Electron — Computers & Electronics
Congr Dig — Congressional Digest
Conservationist — The Conservationist
*Consum Rep — Consumer Reports
*Consum Res Mag — Consumers' Research Magazine
Creat Comput — Creative Computing
Creat Crafts Miniat — Creative Crafts & Miniatures
Curr Health 2 — Current Health 2
Curr Hist — Current History
Current — Current (Washington, D.C.)
Cycle — Cycle

D

Dance Mag — Dance Magazine
Dep State Bull — Department of State Bulletin
Des Arts Educ — Design for Arts in Education
Discover — Discover
Down Beat — Down Beat

E

Earth Sci — Earth Science
*Ebony — Ebony

PERIODICALS INDEXED

All data as of latest issue received

A

*50 Plus. $15. m 50 Plus, 99 Garden St., Marion, OH 43302

Aging. $14. bi-m Superintendent of Documents, U.S. Government Printing Office, Washington, DC 20402
*America. $23. w (except Ja 1, and alternate Saturdays in Jl and Ag) America Press Inc., 106 W. 56th St., New York, NY 10019
American Artist. $19. m American Artist, 1 Color Court, Marion, OH 43302
American Craft. $31.50. bi-m Membership Dept., American Craft Council, P.O. Box 1308-CL, Fort Lee, NJ 07024
American Education. $23. m (bi-m Ja-F, Ag-S) Superintendent of Documents, U.S. Government Printing Office, Washington, DC 20402
*American Heritage. $24. bi-m American Heritage Subscription Office, P.O. Box 977, Farmingdale, NY 11737
American History Illustrated. $16.95. m (except Jl, Ag) American History Illustrated, Box 8200, Harrisburg, PA 17105
American Home. See Redbook
The American Scholar. $15. q The American Scholar, Editorial and Circulation Offices, 1811 Q St., N.W., Washington, DC 20009
Americana. $11.90. bi-m Americana Subscription Office, 381 W. Center St., Marion, OH 43302
Américas. $15. bi-m Américas Subscription Service, P.O. Box 973, Farmingdale, NY 11737
Antiques. $38. m Straight Enterprises, Inc., 551 Fifth Ave., New York, NY 10176
Architectural Digest. $39.95. m Architectural Digest, P.O. Box 2415, Boulder, CO 80322
Architectural Record. $45. m (semi-m Ap, S) Architectural Record, P.O. Box 430, Hightstown, NJ 08520
Art in America. $34.95. m (except Jl) Art in America, 542 Pacific Ave., Marion, OH 43302
Art News. $25.95. m (q Je-Ag) Art News, Subscription Service, P.O. Box 969, Farmingdale, NY 11737
Astronomy. $21. m Astronomy, P.O. Box 92788, Milwaukee, WI 53202
*The Atlantic. $18. m Atlantic Subscription Processing Center, Box 2547, Boulder, CO 80322
Audubon. $16. bi-m National Audubon Society, 950 Third Ave., New York, NY 10022
Aviation Week & Space Technology. $58. w Aviation Week & Space Technology. P.O. Box 1022, Manasquan, NJ 08736

B

*Better Homes and Gardens. $12.97. m Better Homes and Gardens, P.O. Box 4536, Des Moines, IA 50336
BioScience. $52. m (bi-m Jl, Ag) BioScience Subscriptions, AIBS, 1401 Wilson Blvd., Arlington, VA 22209
Black Enterprise. $15. m Black Enterprise, Circulation Service Center, P.O. Box 5500, Bergenfield, NJ 07621
Blair & Ketchum's Country Journal. $16.95. m Country Journal, P.O. Box 392, Mt. Morris, IL 61054
The Bulletin of the Atomic Scientists. $25. m (bi-m Je/Jl, Ag/S) Bulletin of the Atomic Scientists, Circulation Dept., 5801 S. Kenwood, Chicago, IL 60637
Business Week. $39.95. w (except 1 issue in Ja) Business Week, P.O. Box 430, Hightstown, NJ 08520
Byte. $21. m (except 2 issues in Ag and O) Byte Publications, Inc., P.O. Box 590, Martinsville, NJ 08836

C

Car and Driver. $14.98. m Car and Driver, P.O. Box 2770, Boulder, CO 80302
The Center Magazine. $21.50. bi-m Center Magazine, Box 4068, Santa Barbara, CA 93103
Change. $30. m (bi-m Ja/F, My/Je, Jl/Ag, N/D) Change, 4000 Albemarle St., N.W., Washington, DC 20016
*Changing Times. $15. m Changing Times, The Kiplinger Magazine, Editors Park, MD 20782

Channels of Communications. $18. bi-m Channels of Communications, Subscription Service Dept., Box 2001, Mahopac, NY 10541
Charm. See Glamour
Children Today. $14. bi-m Superintendent of Documents, U.S. Government Printing Office, Washington, DC 20402
The Christian Century. $21. w (occasional bi-w issues) Christian Century, Subscription Service Dept., 5615 W. Cermak Rd., Cicero, IL 60650
Christianity Today. $21. semi-m (m Ja, My, Je, Jl, Ag, D) Christianity Today Subscription Services, P.O. Box 1915, Marion, OH 43305
Commentary. $30. m American Jewish Committee, 165 E. 56th St., New York, NY 10022
Commonweal. $24. bi-w (m Christmas-New Year's and Jl, Ag) Commonweal Publishing Co., 232 Madison Ave., New York, NY 10016
Computers & Electronics. $15.97. m Computers & Electronics Circulation Dept., P.O. Box 2774, Boulder, CO 80302

ABBREVIATIONS

+	continued on later pages of same issue		Ltd	Limited
abr	abridged		m	monthly
Ag	August		Mr	March
ann	annual		My	May
Ap	April			
Assn	Association		N	November
Aut	Autumn		no	number
Ave	Avenue			
			O	October
Bart	Baronet			
bi-m	bimonthly		por	portrait
bi-w	biweekly		pseud	pseudonym
bibl	bibliography		pt	part
bibl f	bibliographical footnotes		pub	published, publisher, publishing
bldg	building			
			q	quarterly
Co	Company			
comp	compiled, compiler		rev	revised
cont	continued			
Corp	Corporation		S	September
			sec	section
D	December		semi-m	semimonthly
Dept	Department		Soc	Society
			Sp	Special
ed	edited, edition, editor		Spr	Spring
			Sq	Square
F	February		Sr	Senior
			St	Street
il	illustrated, illustration, illustrator		Summ	Summer
			supp	supplement
Inc	Incorporated		supt	superintendent
int	interviewer			
introd	introduction, introductory		tr	translated, translation, translator
Ja	January		v	volume
Je	June			
Jl	July		w	weekly
Jr	Junior		Wint	Winter
jt auth	joint author			
			yr	year

See the samples on pages 64 and 65 for illustrations of the following:

CROSS-REFERENCES

When you do not find any articles named under a subject heading, you will usually find an instruction to look under another heading. This is called a "see" reference—from a heading not used to the heading used.

Under some subjects you will find "see also" references. These are reminders to look at related subject headings that might also have articles useful to you.

SUBHEADINGS

If the subject is very broad and there are many entries, it will be divided by subheadings. These break down a subject into smaller, specific aspects. They are printed in the middle of the column, instead of at the left side as the main headings are. A particularly important subhead used under several subjects is "Criticisms, plots, etc." This subheading will help you locate reviews under such headings as "Operas," "Dramas," and "Motion picture reviews."

BY AND ABOUT REFERENCES

Sometimes there will be two alphabetical listings under a famous person's name. The first is a list of articles *by* the person as author, and the second is a list of articles *about* the person.

TITLES

Titles of articles are *not* in the index, but titles of stories appear under headings such as "Fiction—Single Works" with a "see" reference to the author's name for full information.

SAMPLE PAGE FROM READERS' GUIDE *(REDUCED)*

JANUARY 1985   103

Fast food restaurants—*cont.*
  Is Frank Perdue chicken? [shying away from chicken restaurant expansion] R. Goydon. il *Forbes* 134:223-4 N 5 '84
Fasteners
    See also
    Nails
    Paper clips
Fasteners industry
    See also
    Hi-Shear Industries Inc.
Fasts and feasts
    See also
    Advent
    Christmas
              Catholic Church
    See also
    Jesus Christ the King, Feast of
Fat
      See also
      Obesity
Fat content of foods *See* Food—Fat content
Fat farms *See* Health resorts, watering places, etc.
Fatal vision [television program] *See* Television program reviews—Single works
Fathers
        See also
        Parent education
        Stepparents and stepchildren
        Support (Domestic relations)
      How are fathers supposed to dress? My five-year-old son has plenty of ideas. B. Lustig. il *Glamour* 82:294 N '84
Fathers, Unmarried
      What about teenage fathers? W. J. Haskins. por *Essence* 15:160 N '84
Fatigue
      See also
      Relaxation
    A case of iron deficiency without anemia. J. V. Wright. bibl *Prevention* 36:67-71 N '84
    Energy crisis [abnormal glycolysis caused by viral diseases; research by George K. Radda and others] *Sci Am* 251:74-5 O '84
Favors
      Personal favors: how much do you owe your boss? B. L. Harragan. *Mademoiselle* 90:124 N '84
FBI *See* United States. Federal Bureau of Investigation
FCC *See* United States. Federal Communications Commission
FDA *See* United States. Food and Drug Administration
Fear
      See also
      Phobias
    Toddler fears. I. Gibson. il *Parents* 59:166 N '84
Feather, Leonard
    John Carter. il por *Down Beat* 51:47 N '84
Federal and provincial relations (Canada)
      See also
      Quebec (Province)—Nationalism
    Setting the economic agenda [meeting of provincial premiers with B. Mulroney] M. Clugston. il por *Macleans* 97:14-15 N 26 '84
Federal Aviation Administration (U.S.) *See* United States. Federal Aviation Administration
Federal Bureau of Investigation (U.S.) *See* United States. Federal Bureau of Investigation
Federal Communications Commission (U.S.) *See* United States. Federal Communications Commission
Federal debt *See* Debts, Public
Federal Duck Stamp *See* Revenue stamps
Federal employees *See* Government employees
Federal lands *See* Public lands
Federal National Mortgage Association
    Fannie Mae is putting co-ops all over the map. T. Thompson and others. il *Bus Week* p166 N 26 '84
    Why Fannie Mae isn't hammering out profits in mortgages. il *Bus Week* p146-7 N 19 '84
Federal regulatory agencies *See* Regulatory agencies
Federal Reserve System (U.S.)
    The Fed may have no choice but to ease policy. B. Riemer. il *Bus Week* p52 N 26 '84
    How the Fed plans to keep recovery going. M. W. Karmin. il *U S News World Rep* 97:88 N 26 '84
    Who's lining up to fill Volcker's shoes. L. Walczak. *Bus Week* p175 N 12 '84
    Why the Fed should resist pressure to push rates down. F. Mervosh. il *Bus Week* p124 N 12 '84
    Will Fed policy knock Reagan off course? P. C. Roberts. il *Bus Week* p20 N 26 '84

Federal Savings and Loan Insurance Corporation
    People's vs. the FSLIC [People's Savings & Loan] S. B. Young. *Black Enterp* 15:28 D '84
Federal spending policy *See* United States—Appropriations and expenditures
Federated States of Micronesia *See* Micronesia (Federated States)
Fedex International Transmission Corporation
    Federal Express forms facsimile unit. *Aviat Week Space Technol* 121:24-5 N 12 '84
Feed supplements, Antibiotic *See* Antibiotic feed supplements
Feedback (Psychology)
      See also
      Biofeedback training
Feeders (Birds) *See* Bird feeders
Feeds
                Medicated feed
      See also
      Antibiotic feed supplements
Fees, Legal *See* Lawyers—Salaries, fees, etc.
Feet *See* Foot
Feibowitz, Marguerite
    What is Canadian style? Design in the Great White North. il *Theatre Crafts* 18:38-41+ N/D '84
Feiwel, Jean
                  about
    Marcus, Feiwel move up at Scholastic Books. pors *Publ Wkly* 226:28-9 O 26 '84
Feldman, Alan
    Along the banks of the Don [poem] *New Yorker* 60:48 D 3 '84
Feldmann, Rodney M.
    (jt. auth) See Babcock, Loren E., and Feldmann, Rodney M.
Fellowships *See* Scholarships and fellowships
Felser, Larry
    Sport interview [D. Shula] pors *Sport Mag* 75:17-18+ N '84
Female impersonators *See* Impersonators, Female
Feminine beauty *See* Beauty, Personal
Feminine hygiene products
                Labeling
    Know your tampon. K. Friefeld. il *Health* 16:71+ O '84
Feminism
    Still different. G. F. Gilder. il *Natl Rev* 36:48-50 N 30 '84
                Language question
      See Sex discrimination in language
Feminist studies *See* Women's studies
La femme de l'hotel [film] *See* Motion picture reviews—Single works
Fences
      See also
      Snow fences
    Give lattice a private look. il *South Living* 19:184 O '84
    Let the garden fence take a turn. il *South Living* 19:103 O '84
Fenders (Boat) *See* Boats and boating—Equipment
Fermentation
      See also
      Glycolysis
Fernandez, Manny
                  about
    The anatomy of a failure. K. K. Wiegner. il *Forbes* 134:42-3 N 5 '84
Ferrari (Automobile) *See* Sports cars
Ferraro, Geraldine A.
    Still headed in the right direction. por *U S News World Rep* 97:33 N 26 '84
    Why I believe that women must exercise their political clout. por *Glamour* 82:134+ N '84
                  about
    A credible candidacy and then some. W. R. Doerner. il por *Time* 124:84-5 N 19 '84
    An exciting choice—then a clumsy gaffe. P. Goldman. il pors *Newsweek* 104 Sp Issue:81-6 N/D '84
    Ferraro: a world of options. M. Beck. il por *Newsweek* 104 Sp Issue:30 N/D '84
    The Ferraro factor. G. Steinem. il pors *Ms* 13:43-4+ O '84
    Ferraro, Mondale make last appeals to voters. il por *Jet* 67:6 N 12 '84
    The importance of being Ferraro. M. McDonald. il por *Macleans* 97:24-5 N 5 '84
    In search of feist. D. Seligman. il *Fortune* 110:171 N 26 '84
    Mondale says goodbye. M. Beck. il pors *Newsweek* 104:50 N 19 '84

Fatigue
    See also
      Relaxation
  A case of iron deficiency without anemia. J. V. Wright.
    bibl *Prevention* 36:67-71 N '84
  Energy crisis [abnormal glycolysis caused by viral diseases;
    research by George K. Radda and others] *Sci Am*
    251:74-5 O '84

Subject entry

Fear
    See also
      Phobias
  Toddler fears. J. Gibson. il *Parents* 59:166 N '84

"See also" references to related material

Will Fed policy knock Reagan off course? P. C. Roberts.
  il *Bus Week* p20 N 26 '84

Illustrated article

Setting the economic agenda [meeting of provincial
  premiers with B. Mulroney] M. Clugston. il por
  Macleans 97:14-15 N 26 '84

Maclean's, Vol. 97, pages 14–15, November 26, 1984

Feeds
               Medicated feed
    See also
    Antibiotic feed supplements

Subheading

Feldman, Alan
  Along the banks of the Don [poem] *New Yorker*
    60:48 D 3 '84

Author entry

Federal debt *See* Debts, Public
Federal Duck Stamp *See* Revenue stamps
Federal employees *See* Government employees
Federal lands *See* Public lands

"See" references from headings not used to headings used

Feather, Leonard
  John Carter. il por *Down Beat* 51:47 N '84

Portrait of person in news story is included in illustrations

Fedex International Transmission Corporation
  Federal Express forms facsimile unit. *Aviat Week Space*
    Technol 121:24-5 N 12 '84

Aviation Week & Space Technology, Vol. 121, pages 24–25, November 12, 1984

Ferraro, Geraldine A.
  Still headed in the right direction. por *U S News World*
    Rep 97:33 N 26 '84
  Why I believe that women must exercise their political
    clout. por *Glamour* 82:134+ N '84
            about
  A credible candidacy and then some. W. R. Doerner.
    il por *Time* 124:84-5 N 19 '84
  An exciting choice—then a clumsy gaffe. P. Goldman.
    il pors *Newsweek* 104 Sp Issue:81-6 N/D '84

"By and about" articles Title entry (referring to main entry under author's name)

Ringed entries enlarged and explained

Other Major Indexes

Poole's Index indexes English and American periodicals from 1802 to 1907, and the *Nineteenth Century Readers' Guide* covers the period from 1890 to about 1922. (The *Readers' Guide to Periodical Literature* covers the twentieth century.) *Poole's*, by the way, was started by a student, William Frederick Poole, who saw the need for it while studying at Yale.

Other indexes are limited to periodicals on special subjects. A *few* examples are:

Applied Science & Technology Index
Art Index
Biological & Agricultural Index
Business Periodicals Index
Education Index
Humanities Index
Public Affairs Information Service
Social Science Index

Indexes exist in most broad subject areas, and there are many more in science, in literature, and in religion and philosophy.

Magazine Index, like the *Readers' Guide*, is an index to popular magazines. However, this index is on microfilm. It quickly locates articles in an alphabetical section (by subject or personal name) and has a numerical listing. Its appeal is the modern format.

CITATION INDEXES

Citation indexes are computer-produced, indexing thousands of journals, and are two-step indexes. These excellent international and interdisciplinary indexes may be used for a straight subject search or as a way of locating related or recent material by finding articles that cite articles written in earlier years. There are several volumes for each year. The *Permuterm Subject Index* volume combines terms and sends the reader to the *Source* volumes for full bibliographic detail. Citation volumes indicate what earlier articles have been cited in recent articles. It is essential to use the guides to citation indexes or ask a reference librarian for assistance. There are three citation indexes: *Arts & Humanities Citation Index*, *Science Citation Index*, and *Social Sciences Citation Index*. (The legal profession also uses citation indexes requiring special knowledge.)

JOURNAL ABSTRACTS

An index cites an article under the subject heading by giving the name of the journal, issue number, pages, and date. An abstract gives the full citation and also a brief summary of the article itself. An abstract may be all the reader sometimes needs in order to get the significant information, and it may also save steps, because from it, the searcher can determine whether tracking down the full article is worth the time. There are abstracting services in most major disciplines. Examples are *Psychological Abstracts* and *Sociological Abstracts*.

ABOUT MAGAZINES

In addition to finding information *in* magazines, there are ways of finding out *about* them. There are directories that list periodicals according to subject (medicine, education, sports, etc.) and give information on subscriptions, circulation, and related material. The *Standard Periodical Directory* lists U.S. and Canadian periodicals and *Ulrich's International Periodicals Directory* is a very comprehensive world list in two volumes. Evaluations of magazines are given in William Katz's *Magazines for Libraries* and Evan Farber's *Classified List of Periodicals for the College Library*.

If you want to know where a certain magazine is indexed, *Ulrich's* indicates that, as does the *Chicorel Index to Abstracting and Indexing Services* for periodicals in the humanities and the social sciences. And of course, the front of each index or abstract carries a list of the periodicals each covers.

NEWSPAPERS

Journalist Walter Lippmann gave this definition of a newspaper's responsibility: "To bring to light the hidden facts, to set them into relation with each other, to make a picture of reality on which men can act."

It is that "picture of reality" written by a person on the scene that makes a newspaper a primary source of current history and, through back issues, brings "ancient" history to life.

Notice certain things when you're reading the newspaper. Look at the dateline because it translates any use of the words "here" and "today" in the story. The dateline will indicate if "here" means your hometown or Moscow, and it will tell you if "today" means yesterday and not the date on which the newspaper is issued (especially possible

(Samples from *The New York Times,* April 3, 1984)

JUSTICES TO DECIDE ON SILENT PRAYER IN PUBLIC SCHOOLS

CLASS 'MOMENTS' AT ISSUE

Court Reaffirms Rulings That Organized Activity Would Violate Constitution

By LINDA GREENHOUSE
Special to The New York Times

WASHINGTON, April 2 — The Supreme Court, reaffirming its rulings that organized prayer in public schools violates the Constitution, agreed today to decide whether "moment of silence" laws are unconstitutional as well.

The decision, announced in a brief, unsigned order, appe~~d likely to shift the ~ of the ~ver ~ ~l
r~

Nicaragua Chooses Council to Supervise Scheduled Elections

MANAGUA, Nicaragua, April 2 (AP) — The Supreme Court named a three-member election council today to supervise the Nov. 4 voting for a president, vice president and 90-member parliament.

Two of the members are lawyers who are considered independents and the third is a peasant who is a member of the leftist Sandinista National Liberation Front that governs Nicaragua.

"With the appointment of members ~e Sup~ Electi~ ~l the

Above: Dateline indicates Managua events of day before, and it is taken from a wire service (AP, which stands for the Associated Press).

Below: By-line of local reporter and current story, so no place or date given

Left: By-line of reporter in another city covering events that took place day before newspaper's date of issue

---

Big Tests for Black Vote Face Jackson in 3 Cities

By RONALD SMOTHERS

The Rev. Jesse Jackson has won as much as 79 percent of the black vote in the Democratic Presidential primaries so far, but three of his biggest tests lie ahead.

As the primaries move into New York today, Pennsylvania next Tuesday and Ohio on May 8, his showing ~ black vo~ ~e mai~
~ v

Voters, elected officials and campaign officials interviewed in the three cities cited the momentum among blacks that Mr. Jackson has built with his previous showings.

The Rev. William Jones, pastor of Bethany Baptist Church in Brooklyn ~~ ~s a Jackson delegate in the pri~ ~ay, told ~ience at his
~ ~~on can

in the case of a morning paper). And notice the source. The story may be written by a local or foreign reporter (and given a by-line) or by a wire service. A newspaper cannot afford to have reporters at every national and international news event, so it buys the services of larger news-gathering organizations called wire services.

Some awareness of how news stories are written is helpful. The pattern of most news stories is almost the reverse of the pattern in fiction. That is, the news story, instead of building to a climax, begins with a condensation of the climax or the important aspects of the event. It then proceeds to present the facts in descending order of importance. This formula saves the reader time. If, after reading the first few paragraphs, you have the information you want, you need not read on, but if it is a subject about which you must know all pertinent facts, they are there for you. A headline is a further abbreviation of the story.

The front page will also tell you what edition you're reading. If there is a lot of developing news, a paper will print several editions in one day to keep the stories up-to-date. The later the edition, the more complete the information given.

Some newspapers are, of course, better than others. Good newspapers offer background articles, pictures, maps, and analysis in addition to an account of the event. A good newspaper keeps opinion out of the news columns and reserves it for the editorial page, where it can be recognized as opinion. Advertisers should not have any influence over the news and editorials.

Libraries keep back files of local newspapers, some of which are preserved on microfilm. In the last ten years, indexes have been done for some major newspapers, and Bell & Howell produces the *Newspaper Index*, which indexes the country's largest newspapers: the *Chicago Sun-Times*, the *Chicago Tribune*, the *Denver Post*, the *Detroit News*, the *Houston Post*, the *New Orleans Times-Picayune*, the *San Francisco Chronicle*, the *Los Angeles Times*, and *The Washington Post*. The combined index began in 1972, and Bell & Howell also produces separate indexes to those newspapers.

The Times of London and *The New York Times* have printed indexes going far back in time. *The New York Times Index*, described here, is very useful in locating material in other newspapers because it gives a clue to the date on which an event might have appeared in the paper.

THE NEW YORK TIMES INDEX

This index is briefly described here because it and the newspaper on microfilm are available in public and university libraries across the United States. And, as mentioned, *The New York Times Index* is useful

HOW TO USE THE NEW YORK TIMES INDEX

The Index is the only service that presents a condensed, classified history of the world as it is recorded day-by-day in The New York Times. It consists of abstracts of news and editorial matter (*entries*) entered under appropriate headings. Headings and their subdivisions, if any, are arranged alphabetically; the entries under them are arranged chronologically. Each entry is followed by a precise reference–date, page and column–to the item which it summarizes. All related headings are covered either by cross-references or by duplicate entries.

SOURCE: The Index encompasses the news and editorial matter in the final Late City Edition of The Times–the same edition that is microfilmed –including the Sunday supplementary sections and including advertisements that are related to the news and likely to be of interest to users. Material is omitted only when it is of such transitory interest as to have no discernible research value.

HEADINGS: Whenever possible, entries are made under "subject" headings (e.g., Agriculture, Housing, Steel). Under geographic headings will be found, usually, only material on the government, general defenses, finances, economy, politics and social conditions of the country; i.e., material too broad to fit under subject headings. Names of persons and organizations are usually covered by cross-references to the subjects of their activities. Entries are made under the most specific heading (e.g., material on the steel industry under Steel, and not under Metals), except where the amount of material is too small or where it is advantageous to collect related material under a single heading. Book reviews, deaths, news of art, crime, entertainment and sports, letters to the editor and some other types of news are generally indexed under subject headings only.

Alphabetization: Headings are alphabetized on the word-by-word basis (New York before Newark). Inverted headings precede uninverted headings (New York, State Univ. of, before New York State). Headings beginning with a prefix are treated as though the prefix were a part of the next word (Pan American after Panama). Abbreviated headings appear alphabetically (CIT before Citizens), not at the start of each letter.

Inversions: Multiple-word headings are inverted if a word other than the first is deemed to be the "key word" in identifying the heading (e.g.,United Steelworkers of America to Steelworkers of America, United). Personal names containing a prefix are entered under the prefix if the person is an American or British national (e.g., de Mille, Agnes), and usually under the word following the prefix for other nationalities (e.g., Gaulle, Charles de). An effort is made to observe national or personal preferences whenever they can be ascertained.

SUBDIVISIONS: Headings are subdivided whenever the amount of material entered there warrants it and the nature of the material permits. Subdivisions consist of **Main Subheads** (set thus in bold-face type) and, where further subdivision is necessary, of *Secondary Subheads* (set thus in italics and preceded by a bullet symbol ●). Both types of subheads are arranged alphabetically. Material that does not lend itself to classification under subheads appears directly under the main heading. Material that does not lend itself to classification under secondary subheads appears directly under the main subhead.

ENTRIES: Entries are by no means limited to a minimal indication of the general content of the item from which they derive; to the contrary, they seek to present concisely all the significant material which is pertinent under a given heading. Entries are made under all headings where the item may be pertinent and which are not covered by appropriate cross-references, and sometimes in addition to such cross-references.

Entries appear in chronological order except in

listings under·Book Reviews, Deaths, Theater–Reviews, and the like, where an alphabetical arrangement is clearly preferable.

Entries for closely related material may be grouped into paragraphs. Where two or more such paragraphs appear, they are arranged chronologically as determined by the date reference of the first entry in each paragraph. (In cross-references to entries in such paragraphs, the paragraphs are identified by the date of their first entry. For example, "Ja 5 in Ja 2 par" refers to an entry dated January 5 contained in a paragraph beginning with an entry dated January 2.)

When a news story is accompanied by the text or transcript of official statements or documents, or by photographs, cartoons, maps, graphs or other illustrative material, the entries specify that such material is included. Entries of unusual interest are set in bold-face type. Under headings containing a large number of entries, these bold-face entries serve as bold guideposts in the search for an item whose date the reader may not know.

DATE, PAGE, COLUMN REFERENCES: Each entry concludes with the date, page and column of the story's publication in The Times (e.g., My 1, 1:8 means that the story was published on May 1, page 1, column 8). Sunday sections other than the main news sections are identified by Roman numerals following the date (e.g., in My 6, IV, 3:4 the numeral IV denotes the News of the Week in Review section).

If an entry summarizes a news story which begins on one page and continues on another, the reference is to the page on which the story begins. If an entry summarizes a news item found only in the continuation, the reference is to the page of the continuation, and not to the beginning of the story.

Since most international, national and general news now appears everywhere almost simultaneously, the date entries indicate·when the news may have appeared in other publications. However, The Index cannot be used to obtain *precise* references to other publications or to editions of The Times other than the final Late City Edition. The reader is also cautioned that the date references in The Index denote the dates of publication in The Times, and not the dates of the events themselves.

CROSS-REFERENCES: Cross-references are arranged in alphabetical order, except that cross-references to general categories of headings (e.g., Food. See ...food names) usually follow the more specific

ones. Cross-references guiding to a single entry under another heading will show not only the heading or subhead where that entry is located but also the date of the entry if necessary.

Cross-references do not indicate the specific content of the entries to which they refer, and should not be so construed. Thus a cross-reference from a person's name to a crime heading cannot and does not indicate whether that person is a defendant, a witness, a prosecutor, or a person merely complaining on the subject but not a party to it.

Many terms are cross-referenced to headings where these terms are used as subheads. Sometimes the cross-reference does not spell out the subhead, when it is obvious, but where it is implied. (For example: **ACCIDENTS and Safety. See also** Airlines. Under the heading Airlines, a subhead Accidents and Safety will be found.)

Sometimes cross-references·are made from names of persons or organizations to entries in which these names are not brought out but implied. Thus the entry "school and board representatives comment on budget" would be applicable to any person from whose name a reference to this entry had been made.

Cross references are made from country names to United Nations and to other international organizations of which the given country is a member. Such cross-references are intended to cover, at times implicitly, the country's participation in all of the organization's activities, whether these are indexed by entries under the organization directly, or by cross-references from the organization's name to subjects.

In converting the Index to the dual role of printed index and data base for an information bank, many changes in subdivisions and cross-references have been made. To conform to thesaurus procedures, "use" references guide. the reader from a synonym or an inverted term to the preferred form. A "see" cross-reference is used when the term from which it runs, although a legitimate search term, is not open for entries. "See also" cross-references guide from headings ·that may be opened for entries to other headings where relevant material is entered.

ADDENDA AND ERRATA: Corrections for current and earlier volumes appear in the back of each Annual. Corrections are also printed when necessary in the back of semi-monthly issues. The publishers work to make The Index as accurate as possible, and will be grateful if subscribers will bring to their attention any·inaccuracies they may find.

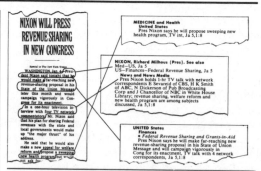

The above instructions appear in each issue of *The New York Times Index.*

in locating items in your local papers (except, of course, strictly local-interest events) because it establishes dates.

The reasons for the availability of *The New York Times* are that it goes far back in time (it began in 1851), it has been preserved on microfilm and carefully indexed for most of its long life, and it has a reputation for reliability and accuracy because it sees itself as a "newspaper of record." And, to risk boasting, some of the finest editors and writers form its staff—a claim supported by many Pulitzer Prizes (annual awards for outstanding achievement in journalism). *The New York Times* also often prints the *full text* of items that are only described in other papers and magazines. The index, under the subject entry, indicates by the words "text" or "excerpts" or "transcript" (for a news conference, etc.) what you will find in the newspaper.

Here is the "How to Use The New York Times Index" page from an index volume. It is best to review this page before using the index.

Though *The New York Times Index* is much more complex, there are similarities between it and the *Readers' Guide*. Both have "see" and "see also" references, subheads under major headings, and abbreviations that are defined in the front of the indexes.

The references are to the date of the newspaper in which the story appears (not necessarily the date of the event), the page number, and the column number. A page has eight columns, numbered 1 on the extreme left to 8 on the far right. If the article appeared in a Sunday paper, a section number (in Roman numerals) may also be given. The citations are preceded by (S), (M), or (L) to indicate that the news item is short, medium, or long.

Ja 11, 1:5   This refers to a story that appeared in the paper of January 11, on page one, column five.

My 1, VI, 33   This refers to a story that appeared on May 1, in section six—the magazine—on page thirty-three. No column number is given because the format of this section of the Sunday paper is different from that of the news section. (*The New York Times Magazine* is also indexed in the *Readers' Guide* because, though part of a newspaper, it is considered a periodical in its own right.)

The Times's index is published twice a month and then cumulated into annual volumes for each year.

One of the special aspects of *The New York Times Index* is that it can be used as a reference tool by itself without necessarily continuing on to the newspaper story. Major news stories are given brief summaries in the index, and the entries are listed chronologically under the subject, so the course of events is clearly seen. The most important events are easily identified by black bold type. Since 1965 the index has included graphs, pictures, maps, and other illustrative material. Here is an example from the 1968 index:

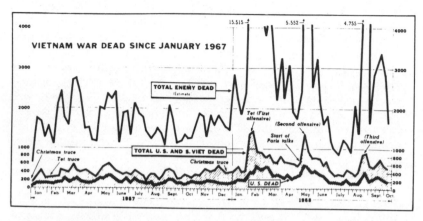

The index all by itself is valuable for finding the names and the spelling of new nations and newly elected officials and for finding sports records, statistics, dates, and the meanings of current initials. Under "Deaths" you'll find a list of prominent persons who have died in a given year; there are other important collective headings such as "Book Reviews." (Some of these collective headings are indicated under appropriate subjects in this guide.)

In the event that the name of one of the Beatles escapes you, a quick check in *The Times*'s index under "Beatles" will show all four names—provided, of course, it's the index for a year when the Beatles were in the news. This is from the 1967 index:

BEATLES, The (George Harrison, John Lennon, Paul McCartney, Ringo Starr). See also Apparel—GB, N 21. Drug Addiction Jl 25. Motion Pictures—Revs, How I Won the War. Music Jl 25. Music—Awards Mr 27. TV—GB, D 27,28 ▲ Lennon illus, Ja 15,II, 13:2; McCartney says group is breaking up, int, Ja 23,29:1; their mgr B Epstein dies, Ag 28,31:4 (see also Epstein, B); they postpone pilgrimage to India, to study with mystic, in order to complete 1-hr TV special; 3 say they have stopped taking drugs, S 11,53:1

There is also a separate *Personal Name Index to "The New York Times Index," 1851–1974.*

As with all reference sources, the best way to familiarize yourself with *The New York Times Index* is to look up a subject you know about and see how it is handled. Become acquainted with the newspaper by looking at the microfilm for the day you were born and see what other important events took place that memorable day. Even the advertisements will help reveal that segment of the past.

ABOUT NEWSPAPERS

There are ways of finding information *about* newspapers as well as *in* them. Two directories that list newspapers by state and then by city, giving publishers, editors, circulation, etc., are the *Editor & Publisher International Yearbook* and the *IMS Ayer Directory of Publications*, which are both published annually. Another is a five-volume set, *The Working Press of the Nation*, which has a newspaper directory; a magazine directory; a TV and radio directory; a directory for feature writers, photographers, and syndicates; and a directory of international publications.

BIBLIOGRAPHY: NEWSPAPERS AND MAGAZINES

Applied Science and Technology Index. New York: H. W. Wilson, 1958 to date. Monthly except August. Annual cumulations.

Arts & Humanities Citation Index. Philadelphia: Institute for Scientific Information, 1976 to date. Annual cumulation.

Art Index. New York: H. W. Wilson, 1929 to date. Quarterly with cumulations.

Biological and Agricultural Index. New York: H. W. Wilson, 1964 to date. Monthly except September. Cumulations. Prior to 1964 was *Agricultural Index, 1916– .*

Business Periodicals Index. New York: H. W. Wilson, 1958 to date. Monthly except August. Annual cumulations.

Chicorel Index to Abstracting and Indexing Services. Periodicals in the Humanities and Social Sciences. 2d ed. Vol. 11 and 11A of the Chicorel Index Series. New York: Chicorel Library Pub., 1978.

Editor & Publisher International Yearbook. New York: Editor & Publisher, 1920 to date. Annual.

Education Index. New York: H. W. Wilson, 1929 to date. Monthly except July and August. Cumulations.

Falk, Byron, and Falk, Valerie. *Personal Name Index to "The New York Times Index," 1851–1974.* Succasunna, N.J.: Roxbury Data Interface, 1976–1981.

Farber, Evan. *Classified List of Periodicals for the College Library.* 5th ed. Westwood, Mass.: Faxton, 1972.

Humanities Index. New York: H. W. Wilson, 1974 to date. Quarterly. Annual cumulations. Formerly *Social Sciences and Humanities Index.*

IMS '84 Ayer Directory of Publications. Fort Washington, Pa.: IMS Press, 1880 to date. Previously published as *N. W. Ayer and Son's Directory of Newspapers and Periodicals.* Philadelphia: N. W. Ayer.

Katz, William. *Magazines for Libraries.* New York: R. R. Bowker, 1982.

Magazine Index. Los Altos, Calif.: Information Access Corp., 1976 to date. Microfilm. Monthly.

The New York Times Index. New York: The New York Times Co., 1913 to date. Semimonthly with quarterly and annual cumulations.

Newspaper Index. Wooster, Ohio: Newspaper Indexing Center, Bell & Howell, 1972 to date. Monthly, quarterly. Annual cumulations.

Nineteenth Century Readers' Guide to Periodical Literature. New York: H. W. Wilson, 1944. 2 vols.

Poole's Index to Periodical Literature. Rev. ed. Boston: Houghton Mifflin, 1891. 2 vols., 5 supplements.

Psychological Abstracts. Lancaster, Pa., and Washington, D. C.: American Psychological Association, 1927 to date. Bimonthly. Annual cumulations.

Public Affairs Information Service. Bulletin of the Public Affairs Information Service. New York: Service, 1914 to date. Semimonthly. Annual cumulations.

Readers' Guide to Periodical Literature. New York: H. W. Wilson, 1900 to date. Semimonthly/monthly. Annual cumulations.

Science Citation Index. Philadelphia: Institute for Scientific Information, 1961 to date. Quarterly. Annual cumulations.

Social Sciences and Humanities Index. New York: H. W. Wilson, 1916 to 1974. Formerly *International Index;* Continued by *Social Sciences Index* and *Humanities Index.*

Social Sciences Citation Index. Philadelphia: Institute for Scientific Information, 1973 to date. (Retrospective indexing provided for 1969–1972.)

Social Sciences Index. New York: H. W. Wilson, 1974 to date. Quarterly. Annual cumulations. Formerly *Social Sciences and Humanities Index.*

Sociological Abstracts. New York: Sociological Abstracts, 1952 to date. Frequency varies.

Standard Periodical Directory: 1983–84. 8th rev. ed. New York: Oxbridge Communications, 1982.

Ulrich's International Periodicals Directory, 1983. 22d ed. New York: R. R. Bowker, 1983. 2 vols. Biennial.

Working Press of the Nation. Burlington, Iowa: National Research Bureau, Inc., 1982. 5 vols.

PART III

REFERENCE BOOKS IN SUBJECT AREAS

CHAPTER 12   ART

Art has been described as an imitation of nature and as a lie that makes us realize the truth. One work of art is a photograph of the "Mona Lisa" upon which a mustache has been drawn. Both this and the original painting are concerned with art. In a diverse subject, filled with contradictions, it is well that there are some excellent books.

Gardner, Helen. *Gardner's Art Through the Ages.* 6th ed. Revised by Horst de la Croix and Richard G. Tansey. New York: Harcourt Brace Jovanovich, 1980.

Gardner's is a one-volume survey beginning with ancient art and concluding with material on modern art. It has a glossary of technical terms, many illustrations, and bibliographies at the end of chapters. Here the reader can find an explanation for Marcel Duchamp's "Mona Lisa" with a mustache. He meant it not as a defacement but as a witty attack on those he felt had betrayed the ideals of art. As daddy of the Dada movement in art, he was dramatizing the view that art had become too precious and too expensive. Years later he signed an unaltered print of the "Mona Lisa," subtitling it "Rasée" (French for "shaved").

Encyclopedia of World Art. New York: McGraw-Hill, 1959–1968. 15 vols. Supplement vol. 1983.

This is a collection of scholarly, monographic articles and detailed bibliographies. The last part of each volume is made up of black-and-white and color plates that are especially good. The index volume is essential for small topics within larger ones. The preface states that the work covers "architecture, sculpture, and painting, and every other man-made object that regardless of its purpose or technique, enters the field of esthetic judgment because of its form or decoration." An example of this thorough treatment may be found under the heading "Table and Food." Here is a discussion of tableware and accessories both as art in their own right and as depicted in famous paintings with a list of the plate numbers for reproductions of the paintings. It includes cross-references to articles on "Ceramics" and "Silverware."

Reinach, Salomon. *Apollo.* Rev. ed. New York: Scribner, 1935.

This is an out-of-print guide, probably not found in all libraries, but it's important to know it exists. Chapters are devoted to the significant art periods to the end of the nineteenth century. It is an English translation of French lectures originally given at the Louvre, and it is illustrated. Here we are given another definition of art:

> A work of art differs in one essential characteristic from those products of human activity which supply the immediate wants of life. Let us consider a palace, a picture. The palace might be merely a very large house, and yet provide satisfactory shelter. Here, the element of art is "superadded" to that of utility. In a statue, a picture, utility is no longer apparent. The element of art is isolated.

Janson, Horst Woldemar, and Janson, Dora Jane. *History of Art: A Survey of the Major Visual Arts from the Dawn of History to the Present Day.* New York: Abrams, 1977.

A handsomely illustrated work, which summarizes Western painting, sculpture, and architecture.

Larousse Encyclopedia of Modern Art, from 1800 to the Present Day. General ed., René Huyghe. New York: Bookthrift, 1981.

One of a series, also translated from the French, which includes *Larousse Encyclopedia of Prehistoric and Ancient Art* (1981), *Larousse Encyclopedia of Byzantine and Medieval Art* (1981), *Larousse Encyclopedia of Renaissance and Baroque Art* (1981). These books show the art of the period in relation to philosophy, literature, science, and social and economic conditions. Illustrated.

Monro, Isabel S., and Monro, Kate M. *Index to Reproductions of American Paintings* and *First Supplement.* New York, H. W. Wilson, 1948, 1964. ——— *Index to Reproductions of European Paintings.* New York: H. W. Wilson, 1956.

These indexes help locate illustrations of paintings in books and exhibition catalogs. Paintings are listed by artist, title of the painting, and subject. When known, the location of the original is given.

Phaidon Dictionary of Twentieth-Century Art. London and New York: Phaidon, 1973.

Articles are brief and useful for ready reference and identification. They describe artists, art movements, and art groups of this century in Europe, the United States, Canada, South America, Israel, and Japan.

The Official Museum Directory: United States, Canada. Washington, D.C.: American Association of Museums; Skokie, Ill.: National Register Publishing, 1971 to date. Annual.

Hudson, Kenneth, and Nicholls, Ann. *The Directory of World Museums.* 2d ed. New York: Facts on File, 1981.

These are sources offering information on and sometimes detailed descriptions of museums and special art collections.

Hamlin, Talbot Faulkner. *Architecture Through the Ages.* Rev. ed. New York: Putnam, 1953.

This illustrated work is an excellent survey of architecture from a social point of view. This history of what has been called the art of the use of space covers primitive and classical architecture and architecture into the first half of the twentieth century. Here is a sample:

592   ARCHITECTURE THROUGH THE AGES

The old tradition of integrity in structure, on which the best Greek Revival architects had so insistently based their work, was breaking down. Romanticism, with its emphasis on the effect and its comparative lack of interest in how the effect was produced, was sapping at the whole integral basis of architecture. These attractive Gothic churches were, all of them, content with lath-and-plaster vaults. In them the last connections between building methods and building form disappeared, and in their very success they did much to establish in America the disastrous separation between engineering

112. INEXPENSIVE WOODEN COUNTRY CHURCH. Richard Upjohn, architect. (*Upjohn's Rural Architecture.*)

and architecture which was to curse American building for two generations. The best of the American Gothic work remains in its simpler, its less ostentatious, monuments: the little churches in which wood was allowed frankly to be itself, as in the small frame chapels which Upjohn designed for country villages and distant mission stations; and the frank carpenter-Gothic of the picturesque high-gabled cottages which rose so bewitchingly embowered in heavy trees along many of our Eastern village streets.

Hitchcock, H. R., and others. *World Architecture.* New York: McGraw-Hill, 1963.

A one-volume work that is well illustrated—everything from a diagram of the Parthenon roof construction, pyramids, and ziggurats to Frank Lloyd Wright's Guggenheim Museum in New York and Charles Eames's Case Study House in Santa Monica.

American Art Directory. New York: R. R. Bowker. Triennial since 1952.

Originally called *American Art Annual,* this work lists museums, art organizations, university art departments, art magazines, art scholarships and fellowships, and other miscellaneous current information on art.

INDEX

Art Index: A Cumulative Author and Subject Index to a Selected List of Fine Arts Periodicals. New York: H. W. Wilson, 1933 to date. Quarterly with cumulations.

Found in larger reference libraries, this cumulative index is a sort of *Readers' Guide* to art magazines, museum bulletins, and art annuals. It includes painting, sculpture, archaeology, architecture, ceramics, and the graphic arts.

BIOGRAPHY

Though most of the works listed in this category include biographical information on artists, there are many individual biographies and biographical dictionaries covering artists, including many translations from French and Italian originals. Examples of titles covering American artists are:

Cummings, Paul. *A Dictionary of Contemporary American Artists.* 3d ed. New York: St. Martin's Press, 1977.

American Federation of Arts, Jaques Cattell Press, ed. *Who's Who in American Art.* New York: Bowker, 1982. Biennial.

Fielding, Mantle. *Dictionary of American Painters, Sculptors and Engravers.* Enl. ed. Green Farms, Conn.: Modern Books and Crafts, 1974.

Only major sources are listed here. Checking the library catalog or *Books in Print* will reveal thousands of books under the names of artists or the subject headings for the types of art. Book publishing has progressed to the point where some of the books on individual artists are themselves works of art. An example:

Taylor, Geoffrey. *The Absurd World of Charles Bragg.* New York: Abrams, 1983.

An intriguing book on the provocative art of Charles Bragg. The display of his work in this handsome book reveals his technical virtuosity as well as his satire and observation of the social scene. The gnomelike characters, in vibrant colors or etched, comment on human frailties, move, and amuse.

GUIDES TO THE STUDY OF ART

Because so much is published in the field of art and some books are themselves works of art, a bibliographic guide is very useful.

Ehresmann, Donald L. *Fine Arts: A Bibliographic Guide to Basic Reference Works, Histories, and Handbooks.* 2d ed. Littleton, Colo.: Libraries Unlimited, 1979.

This guide annotates and names major reference books in many languages. Useful for every aspect of the subject.

Chamberlin, Mary W. *Guide to Art Reference Books.* Chicago: American Library Association, 1959.

Though this is an older work and needs updating, it is a valuable guide to the study of art. It lists more than 2,000 sources from ready reference to very specialized material, arranged by subject and annotated.

COSTUME

Costume and dress are usually considered art, and books on the subject are included with art. Because they also reflect a specific era, they are sometimes included in the history section.

Davenport, Millia. *The Book of Costume.* New York: Crown, 1964.

A chronological survey from early times to the end of the American Civil War. It is profusely illustrated.

Monro, Isabel S., and Cook, Dorothy E. *Costume Index.* Supplement, ed. by I. S. Monro and K. M. Monro. New York: H. W. Wilson, 1937, 1957.

Locates plates and pictures of costumes in books and covers all historical periods and almost all nationalities and classes.

Evans, Mary. *Costume Throughout the Ages.* 3d ed. Philadelphia: Lippincott, 1950. Illustrated.

Includes historical dress as shown in early art and continues through the period of World War II. The second part of the book deals with national costumes of all countries. There are those who believe dress is pretty far out today, but it's plain compared to some other times. Here is a description of the garb of Charles II:

the king and his cavaliers clothed in short doublets, much like modern Eton jackets, displaying generously the fine linen shirt bloused about the waist; in full, be-ribboned rhingraves (a kind of breeches); in low, square-toed shoes with high red heels, and stiff ends of ribbon at the instep; with long stockings of bright silk and a jeweled ribbon garter about the right knee; and in broad-brimmed stiff hats with a profusion of feathers.

CHAPTER 13   BOOKS AND LITERATURE

The first works given below identify, list, or classify published books. The other reference works in this section deal with literature—literature here meaning writing of recognized quality that expresses ideas of permanent and universal interest.

Bibliographies are useful when a reader wants to find out about a book—the publisher, the author's name—or as an aid in the selection of a book for a specific purpose. The list below is short and general. Excluded here, the reader will be happy to learn, are books about books about books, or bibliographies of bibliographies.

United States Catalog. 4th ed. New York, H. W. Wilson, 1928. *Cumulative Book Index.* New York: H. W. Wilson, 1933 to date.

The *U.S. Catalog,* listing all books in print on January 1, 1928, is supplemented and brought up-to-date by the newer title, the *Cumulative Book Index.* Together these two sources list practically every book printed in the United States as well as books published in English in foreign countries. For books too recent to have appeared in *CBI,* current issues of the periodical *Publishers Weekly* can be consulted.

Publishers' Trade List Annual. New York: R. R. Bowker, 1873 to date. Annual.

PTLA is a collection of current lists of American and a few Canadian trade publishers, including some university presses, and scientific and learned societies. It does not include all publishers.

Books in Print. New York: R. R. Bowker, 1948 to date. Annual with supplements.

BIP lists books still in print and available from American publishers, based on the above *PTLA* and augmented by additional sources of new titles.

Subject Guide to Books in Print. New York: R. R. Bowker, 1957 to date. Annual with supplements.

A companion volume to *Books in Print*, this lists the titles by subject. It does not include poetry, fiction, or drama.

Forthcoming Books. New York: R. R. Bowker, 1966 to date. Bimonthly.

This work lists books to be published in the succeeding five months by trade publishers. There is an author and title list here and a companion bimonthly *Subject Guide to Forthcoming Books.* Some of these titles announced for publication are, in fact, never published.

Paperbound Books in Print. New York: R. R. Bowker, 1955 to date. Semiannual.

A work that lists, by author, title, and subject, in-print paperbacks chiefly from U.S. publishers.

There are versions of *Books in Print* for several other countries such as Great Britain, Germany, and France. There are also national bibliographies for many countries, such as our Library of Congress's *National Union Catalog*, which lists, in hundreds of volumes, titles owned by the Library of Congress and titles reported to the Library of Congress by other American libraries.

GENERAL LITERATURE

These are especially interesting reference sources because they're filled with information that reflects not only literary history but also the history of civilization. Besides helping locate and evaluate books and authors, these sources will explain allusions in literature, poetry, and lively conversation. Such references are to characters, places, or events and bring, in a few words, instant recognition and understanding. To be called a Scrooge is immediately comprehensible to any reader of "A Christmas Carol" because Dickens took many pages and great talent to create him.

Benet, William Rose. *The Reader's Encyclopedia.* 2d ed. New York: Crowell, 1965.

This one-volume work contains (in dictionary arrangement) an amazing amount of information on books, literary characters and terms, and authors. If you're called a Babbitt or a Yahoo, a quick check here will explain the term. Also included are references in the fields of art, music, and mythology. A glance down a page indicates the variety. There are entries on:

The Little Foxes, a play
Little John, the Robin Hood character
"Little Lord Fauntleroy," a children's story
Little magazines, a discussion of them
"Little Orphan Annie," the poem, then comic strip

There are two excellent companion books: *The Reader's Encyclopedia of American Literature* (New York: Crowell, 1962) and *The Reader's Encyclopedia of Shakespeare* (New York: Crowell, 1966). See full annotation under Theater, page 176.

Cambridge History of English Literature. Cambridge: University Press, 1907–1932. 15 vols.

This set is a most authoritative, important general history of literature, covering the subject from the earliest times to the end of the nineteenth century. Written by specialists, it is in chapter form and indexed. A companion set is *The Cambridge History of American Literature* (New York: Putnam, 1917–1921. 3 vols.)

Harvey, Sir Paul. *The Oxford Companion to English Literature.* 4th ed. New York: Oxford University Press, 1967.

———. *The Oxford Companion to Classical Literature.* Oxford: Clarendon Press, 1937.

Hart, James D. *The Oxford Companion to American Literature*, 4th ed. New York: Oxford University Press, 1965.

The *Oxford Companions* are one-volume works, and all follow the general format of a dictionary in their alphabetical arrangement. They are reliable and thorough and often include related articles such as one on censorship in the *Companion to English Literature*. In the back of the *Companion to American Literature* is a chronological index showing literary history and social history side by side. Thus a reader can see at a glance that Ernest Hemingway's *Farewell to Arms* and Thomas Wolfe's *Look Homeward, Angel* appeared in 1929, when the stock market collapsed and the Depression began.

The *Cambridge Histories* and the *Oxford Companions* are often confused. On page 87 are examples of how John Donne is treated in a chapter in one volume of a set in the *Cambridge History* and in a brief dictionary entry in the *Oxford Companion:*

CHAPTER XI

JOHN DONNE

FROM the time of Wyatt, Surrey and their contemporaries of the court of Henry VIII, English lyrical and amatory poetry flowed continuously in the Petrarchian channel. The tradition which these 'novices newly crept out of the schools of Dante, Ariosto and Petrarch' brought from Italy, after languishing for some years, was revived and reinvigorated by the influence of Ronsard and Desportes. Spenser in *The Shepheards Calender*, Watson with his pedantic ΕΚΑΤΟΜΠΑΘΙΑ and Sidney with the gallant and passionate sonnets to Stella, led the way ; and, thereafter, till the publication of Davison's *Poetical Rapsody*, in 1602, and, subsequently, in the work of such continuers of an older tradition as Drummond, the poets, in sonnet sequence or pastoral eclogue and lyric, told the same tale, set to the same tune. Of the joy of love, the deep contentment of mutual passion, they have little to say (except in some of the finest of Shakespeare's sonnets to his unknown friend), but much of its pains and sorrows—the sorrow of absence, the pain of rejection, the incomparable beauty of the lady and her unwavering cruelty. And they say it in a series of constantly recurring images : of rain and wind, of fire and ice, of storm and warfare ; comparisons

> With sun and moon, with earth and sea's rich gems,
> With April's first born flowers and all things rare,
> That heaven's air in this huge rondure hems;

allusions to Venus and Cupid, Cynthia and Apollo, Diana and Actaeon ; Alexander weeping that he had no more worlds to conquer, Caesar shedding tears over the head of Pompey ; abstractions, such as Love and Fortune, Beauty and Disdain ; monsters, like the Phoenix and the Basilisk. Here and there lingers a trace of the metaphysical strain which, taking its rise in the poetry of the troubadours, had been most fully elaborated by Guinicelli and

DONNE, JOHN (1571 or 1572–1631), the son of a London ironmonger and of a daughter of J. Heywood (q.v.) the author, was educated both at Oxford and Cambridge, and was entered at Lincoln's Inn. He was in the early part of his life a Roman Catholic. He was secretary to Sir T. Egerton, keeper of the great seal from 1598 to 1602, but alienated his favour by a secret marriage with Anne More, niece of the lord keeper's wife. He sailed in the two expeditions of Essex, to Cadiz and to the Islands, in 1596 and 1597, an episode of which we have a reflection in his early poems 'The Storm' and 'The Calm'. He took Anglican orders in 1615 and preached sermons which rank among the best of the 17th cent. From 1621 to his death he was dean of St. Paul's and frequently preached before Charles I.

In verse he wrote satires, epistles, elegies, and miscellaneous poems, distinguished by wit, profundity of thought and erudition, passion, and subtlety, coupled with a certain roughness of form ('I sing not Syren-like to tempt; for I am harsh'). He was the greatest of the writers of 'metaphysical' poetry, in which passion is interwoven with reasoning. Among his more important poems is the satirical 'Progresse of the Soule', begun in 1601, in which, adopting the doctrine of metempsychosis, he traces the migration of the soul of Eve's apple through the bodies of various heretics. But he left the work uncompleted. His best-known poems are some of the miscellaneous ones, 'The Ecstasie', 'Hymn to God the Father', the sonnet to Death ('Death, be not proud'), 'Go and catch a falling star', etc. They include also a fine funeral elegy (in 'Anniversaries') on the death of Elizabeth Drury, and an 'Epithalamium' on the marriage of the Count Palatine and the Princess Elizabeth, 1613. Thomas Carew described him as

> a king who ruled as he thought fit
> The universal monarchy of wit,

and Ben Jonson wrote of him that he was 'the first poet in some things'.

Imperfect collections of his poems appeared in 1633–49, and 'Letters' by him in 1651. His poems were edited by Dr. Grosart in 1872–3, by C. E. Norton in 1895, by E. K. Chambers in 1896, and by H. J. C. Grierson (Oxford English Texts, 1912; Oxford Poets, 1929), the standard edition. A biography of Donne was written by Izaak Walton, published in 1640, another by E. Gosse in 1899. His name is usually pronounced and was frequently spelt 'Dunne'.

Spiller, Robert E., and others, eds. *Literary History of the United States.* 4th ed. New York: Macmillan, 1974. 2 vols.

The complete history is presented from Colonial times to the present. Influences that shaped authors and their works are discussed in chapters written by experts. Volume II is a fine bibliography to accompany the history. Much insight is given into the writer's works in the context of the age in which he or she lived. Some comments on Stephen Crane's *Red Badge of Courage* are:

> In The Red Badge of Courage Crane marks his artistic advance by moving easily from the description of the countryside, the advance and retreat of armies, the din of battle, and the color of the sky to the alternating hopes and fears of his boy soldier. . . . Crane was far in advance of the psychological knowledge of his contemporaries. . . . Here is a naturalistic view of heroism unknown to the war romances of the time . . .

And on Nathaniel Hawthorne:

> Soon after Hawthorne's birth in 1804, circumstances intensified his innate Puritan characteristics: his analysis of the mind, his somber outlook on living, his tendency to withdraw from his fellows. Yet if, from the first, in the quiet household of his widowed mother at Salem, during a period of lameness which kept him out of sports, or throughout summers in remote Raymond, Maine, he became increasingly introspective, he had few personal problems of mind or spirit.

Magill, Frank Northen. *Cyclopedia of Literary Characters.* New York: Harper & Row, 1963.

This carries brief descriptions of the principal characters of some 1,300 novels and dramas of world literature, arranged by title with a character index (see page 89).

Fleischmann, Wolfgang B., ed. *Encyclopedia of World Literature in the 20th Century.* New York: Ungar, 1967. 3 vols. Supplement and index edited by Frederick Ungar and Lina Mainiero, vol. 4, 1975.

Based on a German work, this encyclopedia includes individual writers, literary movements, genres, and survey articles on national literatures.

Buchanan-Brown, J., general ed. *Cassell's Encyclopaedia of World Literature.* Rev. and enl. London: Cassell, 1973. 3 vols.

The first volume contains histories of national literatures and general

THE MEMBER OF THE WEDDING

Author: Carson McCullers (1917-   )
Time of action: 1945
First published: 1946

PRINCIPAL CHARACTERS

Frances (Frankie) Addams, a twelve-year-old girl. Jealous because she is rejected by other girls and boys in the community, she calls them names, flies into sudden rages against Berenice and John Henry, and bursts into tears of which she is ashamed. She worries over her tall, gawky frame and her big feet. She dreams romantically and excitedly of the adventures she will have with Jarvis and Janice when she accompanies them on their wedding trip, and she fights frantically when she is prevented from going. As the story ends, Frankie appears to be over the worst of her adolescence—she will be Frances from now on.

John Henry West, her six-year-old cousin, a frail child who dies of meningitis. He is Frankie's friend and often her confidant, though he has little understanding of much which she tells him.

Berenice Sadie Brown, the colored cook in the Addams household. She is black, short, and broad-shouldered, and her left eye is bright blue glass. She offers kind, motherly comfort, sharp practical advice and criticism, and affectionate understanding to troubled Frankie and little John Henry. Frankie is unaware that Berenice's pity for the motherless, confused, and unhappy girl has kept her from marrying her suitor, T. T. Williams.

Royal Quincy Addams, Frankie's father, a jeweler, kind to his daughter but too busy with his work to pay much attention to her.

Jarvis, Frankie's brother, an army corporal, a handsome blond.

Janice Evans, the fiancée of Jarvis.

Honey Camden Brown, Berenice's light-skinned, mentally weak foster brother who is jailed for robbing a store while drug-crazed.

A Soldier. He attempts to seduce Frankie but fails.

T. T. Williams, Berenice's middle-aged beau, owner of a colored restaurant.

Aunt Pet and
Uncle Eustace, John Henry's parents.

Evelyn Owen, Frankie's friend who moves to Florida.

Big Mama, an old Negro palm reader.

Mary Littlejohn, Frankie's best, real friend as she enters her fourteenth year.

Barney MacKean, a boy with whom Frankie once committed a "queer sin" and whom she hates.

Uncle Charles, John Henry's great-uncle, a very old man who dies the day before the wedding.

Officer Wylie, a policeman who catches Frankie when she tries to run away.

articles on literary movements, schools, and terms. Volumes two and three contain biographical sketches and some literary works.

Altick, Richard Daniel, and Wright, Andrew. *Selective Bibliography for the Study of English and American Literature.* 6th ed. New York: Macmillan, 1979.

A very useful and respected compilation that intends to provide students of English and American literature with "a reasonably authoritative guide to research materials." There is a glossary of terms and an index.

Magill, Frank N. *Masterplots.* Rev. ed. Englewood Cliffs, N.J.: Salem, 1976. 12 vols.

There are various editions of the basic set and, over the years, there have been changes in format, publishers, and title (*Masterpieces of World Literature in Digest Form* was the former title). Summaries and descriptions of famous books run two or more pages and give details of setting and characters. References to further critical evaluations of a book are listed. The set covers 2,000 basic titles, emphasizing the classics, and includes such books as *Alice in Wonderland, Silas Marner,* and *A Farewell to Arms.*

Logasa, Hannah. *Historical Fiction: Guide for Junior and Senior High Schools, and Colleges, Also for General Reader.* 9th rev. and enl. ed. Brooklawn, N.J.: McKinley, 1968.

Arranged according to periods of history and places (medieval and modern Europe, Latin America, United States) this source lists and briefly annotates historical fiction. It is useful for finding works on certain historical subjects, since fiction titles alone often do not reveal the subject. A typical entry is:

1809–1868 (period covered in the story)
Allen, M. P. *Silver Fox.* McKay, 1951 (author, title, publisher)
Kit Carson and frontier life (subject of story)

Logasa has also done the same thing for nonfiction in *Historical Non-Fiction* (Brooklawn, N.J.: McKinley, 1964).
The works by Logasa are updated by:
Irwin, Leonard B. *A Guide to Historical Fiction.* Brooklawn, N.J.: McKinley, 1971.

Irwin, Leonard B. *A Guide to Historical Reading: Non-Fiction.* Brooklawn, N.J.: McKinley, 1970.

CRITICISM

Criticism is a much maligned occupation. The word has a negative ring. Its purpose, however, is to judge and evaluate. Judgment is often favorable; evaluation is often positive. There is a false impression that criticism is easy. To a conscientious critic, it is not. The best critics will evaluate the successes and the failures of an author's entire output and compare him with writers of similar stature. Naturally no one always agrees with critics, but their opinions often lead the reader to new insights.

Book Review Digest. New York: Wilson, 1905 to date. Monthly. Annual cumulations.

Selected reviews from general magazines are given in digest form in this source. Included are both pro and con reviews, exact citations to the original review, and the number of words of the original review. Main entry is by author of the book reviewed, and there is a title and subject index. This sample from *Book Review Digest* is a good example.

> WEST, ANTHONY. Heritage. 276p pa $4.95 1984 Washing-
> ton Sq. Press
>   ISBN 0-671-50272-7 (pa)
>
> This novel was first published in 1955 (BRD 1955).
> It now appears with a new introduction by the author.
>
> ————
>
> "The son of H.G. Wells and Rebecca West, Anthony
> West was born out of wedlock in 1914, and in 1928
> was formally adopted by his mother, a move which, West
> feels, deprived him of his paternal 'pedigree.'. . . Naomi
> Savage, the egotistical actress who is the mother of the
> boy in [this novel], is a convincing fictional character:
> charming, self-willed, eager to shine, and always, always
> acting, on stage and off. Richard, the youthful narrator,
> loves his mother, but is disappointed by her, time after
> time. It is an affecting, rather wise novel about parent-child
> relationships. No one who has not shared Mr. West's life
> can tell him how he ought to feel about his own experiences.
> But the outpouring of raw anger in the new introduction
> is in somber contrast to the self-discipline of the novelist
> who transformed his unhappiness into a polished and
> stimulating work of art some 35 years ago."
>   *Christ Sci Monit* p26 My 17 '84. Merle Rubin (350w)
>
> *N Y Times Book Rev* p7 My 6 '84. John Gross (900w)

Book Review Index. Detroit: Gale Research, 1965 to date.

This set is more inclusive than the above work but does not offer digests of the reviews. It indexes all reviews in about 300 English-language periodicals and gives bibliographic data: author, title, name of reviewer if known, and exact citation to reviews.

Magill, Frank N. *Magill's Bibliography of Literary Criticism: Selected Sources for the Study of More Than 2,500 Outstanding Works of Western Literature.* Englewood Cliffs, N.J.: Salem, 1979. 4 vols.

This is a good source for literary criticism. Arranged first by literary author and then by individual work, it refers the reader to other sources for the criticism and is quite comprehensive.

Moulton, Charles Wells. *Library of Literary Criticism of English and American Authors.* Buffalo, N.Y.: Moulton Pub. Co., 1901–1905. 8 vols.

This set offers comments and criticism by and about important English and American authors. It includes brief biographical data, followed by personal views of the writer and evaluation of individual works and the general body of writing. There is an index to critics. This unusual work allows the reader to discover, for example, what Thomas Carlyle thought of Robert Burns. Robert Louis Stevenson wrote the following about Walt Whitman:

> . . . Whitman's *Leaves of Grass,* a book of singular service, a book which tumbled the world upside down for me, blew into space a thousand cobwebs of genteel and ethical illusions . . . only a book for those who have the gift of reading.

An extension of this set into the twentieth century with American authors is Dorothy Nyren's *A Library of Literary Criticism: Modern American Literature* (New York: Ungar, 1964. Supplement, 1976).

The New York Times Book Reviews.

The index to *The New York Times* includes book reviews that have appeared in the daily paper and the Sunday *Book Review* section. They are found under the collective heading "Book Reviews" and are listed by author for works by a single author and by title for all other works (anthologies, collaborations, etc.). Also, review citations have been brought together in a separately published collection:

The New York Times Book Review Index, 1896–1970. New York: The New York Times and Arno Press, 1973. 5 vols.

INDEXES

Essay and General Literature Index. New York: Wilson, 1934 to date. Semiannual. Five-year cumulations.

One of the few sources that indexes *parts* of books, this work indexes essays and articles in the English language appearing in collections. The emphasis here is on the humanities, especially on literary criticism.

MLA International Bibliography of Books and Articles on the Modern Languages and Literatures. Chicago: Modern Language Association, 1921 to date. Annual.

An excellent source, arranged by form and national literatures, this work tells readers where to find critical material about authors, linguistics, literature, and so on. Under the national literatures are subdivisions for literary periods, and the names of authors appear in boldface type to facilitate searching.

Arts & Humanities Citation Index. Philadelphia: Institute for Scientific Information, 1978 to date. Published issues covering Jan./Apr. and May/Aug. and an annual cumulation covering Jan./Dec.

This is a multidisciplinary index to journals in the arts and humanities, indexing hundreds of journals in literature, fine arts, drama, poetry, dance, etc.

BIOGRAPHY

In addition to the author information in some of these general sources, the Biography chapter in this guide (page 38) names specific reference books of literary biography.

See also Poetry, page 145.

CHAPTER 14   *BUSINESS, ECONOMICS, AND STATISTICS*

"My own business always bores me to death; I prefer other people's." So said Oscar Wilde. Whether getting down to your own or someone else's business, there are many good reference sources.

There are, in fact, so many sources, and the fields are so complex, that it is best to use a study guide for any extensive search. This chapter will begin with guides and then name some general useful sources.

GUIDES

Wasserman, Paul, Georgi, Charlotte, and Woy, James, eds. *Encyclopedia of Business Information Sources.* 5th ed. Detroit: Gale Research, 1983.

This is an excellent and very comprehensive reference work. The subtitle describes it as "a detailed listing of primary subjects of interest to managerial personnel with a record of sourcebooks, periodicals, organizations, directories, handbooks, bibliographies, on-line data bases and other sources of information on each topic."

Daniells, Lorna M. *Business Information Sources.* Berkeley, Calif.: University of California Press, 1976.

Another excellent work containing chapters on aspects of business (companies, management, marketing, economic trends, investments, etc.) and statistics.

Brownstone, David M., and Carruth, Gordon. *Where to Find Business Information.* New York: Wiley, 1979.

Very helpful information under major and current issues like contracts, affirmative action, the aged and aging, advertising agencies.

GENERAL WORKS

McGraw-Hill Dictionary of Modern Economics. 2d ed. New York: McGraw-Hill, 1973.

This dictionary of terms and organizations includes bibliographies; historical information; and many tables, charts, and diagrams that supplement the text. It lists government and private agencies and non-profit associations concerned with economics and marketing.

Nemmers, Erwin Esser. *Dictionary of Economics and Business.* 4th ed. Totowa, N.J.: Littlefield, Adams, 1978.

Presents brief explanations for more than 5,000 abbreviations, terms, phrases.

Encyclopedia of American Economic History: Studies of the Principal Movements and Ideas. New York: Scribners, 1980. 3 vols.

Five main subject sections contain signed articles by prominent scholars. Most articles have extensive bibliographies.

Editor & Publisher Market Guide. New York: Editor & Publisher, 1924 to date. Annual.

Arranged by state and city, this book gives information under each on population, trade, banks, principal industries, etc. Each state also has summary information and a map. (See the sample entry on page 96.)

INDEX

Business Periodicals Index. New York: H. W. Wilson, 1958 to date. Monthly except August with annual cumulations.

A *Readers' Guide* type of index (see Newspapers and Magazines, page 58) to magazine articles in the field of business.

DIRECTORIES

The Directory of Directories: An Annotated Guide to Business and Industrial Directories, Professional and Scientific Rosters, and Other Lists and Guides of All Kinds. Detroit: Gale Research, 1983.

II-134 Kansas

KANSAS CITY

1 - LOCATION: Wyandotte County (In Kansas City PMSA), E&P Map D-2. County Seat. In NE corner of state. Varied industry. 508 mi. from Chicago; 492 mi. from Indianapolis. On U.S. Hwys. 24, 40, 50, 56, 69, 73, 169; I-70; State Hwys. 5, 35, 29, 435, 10, 32, 58, 132.

2 - TRANSPORTATION: Railroads-AT&SF; CB&Q; CGW; CM&StP; KC Southern; MKT; MP; CRI&P; Frisco; UP; Wabash; GM&P; K.C. Terminal; Norfolk & Western.
Motor Freight Carriers-204 Common Carriers.
Intercity Bus Lines-Greyhound; Trailways; ATA.
Airlines-TWA; Delta; United; Continental; Ozark; Central; Frontier; Midwest; Northwest Orient.

3 - POPULATION:
City 80 Cen. 161,148; Loc. Est. 162,302
County 80 Cen. 172,335; Loc. Est. 173,569
PMSA 80 Cen. 519,031; Loc. Est. 532,711
Demographic Information available from Newspaper. See paragraph 14.

4 - HOUSEHOLDS:
City 80 Cen. 59,655; Loc. Est. 62,911
County 80 Cen. 63,392; Loc. Est. 66,846
PMSA 80 Cen. 184,920; Loc. Est. 198,631

5 - BANKS	**NUMBER**	**DEPOSITS**
Commercial	21	$641,151,000
Savings & Loan	6	$334,273,000

6 - PASSENGER AUTOS: County 87,136

7 - ELECTRIC METERS: Residence 54,924

8 - GAS METERS: Residence 44,885

9 - PRINCIPAL INDUSTRIES: Industry, Number of Wage Earners (Av. Wkly. Wage)-Food Processing 3,400 ($127); Glass, Clay, Stone 4,200 ($183); Equipment Mfg. 15,750 ($131); Chemical 5,400 ($158); Steel Fabricating 1,650 ($122).
Principal Industrial Pay Days-Thu., Fri.

10 - CLIMATE: Min. & Max. Temp.-Spring 45-64; Summer 68-87; Fall 48-67; Winter 10-40. First killing frost, Oct. 2. Last killing frost, Apr. 20.

11 - TAP WATER: Neutral, hard; not fluoridated.

12 - RETAILING: Principal Shopping Center-Indian Springs 87 stores.
Neighborhood Shopping Centers-6 blocks at 17th to 22nd on Quindaro Blvd.; 4 on 5th to 8th on Kansas Ave.; 3 on 6th on Central Ave.; 3 on 9th to 11th on Central Ave.; 6 on 14th to 19th on Central Ave.; 10 on 25th to 34th on Strong Ave.; 3 on 8th to 10th on Southwest Blvd.; 1 on South 34th from Gibbs to Junction Roads; 3 on Brown Ave. from 27th to 30th; 3 on 18th from Armstrong to Nebraska; 2 on Leavenworth Road from 50th to 52nd; Sunset Plaza, 6000 Leavenworth Rd. 22 shops; Wyandotte Plaza, 78th & State 55 stores; Tower Plaza, 38th & State 18 stores; Indian Springs, 4800 State Ave. 60 shops.
Principal Shopping Days-Fri., Sat., Mon.
Stores Open Evenings-Mon., Fri.

13 - RETAIL OUTLETS: Department Stores-Macy's; Montgomery Ward; JCPenney; Sears.
Discount Stores-Venture; K mart; TG&Y.
Variety Stores-Ben Franklin.
Chain Drug Stores-Walgreen; De Goler's 2; ECO Discount 2; Treasury; Skagg's 2; Revco 3.
Chain Supermarkets-Milgram's 6; A&P 5; Thriftway 5; Ball's 5; Lipari's 2; Safeway 4; Foodbarn 2; Sav Mart 2; C. Balls 2; Price Chopper; Aldi's.
Other Chain Stores-Auto: Western Auto, P.N. Hirsch, Firestone; Furniture: Falconers, ABC, Economy, L.A., Singer; Paints: Rickeys, Cook, Great Western, Sherwin-Williams; Shoes: Baker's, McNichols, Robinson; Jewelry: Kreigles, Helzberg, Winklers; Others: Gateway Sporting Goods, Singer Co.

14 - NEWSPAPERS: KANSAN (e-mon to fri; S) 22,468; sworn Sept. 13, 1982.
Local Contact for Advertising and Merchandising Data: Joie Mellenbruch, Adv, Dir, KANSAN, 901 N. Eigth St., Kansas City, KS 66101; Tel. (913) 371-4300.
National Representative: Landon Associates.

Directory of Internships, Work Experience Programs, and On-the-Job Training Opportunities. Thousand Oaks, Calif.: Ready Reference Press, 1976.

Standard & Poor's Register of Corporations, Directors and Executives, United States and Canada. New York: Standard & Poor's Corp., 1928 to date. Annual.

Thomas Register of American Manufacturers. New York: Thomas Publishing, 1906 to date. Annual. 16 vols.

Wasserman, Paul, and McLean, Janice, eds. *Consultants and Consulting Organizations Directory.* 5th ed. Detroit: Gale Research, 1982.

World Wide Chamber of Commerce Directory. Loveland, Colo.: Johnson Publishing, 1965 to date. Annual.

STATISTICS

Pick a number, any number. Assign a meaning to it, and it becomes a statistic. The world today is statistics-happy, probably because of improved and accurate methods of collecting and interpreting numerical information. In addition to the almanacs discussed in an earlier chapter and the general business sources described above, the following are outstanding statistical sources:

U.S. Department of Commerce, Bureau of the Census. *Statistical Abstract of the United States,* Washington, D.C.: Government Printing Office, 1879 to date. Annual.

This single volume, issued every year, gives summary figures on the industrial, social, political, and economic organization of the United States. It serves not only as a source but also as a guide to other sources since the issuing agencies are given for all tables and charts. *Statistical Abstract* deals with the current years, *Historical Statistics,* listed below, deals with the past. But today there are many more statistics gathered than in the past. The current abstract even has figures on cultural activities (more people attend museums than symphonies) and sports and recreation (more people go bowling than play golf).

U.S. Department of Commerce, Bureau of the Census. *Historical Statistics of the United States: Colonial Times to 1970.* Bicentennial ed. Washington, D.C.: Government Printing Office, 1975.

This source covers the same general areas as *Statistical Abstract,* but it summarizes and illustrates historical periods. The reader can clearly see the trends in population, transportation, agriculture, and employment. (The number of blacksmiths has been drastically reduced since 1900, and the price of sweet potatoes has risen.)

American Statistics Index. Washington, D.C.: Congressional Information Service, 1973 to date. Annual with monthly supplements.

As its subtitle indicates, this is a comprehensive guide and index to the statistical publications of the U.S. government.

United Nations, Statistical Office. *Demographic Yearbook; Annuaire Demographique*. New York: United Nations, 1949 to date.

A yearbook with statistics for the world's countries and territories on population trends, marriages, births, deaths, and life expectancy.

United Nations, Statistical Office. *Statistical Yearbook; Annuaire Statistique*. New York: United Nations, 1948 to date. Annual.

World summary statistics on trade, population, consumption, agriculture, etc.

Wasserman, Paul, and Bernero, Jacqueline. *Statistics Sources*. 7th ed. Detroit: Gale Research, 1982.

An excellent subject guide to data on industrial, business, social, educational, and other topics.

Commodity Year Book. New York: Commodity Research Bureau, 1939 to date. Annual.

Statistical data and historical information on more than 100 basic commodities—copper, cotton, gold, hogs, wheat, etc.

U.S. GOVERNMENT INFORMATION

In addition to some of the government titles already named, many government departments publish statistics important to world business and economics. The U.S. Census Bureau publishes much information based on the census, such as the *County and City Data Book*. It also publishes the *Survey of Current Business*, which includes general business indicators, domestic trade, finance, transportation, and so on. The U.S. Department of Labor's Bureau of Labor Statistics issues many works of interest to business, such as the *Monthly Labor Review*. This material is located through the guides to business research and the above-mentioned *American Statistics Index*.

CHAPTER 15   *CUSTOMS AND HOLIDAYS*

In case the Latin proverb is right about custom being a tyrant, it is worth knowing why we celebrate and what habits rule us.

Gregory, Ruth W. *Anniversaries and Holidays.* 4th ed. Chicago: American Library Association, 1983.

This book identifies holidays around the world. In three parts, it lists and describes fixed holidays and movable feasts, and names books relating to anniversaries and holidays.

Chambers, Robert. *Book of Days.* Detroit: Gale Research, 1967. 2 vols. Reprint of 1862 edition.

An old and charming set best described by its subtitle—*A Miscellany of Popular Antiquities in Connection With the Calendar, Including Anecdote, Biography and History, Curiosities of Literature, and Oddities of Human Life and Character.* Under the date of January 28, for example, is a long, fascinating piece on "Court Fools and Jesters," which includes the following:

> It [the custom of keeping professional fools and jesters in palaces] was founded upon, or at least was in strict accordance with, a physiological principle which may be expressed under this formula—The Utility of Laughter. Laughter is favourable to digestion, for by it the organs concerned in digestion get exercise, the exercise necessary for the process. And, accordingly, we usually find an ample meal more easily disposed of where merriment is going on, than a light one which has been taken in solitude, and under a sombre state of feeling.

It may be that this is not exactly a medically sound claim, but it is an interesting one.

Walsh, William Shepart. *Curiosities of Popular Customs.* Detroit: Gale Research, 1966. Reprint of 1898 edition.

Describes the customs of nations and discusses such items as the Blarney stone, lamprey pie at Christmas, Leap Year, and May Day.

Hatch, Jane M. *The American Book of Days.* 3d ed. New York: H. W. Wilson, 1978.

A calendar of religious and historical celebrations which includes birthdays of famous Americans and local American festivals. The book not only tells about such days as Easter and Washington's Birthday but also discusses Cherokee Strip Day in Oklahoma, Daniel Boone Day in Kentucky, and the anniversary of the Blizzard of 1888.

Chase, William D., and Chase, Helen M. *Chase's Annual Events.* Chicago, Ill.: Contemporary Books, Inc. Annual.

This is a slender paperback calendar, issued annually, and often kept in library pamphlet files, so ask for it if you don't find it in the card catalog. It includes National Library Week, Human Rights Week, and some strange local and often commercial events like Biscuit & Muffin Month, Dear Dance Day, and National Mimicry Week. Here's a sample:

May ★ ★ Chase's Annual Events ★ ★ 1984

COPYRIGHT 1983 BY WILLIAM D. CHASE and HELEN M. CHASE

Maye.

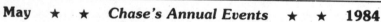

MAY 1 — TUESDAY

122nd Day — Remaining, 244

ADDISON, JOSEPH: BIRTHDAY. May 1. English essayist born Milston, Wiltshire, England on May 1, 1672. Died London, June 17, 1719.

AMERICAN BIKE MONTH. May 1-31. Purpose: To highlight the many pleasures of bicycling by promoting and encouraging local activities & events involving cycling. Sponsor: American Bike Month Committee, 1055 Thomas Jefferson St, NW, #316, Washington, DC 20007.

AMERICA'S LOVE RUN. May 1-31. Purpose: Pledges for each mile run during May with proceeds going to Muscular Dystrophy Assn. Sponsor: Muscular Dystrophy Assn, 810 Seventh Ave, New York, NY 10019.

BELGIUM: PLAY OF ST. EVERMAAR. May 1. Annual performance (for over a thousand years) by the village inhabitants of a "real mystery" play, in its original form.

CHRISTMAS IN MAY. May 1-31. Purpose: To stimulate peoples of the world to visit a handicapped child in their local hospitals or institutions and to take along a gift and some love. Sponsor: Turtles Internatl, Box 96, Westchester, IL 60153.

CORRECT POSTURE MONTH. May 1-31. Purpose: A period of time during which emphasis is placed on correct posture concepts. Sponsor: American Chiropractic Assn, Dept of Communications, 1916 Wilson Blvd, Arlington, VA 22201.

DENMARK: TIVOLI GARDENS SEASON. May 1-Sept 15. Copenhagen, Denmark. World famous for its variety of entertainment, symphony concerts, pantomime and ballet. Beautiful flower arrangements and excellent restaurants.

ENGLAND: FESTIVAL OF ARCHITECTURE. May 1-Dec 31. Events throughout Britain celebrate 150th anniversary of the founding of the Royal Institute of British Architects. Info from: Royal Institute of British Architects, 66 Portland Pl, London WIN 4AD, England.

FESTIVAL OF THE HARE. May 1. Celebrates the official opening of the turtle thoroughbred racing season by honoring the trained exercise rabbits on a job well done in conditioning the mock thoroughbreds for the summer races. Sponsor: Turtles Internatl, Box 96, Westchester, IL 60153.

May 1984

S	M	T	W	T	F	S
		1	2	3	4	5
6	7	8	9	10	11	12
13	14	15	16	17	18	19
20	21	22	23	24	25	26
27	28	29	30	31		

Wasserman, Paul, ed. *Festivals Sourcebook.* Detroit: Gale Research, 1977.

Described by the subtitle: *A Reference Guide to Fairs, Festivals and Celebrations in Agriculture, Antiques, the Arts, Theater and Drama, Arts and Crafts, Community, Dance, Ethnic Events, Film, Folk, Food and Drink, History, Indians, Marine, Music, Seasons, and Wildlife.*

CHAPTER 16   EDUCATION

The mind has been dubbed a muscle. The books below deal with how and where to exercise that muscle.

Lee C. Deighton, ed. *Encyclopedia of Education.* New York: Macmillan/Free Press, 1971. 10 vols.

The articles in this work, many of them lengthy, discuss the history, theory, research, and philosophy of education, with the emphasis on American education. Biographies are included.

World of Learning. London: Europa Publications, 1947 to date. Annual.

World of Learning is a reference book that names under each country, in a world list, the learned societies, libraries, museums, universities, and research institutes. In most instances the officers and faculties are given. There is an international section on world organizations, such as UNESCO.

INDEX

Education Index. New York: H. W. Wilson, 1929 to date. Monthly except July and August. Annual cumulations.

Indexes several hundred English-language journals in education and is especially useful for current information.

COLLEGE AND UNIVERSITY GUIDES

American Council on Education. *American Universities and Colleges.* 12th ed. Hawthorne, N.Y.: DeGruyter, 1983.

————. *American Junior Colleges.* 8th ed. Washington D.C.: American Council on Education, 1971.

The above two works are excellent sources of information. Arranged by state, they list colleges and universities with data on each institution's history, admission requirements, fees, degrees, staff enrollment, student aid, etc. Both also include lists of fields of study, survey articles on education, and encyclopedic information on the subject.

Hawes, Gene, and Novalis, Peter. *The New American Guide to Colleges.* Rev. ed. New York: New American Library, 1977.

Arranged by type of institution—state colleges, liberal arts colleges for men, for women, two-year colleges, U.S., overseas, etc. There is a useful "College Discovery Index" that makes it easier to find colleges that are likely to admit, for example, a C-average student, on a certain budget, in the New England area. The index is arranged by geographic region. It lists colleges according to admission policy and indicates tuition costs.

---

568   COLLEGE DISCOVERY INDEX

2. MIDDLE ATLANTIC
(N J, N Y, Pa)

Highly competitive admis; $1500 & up exp
Albany Medical C of Union U. XIII, N Y, 502
Barnard C (of Columbia U), IV, N Y, 202
Carnegie I of Technology (C of Fine Arts), IX, Pa, 444
Colgate U, III, N Y, 175
Columbia C, III, N Y, 175
Columbia U (School of Law, C of Physicians & Surgeons), p, VIII, N Y, 412
Cornell U (all private undergraduate divisions; graduate studies), VIII, N Y, 413
Dickinson C, I, Pa, 98
Franklin and Marshall C, III, Pa, 178
Hamilton C, III, N Y, 175
Haverford C, III, Pa, 179
New York U (School of Law), p, VIII, N Y, 415

Accepts all C-aver & up admis; $300–600 exp
Broome Technical Community C, a, VI, N Y, 293
Messiah C, e, x, y, I, Pa, 101
Rutgers, The State U (U C), VII, N J, 354
St Joseph's Seraphic S, m, r, XI, N Y, 469
State U of New York Agricultural and Technical C (Alfred), VI, N Y, 296
State U Agricultural and Technical C (Delhi), e, VI, N Y, 297
State U Agricultural and Technical C (Farmingdale), VI, N Y, 297
Syracuse U (State C of Forestry), VIII, N Y, 419

Cass, James, and Birnbaum, Max. *Comparative Guide to American Colleges for Students, Parents, and Councellors.* 10th ed. New York: Harper & Row, 1981.

An alphabetical listing of colleges with information on admission policies, campus life, costs, etc. There is a state index, a selectivity index (not a rating but an indication of the "hurdles a student will face in applying for admission"), and a religion index.

Patterson's American Education. Mount Prospect, Ill.: Educational Directories, 1904 to date. Annual.

This directory, published each year, lists public and private schools, colleges, universities, and special schools in two parts: (1) school systems arranged by states and then by cities; (2) directory of schools, colleges, and universities classified by specialty.

Lovejoy's College Guide. Compiled by Clarence Earle Lovejoy. 16th ed. New York: Simon & Schuster, 1983.

Offers concise information on American colleges. There is a section on costs, scholarships, admissions, etc., followed by descriptions of colleges arranged by state.

Lovejoy, Clarence Earle. *Lovejoy's Career and Vocational School Guide.* 5th ed. New York: Simon & Schuster, 1978.

Lists schools by state and also by trade in a wide variety of occupations. Job titles include nurse, beauty operator, automotive machinist, barber, baker, pilot, radio/TV repairman, sailmaker, sign writer, etc.

Hegner, Karen C., ed. *Peterson's Annual Guides to Graduate Study 1982 Edition.* Princeton, N.J.: Peterson's Guides, 1982.

Book 1: Graduate Institutions of the U.S. and Canada—An Overview. Book 2: The Humanities and Social Sciences. Book 3: Biological, Agricultural, and Health Sciences. Book 4: Physical Sciences. Book 5: Engineering and Applied Sciences.

――――. *Peterson's Annual Guide to Undergraduate Study 1983.* Princeton, N.J.: Peterson's Guides, 1983.

The Peterson annual guides are excellent sources for information on graduate schools and undergraduate study and are very up-to-date.

The College Blue Book. 19th ed. New York: Macmillan, 1983.

A respected five-volume set with various approaches to the information. Volume 1 offers Narrative Descriptions; Volume 2, Tabular Data;

Volume 3, Degrees Offered by College and Subject; Volume 4, Scholarships, Fellowships, Grants, and Loans; Volume 5, Occupational Education.

Fiske, Edward B., with Shelly G. Burtt and the Selective Guide to Colleges Staff. *Selective Guide to Colleges, 1984–85.* New York: Times Books, 1983.

This lively, impressionistic guide, compiled by the Education Editor of *The New York Times,* does not try to cover all colleges and universities but covers "275 of the best and most interesting four-year institutions in the nation." Each entry has a descriptive essay, basic statistics, and ratings.

And before deciding what to study, you might want to look at . . .

U.S. Bureau of Labor Statistics. *Occupational Outlook Handbook.* Washington, 1949 to date. Biennial.

This handbook offers employment information on major occupations. Under such occupational headings as dentists, industrial designers, bus drivers, librarians, and clergy, it gives information on the nature of the work, areas where employment is to be found, training and qualifications needed, outlook, earnings, and working conditions.

SCHOLARSHIPS, GRANTS, AND FINANCIAL AID

Take the money and learn. The following is a selected list of guides to financial aid. Most of them name sources for loans, grants, and scholarships, and some offer advice on writing a grant proposal.

Annual Register of Grant Support, 1982–83. 16th ed. Chicago: Marquis Who's Who, 1982.

Barilleaux, Claude, and Gersumky, Alexis Teitz, eds. *Foundation Grants to Individuals.* New York: Foundation Center, 1982.

Catalog of Federal Domestic Assistance, 1982. Washington, D.C.: Office of Management and Budget; for sale by Superintendent of Documents, U.S. Government Printing Office. Annual basic manual usually issued in May, and update usually issued in December.

The Catalog of Federal Education Assistance Programs, 1980. Washington, D.C.: U.S. Department of Education; U.S. Government Printing Office, irregular.

Coleman, William E. *Grants in the Humanities: A Scholar's Guide to Funding Sources.* New York: Neal-Schuman, 1980.

Directory of Research Grants, 1983. 8th ed. Phoenix: Oryx Press, 1983. Annual.

Federal Council on the Arts and Humanities. *Cultural Directory II: Federal Funds and Services for the Arts and Humanities.* Washington, D.C.: Smithsonian Institution Press, 1980.

Financial Aid for Minorities in . . . Garrett Park, Md.: Garrett Park Press, 1980. 8 vols. Covers the fields of business, education, journalism, communications, law, allied health, engineering, medicine, science.

Foundation Directory. 8th ed. New York: Foundation Center, 1981.

Foundation Grants Index. 11th ed. New York: Foundation Center, 1982. Annual.

Hodson, H. V., consultant ed. *The International Foundation Directory.* 2d ed. London: Europa Publications; distributed by Gale Research, Detroit, 1979, 1982.

Keeslar, Oreon. *Financial Aids for Higher Education Catalog.* 10th ed. Dubuque, Iowa: Wm. C. Brown, 1982.

Lerner, Craig Alan, and Turner, Roland, eds. *The Grants Register, 1983–1985.* New York: St. Martin's Press, 1982.

Mathies, M. Lorraine, ed. *Scholarships, Fellowships, Grants and Loans.* New York: Macmillan, 1982.

Millsaps, Daniel, and editors. *Washington International Arts Letter.* 5th ed. Washington, D.C.: Washington International Arts Letter, 1983.

Public Management Institute. *The Complete Grants Sourcebook for Higher Education.* Washington, D.C.: American Council on Education, 1980.

Research Staff of Public Management Institute. *Corporate 500: The Directory of Corporate Philanthropy.* San Francisco: Public Management Institute, 1980.

Schlachter, Gail. *Directory of Financial Aids for Women.* 2d ed. Santa Barbara, Calif.: ABC-Clio, 1982.

White, Virginia. *Grants for the Arts.* New York: Plenum Press, 1980.

———. *Grants: How to Find Out About Them and What to Do Next.* New York: Plenum Press, 1975.

CHAPTER 17 *GEOGRAPHY*

Travel cheaply, but still go first class—by book. In addition to the atlases described earlier (page 30), here are some important books about places.

Seltzer, Leon E., ed., with the geographical staff of Columbia University Press and with the cooperation of the American Geographical Society. *The Columbia Lippincott Gazetteer of the World.* New York: Columbia University Press, 1962. Supplement.

An outstanding and complete geographical dictionary listing alphabetically cities, towns, lakes, mountains, dams, canals, etc. with considerable relevant detail. It gives pronunciation, location, trade, brief history, natural resources, and other pertinent facts about each place. (Note that the population figures are now out of date.) Odebolt, a town in western Iowa, lists popcorn as its major product and calls itself the "popcorn center of the world." The gazetteer lists:

London, England
A London town in Arkansas
A London city in Kentucky
Two villages by that name

It then goes on to describe London Bridge.

Webster's New Geographical Dictionary. Rev. ed. Springfield, Mass.: Merriam, 1980.

Webster's pronouncing dictionary gives brief information about the world's important places. Included are proper names from biblical times and ancient Greece and Rome to the present. The work also has many full-page and smaller inset maps.

Brewer, James Gordon. *The Literature of Geography: A Guide to Its Organization and Use.* 2d ed. Hamden, Conn.: Linnet Books, 1978.

Presents hundreds of references in subject chapter arrangement, including one in this edition on cartobibliography.

Wasserman, Paul, ed. *Encyclopedia of Geographic Information Sources.* Detroit: Gale Research, 1978.

The subtitle describes this as offering a detailed listing of publications and agencies of interest to managerial personnel, with a record of source books, periodicals, guides to doing business, government and trade offices, directories, handbooks, bibliographies, and other sources of information on each location. A companion volume to *Encyclopedia of Business Information Sources.*

GUIDEBOOKS

Guidebooks are an important source of geographical information whether you're planning a trip or not.

Federal Writers Project of the Works Progress Administration. *American Guide Series.* Various publishers, 1937–1950.

This series covers each state and many principal cities and areas of the United States. Each book contains a section on the historical, ethnic, and artistic background, a section on the cities, and a section on tours through the state. Like the Baedeker guides, this series abounds in interesting details. It is also vividly written. Here's how the article on Gettysburg from the Pennsylvania guide begins:

> Gettysburg, scene of one of the Civil War's most decisive conflicts, lies between two low ridges eight miles north of the Mason-Dixon line. In plan it somewhat resembles a wagon wheel, with ten roads forming the spokes and its Center Square the hub . . .

It is important with books about places to be aware of the publication dates. If the works were published several years earlier, certain statistics, such as population, are out of date, even though the works themselves are still very useful.

Baedeker Guide Books. Leipzig: Baedeker; New York: Macmillan.

Found in larger reference centers, these are splendid volumes even though some are out of date for travel purposes. Old or new, they are extremely useful for detailed plans of cities and minute information on buildings, streets, and works of art. A 1932 guide to Paris, for example, tells how the name Louvre was probably derived from the word for wolfhound kennels that occupied the site at one time. It goes on to describe the Louvre's architectural development, once a castle, once a prison. The floor plans of the museum as well as information on the art are given. The Baedeker guides are filled with fascinating detail.

The older guidebooks are discussed here because they have definite reference value. There are, of course, literally hundreds of current guides for travel available.

PLACE-NAMES

Holt, Alfred H. *American Place Names.* New York: Crowell, 1938. Reprinted 1969.

This is a list of place-names with pronunciation amusingly given, as in these examples.

> **Helena,** Ala., Ark., Mont., Okla. Stress the "hell" in these four states. But in Ohio and Missouri "lee" gets the emphasis.
>
> **La Crosse,** Wis. Just put an *l* in front of "across."
>
> **Lac Vieux Desert** (Mich. and Wis.) According to a letter from President Ellis of the Wisconsin-Michigan Lumber Company, this is "Lac Vo Desar," rhyming with "Mac, row me far." Apparently an American variation of the French-Canadian corruption. Obviously, this does not exhaust the possibilities.

Quimby, Myron J. *Scratch Ankle, U.S.A.: American Place Names and Their Derivation.* South Brunswick, N.J.: A.S. Barnes, 1969.

A discussion of, among others, Ragtown, Texas, Waterproof, Louisiana, Whiskeytown, California, and Scratch Ankle, Alabama.

Stewart, George R. *Names on the Land.* Rev. and enl. ed. Boston: Houghton Mifflin, 1958.

A historical account of place-naming in the United States, with chapters on patterns for street names and how foreign names are used, and some chapters on individual states. There is an index.

NAMES ON THE LAND

Thus in that long period of steady development the names became more English as the strange Indian and Dutch and Swedish words were made over, but in most other ways the names became less like those of England.

>>>-->>>-->>>-->>>-->>>-->>>-->>>-->>>-->>>-->>>-->>>-->>>-->>>--✧--<<<--<<<--<<<--<<<--<<<--<<<--<<<--<<<--<<<--<<<--<<<--<<<--<<<

Chapter XIV ❰ How they took the names into the mountains

Dᴜʀɪɴɢ half a century, there were no new colonies; then in 1732, the fifth year of King George II, the last of the thirteen was merely called in its charter, without explanation: "The Colony of Georgia in America," thus taking the King's name with a Latin ending.

About this time the frontier began to reach the mountains. First of all went the hunters and Indian traders, but their namings often failed to be written down and preserved. Next went most often the surveyors, and the giving and recording of names came to be part of their profession. Their work was to determine the boundaries between colonies, or lay out the lines of grants. With both, they made maps, and wrote on them the names of streams and other easily recognizable features, such as outstanding or strangely shaped hills. By reference to these, other men could locate the surveyors' marks. Once thus written on a map, a name became involved with land-titles, and had a fair chance to survive.

CHAPTER 18   *HISTORY*

Philosopher George Santayana said: "Those who cannot remember the past are condemned to repeat it." . . . condemned in the sense that the horrors of the past are repeated. So a real sense of history is a good thing and is best developed by an "in context" approach to an event. Then a student knows not only the date the Pilgrims landed in America but how they lived, what they wore, what they believed, why they came, and what they found here. The books listed below are basic guides to the remembrance of the past.

GUIDES TO HISTORY

History is another subject so vast that guides to its study play an important role in research. The first two titles are for general history, the third is for American history, and the fourth is an excellent aid to research methods and reference sources, which is of particular help in the evaluation and interpretation of facts and the study of history.

Poulton, Helen J. *The Historian's Handbook: A Descriptive Guide to Reference Works*. Norman: University of Oklahoma Press, 1972.

American Historical Association. Howe, George Frederick, and others, eds. *Guide to Historical Literature*. New York: Macmillan, 1961.

Freidel, Frank, ed. *Harvard Guide to American History*. Rev. ed. Cambridge, Mass.: Belknap Press of Harvard University Press, 1974.

Barzun, Jacques, and Graff, Henry F. *The Modern Researcher*. 3d. ed. New York: Harcourt Brace Jovanovich, 1977.

WORLD HISTORY

Cambridge Ancient History. Cambridge: University Press; New York: Macmillan, 1923–39. 12 vols. 5 vols. Plates, maps.
Cambridge Mediaeval History. Cambridge: University Press; New York: Macmillan, 1911–36. 9 vols.
Cambridge Modern History. Cambridge: University Press; New York: Macmillan, 1902–26. 13 vols. and atlas.
A New Cambridge Modern History. Cambridge: University Press, 1975. 14 vols.

This well-known series has scholarly chapters written by experts and usually includes tables and maps. The *Cambridge Modern History* has an index volume; the others are indexed in the back of each volume. (*Cambridge Histories* on various subjects are often confused with *Oxford Companions* on various subjects. Generally, the *Cambridge* books are done in chapter form, require the use of the index for smaller topics, and are several volumes to a subject such as history, English literature, etc.; the *Oxford Companions* consist of dictionary types of entries, arranged in alphabetical order, in one volume. Examples of this difference are shown in the Books and Literature section, page 84).

Langer, William Leonard. *An Encyclopedia of World History.* 5th ed. Boston: Houghton Mifflin, 1972. 2 vols.

This book is arranged chronologically—Prehistoric Period, Ancient History, Middle Ages, etc.—and within each time period it covers geographical areas—Africa, Europe, North America, etc. It is indexed and has many maps and genealogical tables. Entries are brief and bright like this sample:

> **William IV died** (1837. June 20) and was succeeded by his youthful niece.
> **1837–1901.** **VICTORIA** (1819–1901), then eighteen. Victoria was the daughter of the duke of Kent (d. 1820) and the duchess, a princess of Saxe-Coburg (for the Hanoverian dynasty see p. 469), who had brought up Victoria in England, but surrounded her by German influences, notably that of her brother Leopold (king of the Belgians, 1831, p. 673). Victoria's education had been solid and sensible, and she brought to her heavy duties graciousness and poise rarely associated with one of her age. She was self-willed on occasion, "rebuked" her ministers, but made no serious attempt to invade their rights under the parliamentary system despite the influence of her German adviser, **Baron Christian von Stockmar,** who urged her to take a stand of greater independence.

Larned, Josephus Nelson. *New Larned History for Ready Reference, Reading, and Research.* Springfield, Mass.: Nichols, 1922–24. 12 vols.

The approach here is unusual. It is a dictionary arrangement of universal history, but it uses "the actual words of the world's best historians, biographers, and specialists." Instead of original articles, recognized authorities are quoted under each topic.

Collison, Robert, comp. *Dictionary of Dates and Anniversaries.* New York: Transatlantic Arts, 1967.

This work, with a British emphasis, has two parts. Part I is in alphabetical order by name of place, person, or event. Part II puts the same events in calendar order.

Putnam, George Palmer, and Putnam, George Haven. *Dictionary of Events: A Handbook of Universal History.* New York: Grosset, 1936.

The subtitle describes the book as a "series of chronological tables presenting, in parallel columns, a record of the noteworthy events of history from the earliest times to the present day, together with an index of subjects and genealogical tables." The tabular form is useful and looks like the six columns on pages 114 and 115.

Hayes, Carlton J. H., and others. *History of Western Civilization.* New York: Macmillan, 1962.

Outline history, from the ancient Near East to the present day, covering political, military, literary, and artistic events. Brief entries, illustrated and indexed.

Viorst, Milton. *The Great Documents of Western Civilization.* Philadelphia: Chilton, 1965.

Documents in history from the rise of Christianity to the nuclear age. Brief introductions set the scene and the text of the document follows. Includes such documents as:

Martin Luther's Ninety-five Theses
Magna Carta
Napoleon's Proclamation at Austerlitz
Churchill's Speech after Dunkirk
United Nations Charter

200   TABULAR VIEWS   1851 A.D.-

A.D.	PROGRESS OF SOCIETY, etc.	UNITED STATES.	GREAT BRITAIN
1851	Wyld's monster globe erected in London; employed 300 men nearly 30 days in fitting up the interior. The lord mayor of London, with several of the aldermen and common councilmen, the royal commissioners of the Exposition of Industry, etc., and the executive committee of the royal commissioners, leave England for France, by invitation of the prefect of the Seine.—Aug. 1. The inauguration of the railway between St. Petersburg and Moscow, in Russia, takes place Sept. 1. The town of Lagos, on the coast of Africa, destroyed by an English force, because the native chief refused to sign a treaty for the effectual suppression of the slave trade in his dominions. The chief is deposed, and another substituted in his place, Dec. 26–27.	1851. President issues a proclamation, warning all persons within the jurisdiction of the United States not to aid or engage in any expedition against the Island of Cuba, April 25. Convention of delegates from the Southern Rights Associations of South Carolina meets at Charleston, May 5; and adjourns after resolving that, "with or without co-operation, they are for a dissolution of the Union," May 8. Erie Railroad opened from New York City to Dunkirk, 439 miles, by President Fillmore, Daniel Webster, etc., May 15. Serious conflagrations in California. San Francisco alone suffers by them in May and June to the amount of $12,000,000. "Vigilance committee" at San Francisco. enforces order by summary execution.	1851. The Russell Ministry resign, Feb. 22; but afterwards resume office, the Earl of Derby not having succeeded in forming a Cabinet. Hostilities with the Burmese. 1851. "The great aggregate meeting" of Roman Catholics, from all parts of the United Kingdom, for the inauguration of the Catholic defence association, is held at Dublin, Aug. 19. The American yacht "*America*," at the regatta at Cowes, wins "The cup of all nations," Aug. 22. Kossuth arrives by English steamer from Gibraltar, at Southampton, Eng. Ovations are offered him in various parts of the country. He leaves for the United States, Nov. The submarine telegraph between Dover and Calais completed Oct. 17. Opened for public use, Nov. 13.

Deaths in 1851.

U. S.	Europe.
J. J. Audubon,	Lord Bexley
S. Olin,	Joanna
J. F. Cooper,	Baillie,
T. H. Gallaudet,	Codrington,
3. G. Morton.	Sheil,
	Lingard,
	Daguerre,
	Soult,
	Oersted,
	Jacobi,
	Turner.

Ruskin begins publication of *Stoies of Venice;* Helmholtz invents the ophthalmoscope.

Nicaragua route, between New York and San Francisco, opened, Aug. 12.

Great riot in New Orleans, growing out of the Cuban expedition Houses of Spanish residents attacked. The Spanish consul is obliged to ask protection, and is placed in the city prison for safety, Aug. 21.

Riot, with loss of life at Christiana, Pa., upon an attempt to arrest a fugitive slave, Sept. 11.

U. S. brig *Dolphin* sails on an expedition to run a line of soundings for telegraphic purposes across the Atlantic, Oct.

U. S. steam frigate *Mississippi* sent to Turkey for Kossuth, receives him on board in the Dardanelles. The French government refuses to allow Kossuth to pass through France.

A.D.	FRANCE.	AUSTRIA, PRUSSIA, etc.	THE WORLD, elsewhere.
1851	Revolution: Louis Napoleon by a *coup d'état* seizes the reins of government; dissolves the National Assembly; declares a state of siege; arrests the leaders of the opposition; constitutes an entire new ministry. The president orders the restoration of universal suffrage; an immediate election by people and army of a president to hold office for ten years, to be supported by a Council of State and two houses of Legislature. The vote of the army shows a large majority for Napoleon. Resistance to the usurpation is shown in various parts of France, but the overwhelming power of the army and a "state of siege" in 33 departments crushes all opposition. The election, under various controlling influences, results in the confirmation of Napoleon as president for ten years, by a vote of about seven out of eight millions.—Dec. 2-21.	1851. The Germanic Diet in answer to Lord Palmerston's protest against annexing the non-Germanic provinces of Austria to the Germanic Federation, says, "That no foreign interference should be allowed in a purely German question."—July 17. Marshal Radetzky, by proclamation from Monza, declares the Lombardo-Venetian kingdom to be in a state of siege, July 19. The emperor of Austria urges the minister president to take "into ripe and serious consideration the possibility of carrying out the Constitution of March 4, 1349."—Aug. 20. Louis Kossuth and 35 of his countrymen sentenced to death *in contumaciam*, at Pesth, for not appearing after citation, Sept. 22.	1851. Hawaii:—The difficulties between the Hawaiian and French governments are arranged according to the terms of a "mutual declaration," published at Honolulu, March 25. New Granada:—Congress abolishes slavery in the republic, to take effect January 1, 1852.—May 29. Italy:—An earthquake destroys Melfi, a city of 10,000 inhabitants, about 100 miles S. E. of Naples, and other towns in its vicinity. Seven shocks occurred within 24 hours. Melfi was separated by a ravine from Mount Vulture, upon which are many extinct craters. Not less than 3000 persons supposed to have perished.—July 14. Russia:—Her troops repeatedly defeated by the Circassians.—June. Nicaragua:—Gen. Munoz, ex-minister of war, deposes President Pineda, and sends him and most of his cabinet prisoners to Tigre Islands and makes Albaunaz president. The Senate assembles at Grenada, and elects Montenegro, president Aug. 4. West Indies:— Volcanic eruptions from eight craters in the mountains of Martinique, Aug. 5.

Deford, Miriam A. *Who Was When?* 3d ed. New York: H. W. Wilson, 1976.

A dictionary of contemporaries arranged in tabular form under such headings as literature, science, government, painting, so you can see at a glance the people who made history together. For example, Booker T. Washington, Alfred Dreyfus, and Lizzie Borden were born the same year (1859) that John Brown and Washington Irving died.

Flags of the World. Rev. by E. M. C. Barraclough. New York: Warne, 1982.

Revised many times, this work now has 340 flags in color and 400 text drawings in black and white. Though there is a British emphasis, the book covers all nations.

AMERICAN HISTORY

Adams, James Truslow, ed. *Dictionary of American History.* New York: Scribner, 1976. 8 vols.

Concise articles on a wide variety of subjects in American life and history. Most entries have a brief bibliography of more extensive works on the subject. "Baseball" and "Tin Pan Alley" are treated along with more serious items in U.S. history, and the work includes famous slogans and popular names of laws. (See chapter on Almanacs and Atlases, page 29, for information on *Atlas of American History.* This book can be used as a companion to the dictionary.)

Concise Dictionary of American History. New York: Scribner, 1982.

This work is a one-volume abridgment of the above-listed eight-volume *Dictionary of American History.*

Kane, Joseph Nathan. *Facts About the Presidents.* 4th ed. New York: H. W. Wilson, 1981.

A compilation of biographical and historical data in two parts. Part One has a separate chapter for each President, and Part Two draws comparisons among them along such lines as elections, age when each took office, religious affiliations, etc.

———. *Famous First Facts.* 4th ed. New York: H. W. Wilson, 1981.

A book filled with curious information on such things as the first elevator, balloon, library, and even ice cream sundae. It is arranged alphabetically by subject, and there are chronological and geographical indexes to locate events by years, days, or places.

Mirkin, Stanford M. *What Happened When.* Rev. ed. New York: I. Washburn, 1966.

A calendar of days with each event listed in chronological order by year. Emphasis is on the United States, but there are some others listed. It looks like this:

JULY 18

A.D. 64 Rome burns; Nero fiddles.

1914 The U.S. Army creates an aviation section within the Signal Corps. Six airplanes are made available for aerial training.

1932 A treaty is signed between the United States and Canada for the development of the St. Lawrence River into an ocean lane and power project. (Strong opposition to the project, however, delayed actual construction until the summer of 1954.)

1938 Douglas Corrigan, who left Floyd Bennett Field, New York, on July 17 ostensibly on a flight to California, arrives at Baldonnel Airport, Dublin. (Amused Americans immediately tagged him with the nickname of "Wrong Way Corrigan.")

1940 President Franklin D. Roosevelt is nominated unanimously for a third term by delegates to the Democratic Convention at Chicago. Henry A. Wallace of Iowa is the candidate for Vice President.

1947 President Harry Truman signs the Presidential Succession Act. Under this act, when there is no Vice President, the Speaker of the House of Representatives will succeed to the Presidency, in the case of death. Next in line of succession is the president pro tempore of the Senate, followed by the members of the Cabinet, beginning with the Secretary of State.

1951 The world heavyweight boxing championship is won by Joseph ("Jersey Joe") Walcott in Pittsburgh, Pennsylvania, as he knocks out Ezzard Charles in the seventh round.

1964 The killing of a 15-year-old Negro boy by an off-duty white policeman in New York leads to an outbreak of racial violence in the city's Negro neighborhoods, particularly the Harlem area. Despite the fact that the patrolman claims the boy had threatened him with a knife, crowds of Negroes riot in the streets and hurl rocks and bottles at scores of policemen. (After 4 days, the riots ended, with one man dead, 81 civilians and 35 policemen wounded, 112 stores and commercial establishments damaged or looted.)

Johnson, Thomas H. *The Oxford Companion to American History.* New York: Oxford University Press, 1966.

Like the *Oxford Companions* on other subjects, this is a single volume of brief entries, arranged alphabetically.

1909 *Pres.* THEODORE ROOSEVELT, WILLIAM H. TAFT

SCIENCE; INDUSTRY; ECONOMICS; EDUCATION; RELIGION; PHILOSOPHY.

SPORTS; FASHIONS; POPULAR ENTERTAINMENT; FOLKLORE; SOCIETY.

1909

Henry Ford produced 19,051 **Model T Fords.** He led the auto industry in production and sales by building only 1 model, the "universal" car, which "customers could have any color as long as it was black."

1st **notable animated cartoon** shown in America, *Gertie the Dinosaur,* consisted of 10,000 drawings by Winsor McCay, a cartoonist for the *New York American.*

Suntanned, even redfaced, **Outdoor Girl** replaced the soft, white **Gibson Girl** when women took up automobile driving. "Automobile wrinkles" were soothed by the application of raw, freshly cut cucumbers. New field was opened for hungry fashion designers: special clothes for motoring, including a long veil to keep a lady's hat in place.

Carruth, Gorton, ed. *The Encyclopedia of American Facts and Dates.* 7th ed. New York: Crowell, 1979.

This source does for American History what the Putnams' dictionary does for universal history. It is arranged chronologically in subject columns. The above illustrates how it looks.

Morris, Richard B., and Morris, Jeffrey B. *The Encyclopedia of American History.* 6th ed. New York: Harper, 1981.

Has a basic chronology of the United States by year, a topical chronology (under topics like "Population," "Laws," "Religion," etc.), and a biographical section.

Boatner, Mark M. *Civil War Dictionary.* New York: McKay, 1959.

————. *Encyclopedia of the American Revolution.* New York: McKay, 1980.

These two sources—each a single volume and arranged in alphabetical, dictionary form—contain information on campaigns, battles, laws, and people associated with the two wars.

Commager, Henry Steele. *Documents of American History.* 9th ed. New York: Prentice-Hall, 1974. 2 vols.

Beginning with the king and queen of Spain's "privileges and prerogatives granted to Columbus," this book includes major texts in U.S.

1909 *Pres.* THEODORE ROOSEVELT, WILLIAM H. TAFT

POLITICS AND GOVERNMENT; WAR;	BOOKS; PAINTING; DRAMA;
DISASTERS; VITAL STATISTICS.	ARCHITECTURE; SCULPTURE.

1909

National Association for the Advancement of Colored People founded to promote the rights and welfare of American Negroes.

Jan. 28 2nd military occupation of Cuba by U.S. troops ended. Last troops left island Mar. 31.

Feb. 19 Revised Homestead Act permitted entry on twice as many acres of grazing land where irrigation would not work.

Jack London's tempestuous life on the Pacific coast formed the basis of a semi-autobiographical novel, *Martin Eden.* Here is the story of a laborer, a seaman, who drives himself mercilessly to the heights of authorship and fame, but after overcoming all obstacles finds himself "burned out" and gives up his life to the sea.

---

history, famous court decisions, speeches, treaties. Some of these documents make history very lively. Here is part of the "Seneca Falls declaration of sentiments and resolutions on Woman's Rights," July 19, 1848:

> The history of mankind is a history of repeated injuries and usurpations on the part of man toward woman, having in direct object the establishment of an absolute tyranny over her. To prove this, let facts be submitted to a candid world.
>
> He has never permitted her to exercise her inalienable right to the elective franchise.
>
> He has compelled her to submit to laws, in the formation of which she had no voice.
>
> He has withheld from her rights which are given to the most ignorant and degraded men—both natives and foreigners.
>
> Having deprived her of this first right of a citizen, the elective franchise, thereby leaving her without representation in the halls of legislation, he has oppressed her on all sides.
>
> He has made her, if married, in the eye of the law, civilly dead.
>
> He has taken from her all right in property, even to the wages she earns.

INDEXES

America: History and Life. Santa Barbara, Calif.: ABC-Clio, 1964 to present. Quarterly with cumulations.

An index leading to periodical articles on American history, this is a useful and important source.

Historical Abstracts. Santa Barbara, Calif.: ABC-Clio with the International Social Science Institute, 1955 to date. Quarterly with cumulations.

This abstracting service locates articles in periodicals. Part One covers the period from 1450 to 1914, and Part Two covers 1914 to the present.

CHAPTER 19   MATHEMATICS

There was a young fellow from Trinity
Who took $\sqrt{\infty}$
But the number of digits
Gave him the fidgets.
He dropped math and took up divinity.
    —George Gamow, *One, Two Three . . . Infinity*

Mathematics developed from a primeval need. People wanted to know things like the number of animals in their flocks and had an impulse to keep track of the passage of time, most likely leading them to record the changing face of the heavens. The library will have individual books on arithmetic, algebra, geometry, etc. Count on those listed here for general information on all aspects of math.

Dick, Elie M. *Current Information Sources in Mathematics: An Annotated Guide to Books and Periodicals, 1960–1972.* Littleton, Colo.: Libraries Unlimited, 1973.

Provides students, instructors, and researchers with a bibliography of sources in mathematics. The emphasis is on monographic materials.

Dorling, Alison Rosemary. *Use of Mathematical Literature.* Woburn, Mass.: Butterworths, 1977.

Offers chapters on topical areas of mathematics, as well as on the history of math, education, and organizations.

Beyer, William H. *CRC Handbook of Mathematical Sciences.* 5th ed. West Palm Beach, Fla.: CRC Press, 1978.

This is a revised edition of the *Handbook of Tables for Mathematics*. Some tables have been made more concise, and new material has been added.

Newman, James R., ed. *The World of Mathematics.* New York: Simon & Schuster, 1956–1960. 4 vols.

This is a small library of the famous literature of mathematics from A'h-mosé the Scribe to Albert Einstein. It includes discussions of all aspects of math, ranging from mathematical ways of thinking to the laws of probability and chance. These four volumes convey "the diversity, the utility and the beauty of mathematics." The historical and biographical material will be useful to all, but some of the literature included is of use only to those with special interest in the subject. There is an article, for example, by Archimedes, whose fascination with large numbers is revealed in his "cattle problem" solution. This consisted of eight numbers which, when written out, would require almost 700 pages. The material is fascinating, but this is not a set for someone boning up on math.

Universal Encyclopedia of Mathematics. Foreword by James R. Newman. New York: Simon & Schuster, 1964.

A compact one-volume work which, in Part I, has articles arranged alphabetically by subject. Part 2 contains mathematical formulas; Part 3, mathematical tables. Covers mathematics from arithmetic through calculus.

Hogben, Lancelot. *Mathematics for the Million.* 4th rev. ed. New York: Norton, 1968.

Here are the lore and theory of mathematics, including such aspects as mathematics for the mariner. There are those who will think it appropriate that an article on how algebra began is titled "The Dawn of Nothing." Shown on page 123 are illustrations from Hogben's book that deal with the early history of math.

James, Glenn, and James, Robert C. *Mathematics Dictionary.* (Multilingual) 4th ed. New York: Van Nostrand Reinhold, 1976.

Definitions range from terms in high school geometry and algebra to more advanced university topics. It is designed to meet the needs of both students and scholars.

Turnbull, Herbert Westren. *The Great Mathematicians.* New York: New York University Press, 1961.

These brief biographies of men like Descartes and Isaac Newton reveal the history of math through interesting lives.

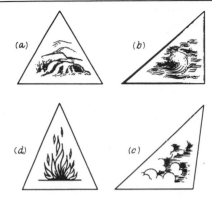

Fig. 2. Plato took Measurement out of the Geometry of his
Predecessors and Reinstated the Superstitions of their
Ancestors

The real world of Plato was a world of form from which matter was
banished.

(*a*) An *equilateral* triangle (i.e. one of which all three sides are
equal) is the elemental earth form.

(*b*) A *right-angled* triangle is the spirit of water. (To find spirit in
water is the most advanced kind of magic.)

(*c*) A *scalene* triangle with no equal sides is the spirit of the air.

(*d*) An *isosceles* triangle (i.e. one of which only two sides are equal)
is the elemental fire.

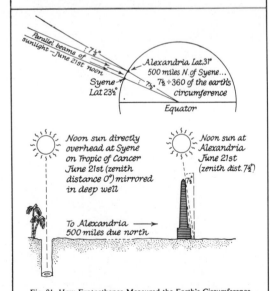

Fig. 81. How Eratosthenes Measured the Earth's Circumference

Note that at noon the sun lies directly over the observer's meridian
of longitude. Syene and Alexandria have nearly the same longitude. So
the sun, the two places, and the earth's center may be drawn on the
same flat slab of space.

Mathematical Reviews. Providence, R.I.: American Mathematical Society, 1940 to date. Monthly with cumulations.

An abstracting service, this publication offers comprehensive coverage of the literature of pure and applied mathematics.

CHAPTER 20   *MINORITIES*

It may be a good thing that America is not literally a melting pot because "melting" implies a loss of identity. And this country seems to allow diversity and appreciate the cultural contributions and ethnic heritage of special Americans.

GENERAL

Wasserman, Paul, ed. *Ethnic Information Sources of the United States.* 2d ed. Detroit: Gale Research, 1983. 2 vols.

Under various ethnic groups, this work lists fraternal, religious, cultural, and educational organizations, as well as books, magazines, museums, special libraries, and other sources of information (see page 126).

Thernstrom, Stephen, ed. *Harvard Encyclopedia of American Ethnic Groups.* Cambridge, Mass.: Harvard University Press, 1980.

Defines and identifies groups from Aleuts and Gypsies to Zoroastrians. Also contains tables and maps and thematic essays on, for example, ethnicity, folklore, immigration.

Miller, Wayne Charles. *A Comprehensive Bibliography for the Study of American Minorities.* New York: New York University Press, 1976. 2 vols.

This very comprehensive work offers sections covering minorities from Africa and the Middle East, from Eastern Europe and the Balkans, from Europe, from Asia, from Puerto Rico and Cuba, and Native Americans.

ASIANS
(Includes BUDDHISTS)
See also: Individual Asian Peoples

Fraternal Organizations

PAN PACIFIC AND SOUTHEAST ASIA WOMEN'S ASSOCIATION OF THE U.S.A.
Two Times Square
New York, New York 10036   (212) 944-0045
President: Barbara Tuber   Founded 1928

To further international understanding and friendship among the women of Asia, the Pacific and women of the United States of America. Provides hospitality to temporary residents and visitors from Pacific and Asian areas. Offers assistance with study and travel programs to such visitors when referred by United States Department of State, Missions to the United Nations and Consulates General. Fosters international friendships. Conducts classes in English, French and Japanese conversation, American history and other subjects. Operates Asian and Pacific Women's Center. Formerly: (1955) Pan Pacific Women's Association of U.S.A.
Publications: Newsletter, quarterly.

Professional Organizations

ACUPUNCTURE INTERNATIONAL ASSOCIATION
2330 South Brentwood Boulevard
Saint Louis, Missouri 63144
Executive Officer: Dr. Robert   (314) 961-9826
X. Adams   Founded 1949

Doctors of medicine, chiropractic and osteopathy who practice acupuncture. Conducts professional education and public health programs and seminars. Maintains library of 686 volumes. Bestows awards and conducts charitable programs. Publishes newsletters, bulletins, proceedings and abstracts.

ASIAN/PACIFIC AMERICAN LIBRARIANS ASSOCIATION
c/o Kingsborough Community
  College Library
Oriental Boulevard
Brooklyn, New York 11235
President: Dr. Sharad Karkhanis   Founded 1980

Librarians and information specialists of Asian Pacific descent working in the United States; other interested persons. Seeks to provide a forum for discussing problems and concerns; to support and encourage library services to Asian Pacific communities; to recruit and support Asian Pacific Americans in the library and information science professions. Offers placement service.
Publications: Newsletter, quarterly; Membership Directory, annual.

ASIAN POLITICAL SCIENTISTS GROUP IN USA
c/o Dr. Chun-Tu Hsueh
Department of Politics
University of Maryland
College Park, Maryland 20742
Chairman, Executive Committee: (301) 454-6706
  Chun-Tu Hsueh   Founded 1973

Political scientists of Asian descent in the United States. Purpose is to promote the professional and ethnic interests of the group. Activities include organization of panels for the annual meeting of the American Political Science Association. Maintains placement service. Publishes books.

ASSOCIATION OF ASIAN/PACIFIC AMERICAN ARTISTS
6546 Hollywood Boulevard, Suite 201
Hollywood, California 90028   (213) 464-8381
President: Sumi Haru   Founded 1975

Active members are individuals in the entertainment industry, including performers, producers, designers, directors, technicians, and writers. Supporting members include students, indivuals and organizations. Encourages equal employment opportunities in all aspects of the entertainment industry in order to assure realistic images and portrayals of Asian/Pacific peoples as they exist in real life and in the mainstream of America. Speaks with decision makers in the industry to fulfill goals. Sponsors business and professional seminars with industry leaders to expand members' knowledge of theatre, motion pictures and television. Maintains library; offers specialized education.
Publications: Newsletter, quarterly.

INDEPENDENT SCHOLARS OF ASIA
260 Stephen Hall
University of California
Berkeley, California 94720
National Director: Dr. Ruth-Inge   (415) 849-3791
  Heinze   Founded 1981

60

Cole, Katherine, ed. *Minority Organizations: A National Directory.* Garrett Park, Md.: Garrett Park Press, 1978.

    This is a directory with brief descriptions of organizations, a geographical index, a functional index, and miscellaneous information.

Oaks, Priscilla. *Minority Studies: A Selected Annotated Bibliography.* Boston: G. K. Hall, 1975.

A work divided into sections on general studies, Native Americans, Spanish-Americans, Afro-Americans, and Asian-Americans. Under each are listed bibliographies on such topics as history, culture, community life, literature, and education.

AFRO-AMERICANS

Newman, Richard. *Black Access.* Westport, Conn.: Greenwood Press, 1984.

This is a bibliography of Afro-American bibliographies, arranged alphabetically by author with a chronological index and a subject index.

Blazek, Ron; Dennell, Janice; and McKinney, Frances Masterson. *The Black Experience: A Bibliography of Bibliographies, 1970–1975.* Compiled for the Adult Library Materials Committee, Reference and Adult Services Division. Chicago: American Library Association, The Division, 1978.

Contains bibliographies, an annotated author listing of monographs, an annotated list of bibliographic journal articles, and unexamined bibliographies.

Smythe, Mabel M., ed. *The Black American Reference Book.* Englewood Cliffs, N.J.: Prentice-Hall, 1976.

Presents essays with graphs, tables, and bibliographies on black American workers, women, and politicians, and black participation in sports, the armed forces, the media, theater, and the arts.

Editors of *Ebony. The Ebony Handbook.* Chicago: Johnson, 1974.

Essays (blacks in film, black music, etc.) with charts and tables, and a government/politics chronology for 1969–1973.

Low, W. Augustus, and Cliff, Virgil A., eds. *Encyclopedia of Black America.* New York: McGraw-Hill, 1981.

An A to Z alphabetical arrangement, including lots of people and organizations along with subjects, often with accompanying illustrations and tables.

Miller, Elizabeth W. *The Negro in America: A Bibliography.* 2d. ed., rev. and enl. Compiled by Mary L. Fisher. Cambridge, Mass.: Harvard University Press, 1970.

A listing of books and periodicals under such headings as history, intergroup relations, political rights and suffrage, employment, education.

Ploski, Henry A., and Williams, James, eds. *The Negro Almanac: A Reference Work on the Afro-American.* New York: Wiley, 1983.

A huge one-volume work covering black musicians, black athletes, the black family, the press, documents in Afro-American history, and many biographies of prominent black Americans. Also has a selected bibliography.

ASIAN-AMERICANS

Rj Associates. *Asian American Reference Data Directory.* Washington, D.C.: U.S. Department of Health, Education and Welfare, Office for Asian American Affairs, 1976.

Emphasizes data developed by federal and state agencies, universities and individuals, on such topics as the current health, education, and social welfare of the Asian-American population.

NATIVE AMERICANS

Hodge, Frederick Webb. *Handbook of American Indians North of Mexico.* Washington, D.C.: Government Printing Office, 1907–1910, reissued 1912. 2 vols. (U.S. Bureau of American Ethnology. Bull. 30) Reprint: New York: Pageant Books, 1969.

Contains a descriptive list of the tribes, tribal divisions, and settlements north of Mexico, with biographies, histories, archaeology, arts, customs, and manners. Includes bibliographies.

Hodge, William H. *A Bibliography of Contemporary North American Indians.* Selected and partially annotated with study guide. New York: Interland Publishing, 1976.

Intended to complement rather than supplant other bibliographies. The chief focus is on contemporary Indian activities.

Klein, Barry. *Reference Encyclopedia of the American Indian.* 3d. ed. Rye, N.Y.: Todd Publications, 1978. 2 vols.

Rather than a straight encyclopedia, this is a compilation of directories, listings of government agencies, museums, libraries, associations, reservation tribal councils, and schools. Has extensive bibliography and biographical section.

Leitch, Barbara A. *A Concise Dictionary of Indian Tribes of North America.* Algonac, Mich.: Reference Publications, 1979.

Describes individual tribes, their languages and religions, organization, and customs. Brief bibliographies accompany most articles.

Hirschfelder, Arlene B., Byler, Mary Gloyne, and Dorris, Michael A. *Guide to Research on North American Indians.* Chicago: American Library Association, 1983.

A detailed and scholarly work covering many sources in history, economic and social aspects, religion, arts and literature. This bibliography is a basic guide to the growing body of literature about Native Americans.

Prucha, Francis Paul. *A Bibliographical Guide to the History of Indian-White Relations in the United States.* Chicago: University of Chicago Press, 1977.

————. *Indian-White Relations: A Bibliography of Works Published 1975–1980.* Lincoln: University of Nebraska Press, 1982.

These valuable works offer guides to sources and reference books and a classified bibliography of published works.

SPANISH-SPEAKING AMERICANS

Herrera, Diane. *Puerto Ricans and Other Minority Groups in the United States: An Annotated Bibliography.* Detroit: Blaine Eldridge Books, 1979.

Originally published as *Puerto Ricans in the United States,* this work focuses on bilingual and bicultural education and includes sociological, psychological, and literary studies of the Puerto Rican experience.

Robinson, Barbara J., and Robinson, J. Cordell. *The Mexican American: A Critical Guide to Research Aids.* Greenwich, Conn.: JAI Press, 1980.

Part One is an annotated bibliography of general works; Part Two presents subject bibliography (education, folklore, literature, history, etc.). There are author, title, and subject indexes.

Talbot, Jane Mitchell, and Cruz, Gilbert R. *A Comprehensive Chicano Bibliography, 1960–1972.* Austin, Texas: Jenkins, 1973.

A classified bibliography covering history, economics, migrant labor, the role of churches, and other aspects of Mexican-American life. Lists Chicano newspapers and journals.

CHAPTER 21   *MUSIC*

Hear with your eyes. That's the opportunity offered by some books on the subject of music.

Duckles, Vincent Harris. *Music Reference and Research Materials: An Annotated Bibliography.* 3d ed. New York: Free Press, 1974.

The guide is very useful, listing more than 1,900 items, annotated and arranged by categories such as dictionaries, encyclopedias, bibliographies, and so on.

Sadie, Stanley, ed. *The New Grove Dictionary of Music and Musicians.* London: Macmillan, 1980. 20 vols.

This wonderful new set is based on *A Dictionary of Music and Musicians* by Sir George Grove but contains much more new material. It covers the whole field of music from 1450 on and includes musical and related terms such as "buffo" and subjects like the Berkshire festivals, music history, theory and practice, and musical instruments. Bibliographies are given, and the complete catalogs of works of major musicians. Biographies are comprehensive for major figures such as Wagner and brief for obscure people such as Wynkyn de Worde, an Alsatian printer who was the first to print music in London. *Grove's* is illustrated with photographs and drawings.

Scholes, Percy Alfred. *The Oxford Companion to Music.* 10th ed. New York: Oxford University Press, 1970.

The work is a comprehensive alphabetical dictionary on all phases of music. Includes biographies and many encyclopedic articles.

Kobbé, Gustave. *The New Kobbé's Complete Opera Book.* Lord Harewood, ed. and rev. New York: Putnam, 1976.

W. H. Auden once said that no good opera plot can be sensible, for people do not sing when they are feeling sensible. Sensible or not,

Kobbé's is the place to go for plot summaries and general information. Music for the important motifs is usually given. The period covered includes modern times, concluding with Menotti and George Gershwin's *Porgy and Bess.*

Lubbock, Mark H. *Complete Book of Light Opera.* Des Moines, Iowa: Appleton-Century-Crofts, 1963.

Intended as a companion to Kobbé's opera book, this source covers light opera in Paris, Vienna, Berlin, and London from 1850 to 1961. There is an American section by David Ewen, which includes works like *Cabin in the Sky* and *The Sound of Music.* Musical themes are given along with plot—as shown in this example, the conclusion to a description of the 1903 London production of *A Princess of Kensington:*

Having settled her own love affair happily, Kenna asks Puck to straighten out the situation between poor Brook Green and Joy. Brook Green has come to Winklemouth, disguised as a boatman, to find Joy. Here he sings of his longing for her:

My heart a ship at an- chor lies up-on the a - zure of thine eyes.

But although Joy is pleased to see Brook, she teases him and they have a quarrel. In despair Brook finds the Recruiting Sergeant and joins the Marines. Joy is dreadfully upset when she hears this, but when Sir James Jellicoe himself appears he rectifies matters by explaining that Brook Green is in his employ and may not enlist without his permission. So Joy's lover is restored to her. Nell decides to marry Uncle Ben and that is the happy end to the Midsummer Day.

Light opera may be dead.

Fuld, James J. *Book of World-Famous Music: Classical, Popular, and Folk.* Rev. and enl. ed. New York: Crown, 1971.

Data on thousands of songs, tunes, etc. They are alphabetically indexed with musical theme, words, date of first appearance, and brief biographical information on composers and lyricists.

Shapiro, Nat. *Popular Music, An Annotated Index of American Popular Songs.* New York: Adrian Press, 1964–1973. 6 vols.

Listing popular songs published 1940 to 1967, this index is arranged by year and then by title. It gives author, title, composer, publisher, and first or best-selling record with performer and record company.

Baker, Theodore. *Baker's Biographical Dictionary of Musicians.* 6th ed. Nicolas Slonimsky, ed. New York: Schirmer, 1978.

This reliable dictionary compactly gives biographies of musicians of all ages and nations. Informative and useful, it reveals, for example, that Irving Berlin received no formal music training and never learned to read or write music, and the anguish of Beethoven, who, in the isolation of his deafness, created some of the world's great music.

Sears, Minnie Earl. *Song Index.* New York: Wilson, 1926, and supplement, 1934. Hamden, Conn.: Shoe String Press, 1966. 2 vols. in 1.

The *Song Index* gives references to thousands of songs, which may be found in more than 150 collections. It contains titles, first lines, authors' names, and composers' names in one alphabet. Useful for locating the music and words of a song and lists of songs by an author or composer.

Thompson, Oscar. *International Cyclopedia of Music and Musicians.* 10th rev. ed. Bruce Bohle, ed. New York: Dodd, 1975.

Here is an excellent one-volume encyclopedia on music. It covers a wide range of topics from the Braille system to black music to music criticism.

Lawless, Ray M. *Folksingers and Folksongs in America.* 2d ed. New York: Duell, 1981. Reprint of 1965 edition.

This guide to folk music includes biographies and an annotated bibliography of collections of folk songs. It is illustrated with paintings by Thomas Hart Benton and photographs such as one that shows the log cabin where "Home on the Range" was written in 1873. It even takes on the definition of a folk song:

> But a folksong is not easily defined. A ballad is a folksong, but a folksong is not a ballad unless it tells a story . . . the Shanty . . . is a folksong. A spiritual is a religious folksong. The blues, a predominantly melancholy type of jazz, may be a folksong. . . . But the specific characteristics of a general, traditional folksong . . . are these: it is music that has been submitted to the process of oral transmission; it is the product of evolution and is dependent on the circumstances of continuity, variation, and selection.

Feather, Leonard. *The Encyclopedia of Jazz.* Rev. ed. New York: Horizon Press, 1960.

In the introduction to this work, Benny Goodman says that he believes jazz is one of our most original contributions to twentieth-century culture and seems likely to go down in history as the real folk music of our country. The encyclopedia is primarily made up of biographies of famous jazz musicians (Dave Brubeck, Ella Fitzgerald, Charles Mingus), but it also has a historical survey, a chronology of jazz, and related articles.

———. *The Encyclopedia of Jazz in the Sixties.* New York: Horizon Press, 1966.

———. *Encyclopedia of Jazz in the Seventies.* New York: Horizon Press, 1976.

These two titles bring *The Encyclopedia of Jazz* up-to-date.

Chujoy, Anatole, and Manchester, P. W. *The Dance Encyclopedia.* Rev. ed. New York: Simon & Schuster, 1978.

A guide that has long, signed articles as well as brief references to many subjects connected with dance. Includes information on various ballet companies, biographies, and material on national dances (American, Oriental, Soviet, etc.).

Ewen, David. *The Complete Book of the American Musical Theater.* Rev. ed. New York: Holt, 1970.

A subtitle describes this as a guide to more than 300 productions of the American musical theater, listing stars, songs, composers, etc. and giving the plots. This same author, David Ewen, has edited several other books about music and musicians, which vary in usefulness.

Bordman, Gerald Martin. *The American Musical Theatre: A Chronicle.* New York: Oxford University Press, 1978.

This lively chronicle describes almost every musical to appear on Broadway and, after the World War I period, includes the musical theater in Boston, Philadelphia, and Chicago. The pre-1866 period is summarized, and then arrangement is by theater season.

The following three titles are examples of current material on music by special subject:

Stambler, Irwin. *Encyclopedia of Pop, Rock and Soul.* New York: St. Martin's Press, 1975.

Cohn, Nik. *Rock from the Beginning.* New York: Stein and Day, 1969.

Malone, Bill C. *Country Music U.S.A.: A Fifty Year History.* Austin: University of Texas Press, 1968.

CHAPTER 22   MYTHOLOGY

Myths are entertaining, and, as the science, religion, and literature of primitive people, they are important. Beyond that, think how deprived our language would be without the elegance and instant recognition of stories and names like Pandora, Cupid, and the Lotus Eaters.

Mythology of All Races. New York: Cooper Square, 1964. 13 vols. Reprint of 1916–1932 edition.

A leading reference work in the field, this set is arranged by race and has a general index. It discusses myths surrounding thunder, fire, and wind, etc. in the view of various races.

Gayley, Charles Mills. *The Classic Myths in English Literature and Art.* Boston: Longwood, 1977. Reprint of 1911 edition.

This one-volume work treats classical myths in relation to English literature and art. Based originally on *Bulfinch's Age of Fable*, it includes chapters on Norse and German myths. It is filled with notes like the one that Venus, goddess of love and beauty, was called Aphrodite by the Greeks because the word means "foam-born" and they believed she arose from the foam of the sea. It then places her in literature and art (the "Venus de Milo," for example).

Frazer, Sir James G. *New Golden Bough: A New Abridgment of the Classic Work.* Theodor H. Gaster, ed. New York: S. G. Phillips, 1959.

Description and interpretation of beliefs and customs related to magic and religion. This is an abridgment of the comprehensive original twelve-volume set.

Bulfinch, Thomas. *Bulfinch's Mythology: The Age of Fable; The Age of Chivalry; Legends of Charlemagne.* 2d rev. ed. New York: Crowell, 1970.

Bulfinch's presents the stories of King Arthur and Charlemagne as well as Greek and Roman myths. A "dictionary index" (see sample below) is useful for quickly identifying references from mythology.

Gor'gons, three monstrous females, with huge teeth, brazen claws and snakes for hair, sight of whom turned beholders to stone; Medusa, the most famous, slain by Perseus (which *See*), 115.

Gor'lois, Duke of Tintadel, 397, 398.

Gou-ver-nail, squire of Isabella, queen of Lioness, protector of her son Tristram while young, 449, and his squire in knighthood, 463.

Graal, the Holy, cup from which the Saviour drank at Last Supper, taken by Joseph of Arima-
thea to Europe, and lost, its recovery becoming a sacred quest for Arthur's knights, 392, 475, 487.

Graces, three goddesses who enhanced the enjoyments of life by refinement and gentleness; they were Aglaia (brilliance), Euphrosyne (joy), and Thalia (bloom), 4, 8.

Gra-das'so, king of Sericane, 672, 700, 702, 737, 740, 765, 768-769, 784-788.

Græ'æ, three gray-haired female watchers for the Gorgons, with one movable eye and one tooth between the three, 115-116.

Grimal, Pierre, ed. *Larousse World Mythology*. Patricia Beardsworth, tr. New York: Book Thrift, 1981.

This handsomely illustrated book presents chapters on the mythologies of geographical regions throughout the world. They are all here—the god Gou of Dahomey and the magic animals of the Uralian peoples, for example. The *Larousse* is a work that will be of interest to the art and literature student because of its emphasis on "myths which have been important in the life and literature of man from prehistoric times to the present."

Hamilton, Edith. *Mythology*. Boston: Little, 1942.

The Hamilton work includes both classic and Norse myths with comparisons of the original and the later versions. Family charts are also included.

Campbell, Joseph. *The Masks of God*. New York: Viking Press, 1959–1968.

This is the title of an excellent series of four books on different mythologies. Volume one: Primitive Mythology. Volume two: Oriental Mythology. Volume three: Occidental Mythology. Volume four: Creative Mythology.

Harnsberger, Caroline Thomas. *Gods and Heroes: A Quick Guide to Occupations, Associations and Experiences of the Greek and Roman Gods and Heroes.* Troy, N.Y.: Whitston, 1977.

The main section of the book is arranged alphabetically by terms denoting occupations, characteristics, attributes, etc. There is also an index by names of gods and heroes.

Cotterell, Arthur. *A Dictionary of World Mythology.* New York: Putnam, 1980.

The arrangement is geographic according to "the seven great traditions of world mythology: namely, West Asia, South and Central Asia, East Asia, Europe, America, Africa, and Oceania." Essays are followed by dictionary entries.

CHAPTER 23   *PARLIAMENTARY PROCEDURE*

There is no escaping it. Books on "rules of order" seem to lack order. Well, the rules are listed in an orderly way, but the language is unruly. The standard works are based on the rules and practice of Congress (a body not noted for its orderly behavior), and though they have been revised and simplified, they are still essentially what they were in 1876. Try reading the section on "Quasi Committee of the Whole (Consideration as if in Committee of the Whole)" or the instructions on "Creating a Blank." And if you think you're tired now, read the following on the "Exhaustion of the Previous Question."

EXHAUSTION OF THE PREVIOUS QUESTION. The *Previous Question* is said to be *exhausted* (in reference to a particular order for it) when all of the motions on which it was ordered have been finally disposed of, or when any motions not yet finally disposed of are no longer affected by the order. The conditions for exhaustion of the *Previous Question* are the same as for an order limiting or extending limits of debate—that is: (1) when all motions on which the *Previous Question* was ordered have been voted on; (2) when those not yet voted on have either been committed or postponed indefinitely; or (3) at the end of the session in which the *Previous Question* was ordered—which occurs first. After the *Previous Question* is exhausted, any remaining questions that come up again are open to debate and amendment just as if there had been no order for the *Previous Question*.

Of course, it's not quite fair out of context, and alas, no meeting can function without guidelines. There are revised editions that help a lot. One, for example, is:

Robert, Henry Martyn. *The Scott, Foresman Robert's Rules of Order.* New and enl. ed. Sarah Corbin Robert, ed. Glenview, Ill.: Scott, Foresman, 1981.

CHAPTER 24   *PHILOSOPHY AND RELIGION*

Beliefs, life-styles, and views of the universe are the topics in these sources.

DeGeorge, Richard T. *The Philosopher's Guide to Sources, Research Tools, Professional Life, and Related Fields.* Lawrence: Regents Press of Kansas, 1980.

A guide to reference sources, it covers related fields like religion, social science, and fine arts in addition to philosophy.

Encyclopedia of Philosophy. New York: Macmillan, 1973. 8 vols. in 4.

This very scholarly set covers both Oriental and Western concepts and philosophers for all periods. It gives summaries of philosophies, and the articles are long and followed by bibliographies.

Magill, Frank N., ed. *Masterpieces of World Philosophy in Summary Form.* New York: Salem Press, 1961.

This book includes brief summaries of all major philosophies and religions, both Eastern and Western. It ranges from Plato to Martin Buber, to Confucius, St. Augustine, and Jean-Paul Sartre. Each summary begins with a short description of the "principal ideas advanced" and then elaborates (see page 141).

Dictionary of the History of Ideas: Studies of Selected Pivotal Ideas. Philip P. Wiener, ed.-in-chief. New York: Scribner, 1974. 4 vols and index.

An international roster of scholars contributed to the set, which has long articles on topics in intellectual history. Relates ideas in history, psychology, religion, anthropology, literature, and art and shows how they developed. Through the index volume, one can follow concepts of peace or war from the early Greeks to St. Augustine to the present day. This is a valuable, fascinating work.

I AND THOU

Author: Martin Buber (1878-   )
Type of work: Theology, epistemology
First published: 1923

Principal Ideas Advanced

There is no independent "I" but only the I existing and known in objective relation to something other than itself, an "It," or as encountered by and encompassed by the other, the "Thou."

Just as music can be studied analytically by reference to its notes, verses, and bars, or encountered and experienced in such a manner that it is known not by its parts but as a unity, so the I can relate itself analytically to something other, "It," or it can encounter the other, "Thou," so as to form a living unity.

The "Thou" stands as judge over the "It," but as a judge with the form and creative power for the transformation of "It."

Each encountered "Thou" reveals the nature of all reality, but finally the living center of every "Thou" is seen to be the eternal "Thou."

The eternal "Thou" is never known objectively, but certitude comes through the domain of action.

Gaer, Joseph. *What the Great Religions Believe.* New York: Dodd Mead, 1963.

Describes Eastern religions as well as Judaism and Christianity. Kipling may have been wrong about "East is East, and West is West, and never the twain shall meet." Today there seems to be a lot of interest, for example, in Zen, which this book describes this way:

> To comprehend Zen one must first discipline and restrain the mind through meditation and introspection, without the use of logical thinking, avoiding the pitfalls of verbalization. The ultimate aim is to obtain an entirely new view of all experience. And the key word is Satori (enlightenment) . . . Zen encourages search *into* rather than *outside* oneself for enlightenment. If the question is properly "felt" the answer is instantly received.

Mead, Frank S. *Handbook of Denominations in the United States.* 7th ed. Nashville, Tenn.: Abingdon Press, 1980.

Factual and historical information arranged by denomination and giving basic beliefs of each. It also indicates different groups within a major denomination.

Yearbook of American and Canadian Churches. New York: National Council of Churches of Christ in the U.S.A., 1916 to date. Annual.

Directory and statistical information on all faiths. Includes religious agencies and organizations. (In addition there are yearbooks put out by individual religions such as *The Jewish Yearbook* [London: Jewish Chronicle Publications, Annual] and *The Official Catholic Directory* [New York: P. J. Kennedy & Sons, Annual].)

Geisendorfer, James, ed. *Directory of Religious Organizations in the United States.* 2d ed. Falls Church, Va.: McGrath, 1982.

Chapters, arranged by type (academic, educational, evangelical, etc.), describe organizations, giving name, address, description, publications, meetings, name of director.

There are works covering specific religions such as:

Encyclopedia of Islam. New ed. Leiden, Brill; London: Luzac, 1954–. 5 vols. and index (in progress).

This is a most important work in English on Islamic subjects, not just religion. The set is scholarly with signed articles and bibliographies.

New Catholic Encyclopedia. Prepared by an editorial staff at the Catholic University of America. Palatine, Ill.: Publishers Guild, 1981. 17 vols. Reprint of 1967 edition.

The New Catholic Encyclopedia and the encyclopedias listed below are broad enough for general use as well as religious reference. The fine *New Catholic Encyclopedia* has scholarly and readable articles, signed and with select bibliographies. In line with today's ecumenical trends some of the articles are written by non-Catholics, such as the one on Christian Science, written by E. D. Canham, former editor of *The Christian Science Monitor.* The encyclopedia covers doctrine, religious institutions, philosophies and scientific and cultural developments affecting the Catholic Church from its beginning to the present.

Jewish Encyclopedia. Bowling Green, N.Y.: Gordon Press, 1976. 12 vols. Reprint of 1901–1906 edition.

"A descriptive record of the history, religion, literature, and customs of the Jewish people from the earliest times to the present day." Though old, this scholarly set is very useful for its biographies and historical information. The brief article on "Apple" is an example of its unique and learned approach. The apple is discussed in terms of biblical data, in terms of its symbolic meaning in rabbinical literature, and from a botanical point of view. And there is a separate, shorter article on the Apple of Sodom, or Dead Sea Apple, which was "externally of fair appearance, but turning to smoke and ashes when plucked with the hands."

Roth, Cecil, and Wigoder, Geoffrey, eds. *The New Standard Jewish Encyclopedia.* 4th ed. Garden City, N.Y.: Doubleday, 1978.

Presents historical events and all phases of Jewish life in one volume. More up-to-date than the encyclopedia listed above, and it emphasizes American subjects and life.

Encyclopaedia Judaica. Jerusalem: Encyclopaedia Judaica; New York: Macmillan, 1972. 16 vols.

Presents a comprehensive view of world Jewry, in English, by an international list of scholars.

Malalasekera, G. P., ed. *Encyclopaedia of Buddhism.* Colombo, Sri Lanka: Government Press, 1961– . Vols. in progress.

This scholarly work is produced under the aegis of the government of Sri Lanka. It is arranged in dictionary form with articles on all aspects of Buddhist thought, history, and civilization.

Suzuki, Shunryu. *Zen Mind, Beginner's Mind.* New York: Weatherhill, 1970.

A work consisting of informal talks on Zen meditation, it is about Zen practice, about posture and breathing, about the basic attitudes and understanding that make Zen practice possible.

THE BIBLE

There are all kinds of aids to Bible study—atlases, concordances, and Bible quotation books. Examples are:

Hastings, James. *Dictionary of the Bible.* Rev. ed. Frederick C. Grant and H. H. Rowley, eds. New York: Scribner, 1963.

Contains maps and chronologies in addition to the dictionary entries under headings such as "Dreams" and "Good Samaritan." Cites exact references to chapter and verse in the Bible where story or subject appears. It is both specific and detailed. For example, under "Ant" it points out that ants are mentioned only twice in the Bible and then cites the instances.

May, Herbert G., and others. *Oxford Bible Atlas.* 2d. ed. New York: Oxford University Press, 1974.

Stevenson, Burton E. *Home Book of Bible Quotations.* New York: Harper & Row, 1949.

Cruden, Alexander. *Cruden's Unabridged Concordance to the Old and New Testaments and the Apocrypha.* Grand Rapids, Mich.: Baker Book House, 1953.

INDEXES

There are several indexes and abstracts in philosophy and religion. Among them are: *Philosopher's Index, Index to Religious Periodical Literature, Index to Jewish Periodicals,* and *Catholic Periodical Index.*

CHAPTER 25   POETRY

There is an ugly rumor that nobody reads poetry anymore, but still it continues to be written and quoted. Certainly poetry is elusive and probably was best described by poet Maxwell Bodenheim, who called it the attempt to paint the color of the wind.

Smith, Wm. J., ed. *Granger's Index to Poetry*. New York: Columbia University Press, 1982.

This is the most complete index to individual poems in collections of poetry. It has three indexes: one by author (where you will find under the author's name a useful alphabetical list of his poems), a subject index, and a title and first-line index. The title index is the main entry and looks like this:

> Schoolroom on a Wet Afternoon. Vernon Scannell.
> HaMU.

"Schoolroom . . ." is the title, Scannell is the author, and "HaMU" is the symbol for a collection of poetry in which the poem will be found. In this case the symbol stands for *The Harrap Book of Modern Verse*. (A key to the symbols is located in the front of *Granger's*.) This poem is also indexed under its first line, by author, and in the subject index under "Schoolroom."

Preminger, Alexander *et al. Princeton Encyclopedia of Poetry and Poetics*. Rev. ed. Princeton, N.J.: Princeton University Press, 1975.

A lively book with signed articles usually accompanied by bibliographies. The work includes articles you would expect to find, like those on rhyme and meter, but also some unusual ones—for example, "The Fleshly School of Poetry"—and here's how the one on "Poetic Madness" begins:

POETIC MADNESS. In *Phaedrus* 245 Socrates asserts that poets are suscepti- ble to madness and, in fact, cannot succeed without it. In the *Ion* both poet and critic are described as possessed by a frenzy so that they do not con- sciously control their words. In Aristotle's *Problemata* 30 it is said that poets and philosophers are inclined to excessive melancholy. Roman poets are possessed by spirits or demons (Ovid: "Deus est in nobis/Agitante calescimus illo"—"A god is within us; when he urges, we are inspired"); write best when tipsy (Horace); are filled with the divine afflatus (Cicero); or are literally mad (the tradition that Lucretius was driven insane by a love potion). The concept of p.m., which can be found *passim* in European poetry and criticism, is summed up in two familiar quotations: "The luna- tic, the lover, and the poet/Are of imagination all compact" (Shakespeare); and "Great wits are sure to madness near allied/And thin partitions do their bounds divide" (Dryden).

The parallel between poets and madmen is extremely primitive. It ap- parently goes back to the time when the poet, the prophet, and the priest were one and the same . . .

It is well cross-referenced, too. Under a brief article on "Haiku" (three-line poems that must state or imply a season and use natural images) there is a "see" reference to a long article on "Japanese Poetry," which has a few examples of haiku. Here is one:

> The moon passes
> In splendor through its central heavens
> And I through wretched streets.

Deutsch, Babette. *Poetry Handbook.* 4th ed. New York: Funk & Wagnalls, 1974.

A dictionary of terms with illustrations from English poetry and po- etry in translation. The author is a poet, critic, and teacher.

Magill, Frank N. *Critical Survey of Poetry: English Language Series.* Walton Beacham, academic director. New York: Salem Press, 1982. 8 vols.

Provides critical analysis of the principal poetic works of three hun- dred forty English-language poets. Each poet is discussed in an article of about ten pages covering principal poems, biographical data, achievements, and analysis of individual works. A companion *Foreign Language Series* was published in 1984.

Kunitz, Joseph Marshall, and Martinez, Nancy C. *Poetry Explication.* 3d. ed. Boston: G. K. Hall, 1980.

Subtitled *"A checklist of Interpretation since 1925 of British and American Poems, Past and Present,"* this work indexes literary periodicals and composite books. Under authors and then by individual poems, it gives citations to explication and criticism.

Shapiro, Karl, and Beum, Robert, eds. *A Prosody Handbook*. New York: Harper & Row, 1965.

This is a compact manual dealing with the elements of prosody—line, meter, rhythm, and its uses, stanza forms, etc.

There are many fine collections of poetry. A few of the best-known general collections are:

Stevenson, Burton Egbert. *Home Book of Verse, American and English*. 9th ed. New York: Holt, 1953. 2 vols.

——. *Home Book of Modern Verse*. 2d ed. New York: Holt, 1953.

Matthiessen, F. O., ed. *Oxford Book of American Verse*. New York: Oxford University Press, 1950.

Ellmann, Richard, ed. *New Oxford Book of American Verse*. New York: Oxford University Press, 1976.

Quiller-Couch, Sir Arthur, ed. *Oxford Book of English Verse*. Oxford: Clarendon Press, 1939.

Gardner, Helen Louise, ed. *New Oxford Book of English Verse*. New York: Oxford University Press, 1972.

Untermeyer, Louis. *Modern American Poetry*. 8th ed. New York: Harcourt, 1962.

——. *Modern British Poetry*. New and enl. ed. New York: Harcourt, 1962.

Lask, Thomas, ed. *The New York Times Book of Verse*. New York: Macmillan, 1970.

To end, a bit of poetry that has spanned time, from Kabir in India around 1400 to contemporary poet Robert Bly in Minnesota.

Are you looking for me? I am in the next seat:
your shoulder is against mine.
You will not find me in stupas, nor in Indian shrine rooms,
    nor in the synagogue, nor in cathedrals,
not in masses, nor kirtans, not in legs twisting around the neck,
    nor in eating nothing but vegetables.

When you look for me, you will find me instantly.
You will find me in the tiniest house of time.
Kabir says, "Student, tell me, what is God?
He is the breath inside the breath."

CHAPTER 26 POLITICS, GOVERNMENT, AND CURRENT EVENTS

Though many of the books listed here include historical information, most are annuals or are often revised and so contain up-to-date information on countries and governments. The following sources deal with the "necessary evil," as Thomas Paine called government.

Holler, Frederick L. *The Information Sources of Political Science.* 2d ed. Santa Barbara, Calif.: ABC-Clio, 1975.

Contains sources for reference in political science and related fields, politics, public administration, international relations, government information, etc.

THE WORLD

Council on Foreign Relations, Inc. *Political Handbook of the World.* New York: McGraw-Hill, 1975–. Annual. Supersedes the council's *Political Handbook and Atlas of the World,* issued from 1927.)

A work that treats the independent governments of the world and gives chief government officials, party programs and leaders, the press, and political events. Information is complete and compact.

The Worldmark Encyclopedia of Nations. 5th rev. ed. New York: Worldmark Press, Harper & Row, 1976. 5 vols.

The five volumes in this set cover (1) the United Nations, (2) Africa, (3) the Americas, (4) Asia and Australia, (5) Europe. All aspects of a country are treated—trade, mining, forestry, banking, judicial system, etc. Though not issued annually (so note the copyright date for year of publication), it is a "practical guide to the geographic, historical, political, social and economic status" of nations and the UN. There are some illustrations and small maps.

Europa Year Book. London: Europa Publications, 1946 to date. 2 vols. Annual.

Volume one includes international organizations and Europe. Volume two covers Africa, the Americas, Asia, Australia. Statistical information, constitution, diplomatic representation, the press, etc. are given for each country. For the tiny kingdom of Sikkim, for example, under the heading "Transport and Tourism" one learns that there is no railway or airport in Sikkim but there is an "aerial ropeway"—a ropeway, thirteen miles long, which links the town of Gangtok to the foot of the Nathula Pass. (For complete information on education and learned societies see Europa's *World of Learning*, which is discussed in the Education section, page 102.)

International Yearbook and Statesmen's Who's Who. London: T. Skinner, 1953 to date. Annual.

Includes information on international organizations and gives political, statistical, and directory information on every country in the world. Biographical section contains sketches of world leaders.

Statesman's Year-Book. London, New York: Macmillan, 1864 to date. Annual.

Much statistical information and reliable facts on constitution, government, employment, finance, commerce, religion, education, diplomatic representation, etc. for all the countries of the world.

Egan, E. W., et al. *Kings, Rulers and Statesmen.* New York: Sterling, 1976.

An illustrated handbook giving, under each country's name, a chronology of rulers and sometimes brief biographies.

Kurian, George Thomas. *The Encyclopedia of the Third World.* New York: Facts on File, 1978. 2 vols.

A very useful source for third world countries, this set offers information in each in several categories: map, basic fact sheet, weather, population, language, religions, government, finance, and other topics. There is also a selected bibliography for each country.

Yearbook of the United Nations. New York: United Nations Department of Public Information, 1947 to date. Annual.

A summary of the year's activities of the UN and its specialized agencies. It has a subject and a name index.

Facts on File. New York: Facts on File, 1940 to date. Weekly. Annual cumulations.

This digest of news is arranged under such headings as "World Affairs," "National Affairs," "Finance," "Economy," "Science," "Education," etc. It also covers events in the arts, listing books published and theater openings, has obituaries, and includes the latest in sports. An important and useful guide to current information.

International Affairs

Soviet Union withdraws from Los Angeles Olympics; Bulgaria, East Germany follow; security concerns, U.S. stance cited; move provokes anger, regret.

Moderate, rightist both claim Salvador election victory; D'Aubuisson charges 'irregularities'; unofficial tally gives Duarte 55%; Duarte vows death squad probe; CIA said to aid moderates.

Reagan warns of communist victory in El Salvador; House approves aid hike; Democrats score military solution; World Court favors Nicaragua; text of Reagan's speech.

Lebanese cabinet formed; militia clashes continue; U.S. cleric abducted.

Pages 329–335

U.S. Affairs

Hart revives campaign with wins in Ohio and Indiana; Mondale has commanding delegate lead; Senate runoff slated in Texas; Rep. Hall defeated in Indiana; other primary results.

Vietnam veterans, chemical companies settle Agent Orange suit; $180 million fund set up.

Interest rate rise prompts White House criticism of Fed; Feldstein sets return to Harvard; Treasury note rates rise at auction; Fed attack, election worries linked; April jobless rate steady at 7.7%.

Senate debates plans to cut budget deficits; Democrats' plan loses on tie vote; GOP plan also loses; Weinberger outlines Pentagon cuts.

Supreme Court backs broad reviews of libel appeals; other actions.

CBS, Wall Street Journal in insider trading probes.

Pages 335–339

Keesing's Contemporary Archives. London: Keesing's, July 1, 1931 to date. Weekly.

A service similar to *Facts on File*. *Keesing's* has a British emphasis, and its coverage is more in depth than and not quite as brief as *Facts on File*. *Keesing's* is a weekly diary of important events and frequently includes the full texts of speeches and documents.

THE UNITED STATES

U.S. Congress. *Official Congressional Directory.* Washington, D.C.: Government Printing Office, 1809 to date.

An indispensable work containing information on congressional organization and personnel. Contains biographical sketches of congress men and officials, lists by state, committee memberships, and information on various government commissions and boards. The directory also has maps of congressional districts.

U.S. Congress. *Biographical Directory of the American Congress, 1774–1971.* Washington, D.C.: Government Printing Office, 1971.

This directory lists Presidents, cabinet officers, and members of Congress, with brief biographies of each, from the First through the Eighty-sixth Congress.

United States Government Organization Manual. Washington, D.C.: Government Printing Office, 1935 to date.

An annually revised manual on the federal government. It describes the creation, activities, organization (with charts of the more complex agencies), and chief officials of various departments and offices. It also includes quasi-official agencies, like the National Academy of Sciences and the American National Red Cross.

The Book of the States. Lexington, Ky.: Council of State Governments, 1935 to date.

Published every two years, this work gives information on state constitutions, elections, legislatures, etc. Also given are the nickname, motto, flower, bird, and song for each state. (North Carolina's interesting state motto is "Esse Quam Videri"—To Be Rather Than to Seem; the Pennsylvania state bird is the ruffed grouse; and Oklahoma's state flower is mistletoe . . . all year.) Supplements to *The Book of the States* are issued to keep the lists of officials up-to-date.

Municipal Year Book. Chicago: International City Managers Association, 1934 to date.

Contains statistical data and information on U.S. cities. It discusses municipal problems and activities and gives a directory of chief officials for cities of 10,000 population or over and of mayors and clerks for those of 5,000 to 10,000 populations.

Mitchell, Edwin Valentine. *An Encyclopedia of American Politics.* Westport, Conn.: Greenwood Press, 1969. Reprint of the 1946 edition.

Useful for its identification of terms, slogans, nicknames, biographies of political figures. The work also has excerpts from significant documents.

Plano, Jack C., and Greenberg, Milton. *The American Political Dictionary.* 6th ed. New York: Holt, Rinehart & Winston, 1982.

Under eighteen topics such as "U.S. Constitution" and "National Defense," this book identifies terms, cases, agencies, and so on. There is also an index.

Safire, William L. *Safire's Political Dictionary.* New York: Random House, 1978.

This is an enlarged and updated edition of *The New Language of Politics.* The dictionary discusses the origin and development of terms relating to politics.

Scammon, Richard M., ed. *America Votes; A Handbook of Contemporary American Election Statistics.* Vols. 1–2, New York: Macmillan, 1956, 1958. Vols. 3–6, Pittsburgh: University of Pittsburgh Press, 1959–1966. Vols. 7– , Washington, D.C.: Congressional Quarterly, 1968– . Biennial.

Arranged alphabetically by state, the Scammon books contain valuable statistics on the vote since 1945 for President, governor, senator, and congressman. These volumes include maps of state counties and congressional districts and of assembly districts for large cities.

Petersen, Svend. *A Statistical History of the American Presidential Elections: With Supplementary Tables Covering 1968 to 1980.* Westport, Conn.: Greenwood Press, 1981. Reprint of 1963 edition with additions.

Statistical compilations of various aspects of the vote for each presidential election from 1789 to 1960 are found in this work. Tables are arranged by election year, by state, by political party, etc., as illustrated below.

Election of 1860

TABLE 21 — Electoral and Popular Vote

States	L	Br	Bl	D	Lincoln	Douglas	Breck.	Bell	Smith
Alabama		9				13,651	48,831	27,875	
Arkansas		4				5,227	28,732	20,094	
California	4				39,173	38,516	34,334	6,817	
Connecticut	6				43,486	17,364	16,558	3,337	
Delaware		3			3,816	1,069	7,344	3,868	
Florida		3				367	8,543	5,437	
Georgia		10				11,613	52,131	43,050	
Illinois	11				172,171	160,205	2,402	4,913	35
Indiana	13				139,033	115,509	12,295	5,306	
Iowa	4				70,409	55,111	1,048	1,763	
Kentucky				12	1,364	25,651	53,143	66,058	
Louisiana		6				7,625	22,681	20,204	
Maine	8				62,811	26,693	6,368	2,046	
Maryland		8			2,895	5,953	42,511	41,875	
Massachusetts	13				106,649	34,492	6,277	22,536	
Michigan	6				88,480	65,057	805	405	
Minnesota	4				22,069	11,920	748	62	
Mississippi		7				3,283	40,797	25,040	
Missouri				9	17,028	58,801	31,317	58,372	
New Hampshire	5				37,519	25,881	2,112	441	
New Jersey	4		3		58,346	62,869			
New York	35				362,646	312,510			
North Carolina		10				2,701	48,539	44,990	
Ohio	23				231,610	187,232	11,405	12,194	136
Oregon	3				5,496	4,127	5,342	976	
Pennsylvania	27				268,030	16,765	178,871	12,776	
Rhode Island	4				12,240	7,753			1
South Carolina		8							
Tennessee				12		11,428	66,440	70,706	
Texas		4					47,548	15,438	
Vermont	5				33,888	8,748	1,859	217	
Virginia			15		1,929	16,292	74,379	74,701	
Wisconsin	5				86,110	65,021	888	161	
TOTALS	180	72	39	12	1,867,198	1,379,434	854,248	591,658	172

Congressional Quarterly Weekly Report. Washington, D.C.: Congressional Quarterly, Inc., 1945 to date.

CQ is a weekly service (with a quarterly index) giving information on U.S. congressional activities. It also publishes a yearly almanac which "distills, reorganizes and cross-indexes" the year in Congress. It is very helpful when one searches for action on bills, the voting records of members of Congress, presidential messages, etc.

LAWS

U.S. Congress. House of Representatives. *How Our Laws Are Made.* Washington, D.C.: Government Printing Office, 1981.

This best-selling government pamphlet (available from the Superintendent of Documents, U.S. Government Printing Office, Washington, D.C. 20402) gives a careful explanation of the complicated legislative process. Because it is in paperback, it may be kept by libraries in the pamphlet file (called a vertical file), so if it is not found in the catalog, ask the librarian for it. (A simple and graphic explanation of this subject is also given in the *World Book Encyclopedia* under "United States, Government of" in an article titled "How a Bill Becomes a Law.")

When laws are passed by Congress, they are first printed individually in pamphlet form known as slip laws. At the end of each year they are published by the Government Printing Office as *United States Statutes at Large*. These are primarily of research interest because many laws modify earlier ones and are themselves modified by later legislation.

To find current laws, use:

U.S. *Laws, Statutes, etc. United States Code, 1976 edition.* Washington, D.C.: Government Printing Office, 1977.

This multivolume set is the official compilation of all laws in force as of January 3, 1965. The *U.S. Code* is usually issued every six years, and cumulative supplements are issued after each session of Congress. (There are commercially published editions known as *United States Code Annotated.* These editions include notes on judicial interpretation as well as the law itself.)

U.S. Congress. *Congressional Record.* Washington, D.C.: Government Printing Office, 1873 to date.

The *Record* is a newspaper issued every day Congress is in session, and there is nothing quite like it. It is all things—funny, serious, lofty, and low-down. It contains words spoken on the floors of both chambers (such as speeches and debate on legislation) and much that is not said since members may add revised and extended remarks and letters, new articles, and other items. Often things are included by Representatives so they can have them reprinted and distributed back home under the *Congressional Record* banner. The *Record* is bound and indexed (by name and subject) at the end of each session, and a "History of Bills and Resolutions" index is included.

INDEXES

In addition to the general *Social Sciences Index* and the *Social Sciences Citation Index* (see page 66), some indexes of particular note are:

Public Affairs Information Service. *Bulletin.* New York: Public Affairs Information Service, 1915 to date.

Known as *PAIS*, this is a subject index (somewhat like the *Readers' Guide)* to periodicals, pamphlets, government documents, and even mimeographed material in economics, sociology, political science, government, and legislation. It is issued semimonthly, cumulated at intervals, and then issued in annual volumes.

U.S. Superintendent of Documents. *Monthly Catalog of United States Government Publications.* Washington, D.C.: Government Printing Office, 1895 to date. Monthly with varying cumulations.

This remarkable index goes way back (the title varies in earlier years) and lists publications issued by all branches of the government, including congressional and department and bureau publications. Each issue contains general instructions for ordering copies of documents. Covers an enormous range of subjects.

CIS Congressional Information Service. Index to publications of the United States Congress. Washington, D.C.: Congressional Information Service, 1970 to date. Monthly with varying cumulations.

CIS offers brief abstracts of congressional publications, such as committee hearings, House and Senate documents and reports, executive reports, and miscellaneous publications. The annual volume provides brief descriptions and legislative histories of public laws enacted during the period covered.

NOTE: Government documents represent an enormous source of information, and many, many titles are listed throughout this guide along with nongovernmental sources. For comprehensive discussions of government publications see works by W. Philip Leidy and by Joe Moorehead recommended in the bibliography to this book on page 218.

CHAPTER 27   PSYCHOLOGY

For anyone who wonders why we are the way we are, here are some books offering help with the search.

Bell, James Edward. *A Guide to Library Research in Psychology.* Dubuque, Ia.: W. C. Brown, 1971.

Aimed at undergraduates, this guide has chapters on using the library and writing a research paper, followed by psychology sources and selected reading lists for aspects of psychology.

Wolman, Benjamin B., ed. *International Encyclopedia of Psychiatry, Psychology, Psychoanalysis, and Neurology.* New York: Produced for Aesculapius Publishers by Van Nostrand Reinhold Co., 1977. 12 vols. Progress volume, 1983.

An authoritative encyclopedia with survey articles covering several disciplines. Bibliographies follow articles, and there is a detailed index.

Corsini, Raymond J., ed. *Encyclopedia of Psychology.* New York: Wiley, 1984. 4 vols.

This is a general encyclopedia for psychology, with bibliographies following most articles and carrying many biographical entries. Volume four is the index.

Eysenck, H. J., Arnold, W., and Meili, R., eds. *Encyclopedia of Psychology.* London: Search Press; New York: Herder and Herder, 1972. 3 vols.

This source has a roster of international contributors and has been published in many languages. It covers important concepts and terms in psychology and has a limited number of biographies.

There are two up-to-date one-volume dictionaries:

Goldenson, Robert M., ed. *Longman Dictionary of Psychology and Psychiatry.* New York: Longman, 1984.

Harré, Rom, and Lamb, Roger, eds. *The Encyclopedic Dictionary of Psychology.* Cambridge, Mass.: MIT Press, 1983.

INDEX

Psychological Abstracts. Lancaster, Pa.: American Psychological Association, 1927 to date. Monthly. Annual cumulations.

This very important service offers current indexes for journal articles in psychology and provides bibliographic information on books and technical reports. There is an author index, and subject cumulations covering more than one year have been issued.

> 2822. **Epstein, Arthur W.** (Tulane U School of Medicine) **Observations on the brain and dreaming.** *Biological Psychiatry,* 1982(Nov), Vol 17(11), 1207–1215. —Outlines Freud's and Jung's ideas on dreams, research on uncinate seizures, the role of dreams in memory processing, and the dissolution of the dream mechanism. Research into the relationship of dreams to the cerebral hemispheres may yield insights into psychopathology and the evolution of mentation. Since dreaming is a linguistic form involving the sequencing, combining, and modulation of images that have symbolic significance, it must be closely related to the brain's other language functions. Studies have shown that aphasic patients with dominant (left) hemisphere lesions show dreaming loss and that posterior lesions affecting visual and visual-associative areas may produce dream cessation. The same has been reported for individuals with frontal lobotomy. In view of the theory that the dream is a reflection of the brain's memory-processing function, the effect of such disorders as transient global amnesia on dreaming should be investigated. Metabolic studies of the brain during sleep could be used to explore whether typical or other affect-laden dreams show a different metabolic pattern than higher-level dreams. (18 ref) —*C. H. Bartlett.*

This is a sample entry from *Psychological Abstracts.*

The *Social Science Index* and *Social Science Citation Index* are also very useful for psychology.

CHAPTER 28   QUOTATIONS

Quotations are best used sparingly amid original thought. Books of quotations are reference works in which one can find the sayings of a particular person, verify or identify a particular quotation, and find quotations on a particular subject. These books are especially "democratic," including something as familiar as "snug as a bug in a rug" along with the lofty expressions of a Supreme Court justice. A few of the basic, general sources are described here.

Bartlett, John. *Familiar Quotations*. 15th ed., rev. and enl. Boston: Little, Brown, 1980.

One of the best standard collections, Bartlett's is arranged chronologically by authors quoted and has an excellent key word index. The following quotation by Benjamin Franklin can be found in the index under several key words—"eagle," "turkey," "bird," "moral," and "material welfare."

> I wish the bald eagle had not been chosen as the representative of our country; he is a bird of bad moral character; like those among men who live by sharping and robbing, he is generally poor, and often very lousy.
> The turkey is a much more respectable bird, and withal a true original native of America.
>
> *Letter to Sarah Bache*
> *(January 26, 1784)*

Stevenson, Burton Egbert. *Home Book of Quotations*. Rev. ed. New York: Dodd, 1967.

This is a very comprehensive quotation book arranged by subject and with an index. It covers classical and modern quotations. If you look under the heading "Study," you will find the following advice from J. M. Barrie: "Concentrate though your coat-tails be on fire." The same editor has compiled several other quotation books, such as the *Home Book of Shakespeare Quotations* (New York: Scribners,

1937), the *Home Book of Bible Quotations* (New York: Harper, 1949), and the *Home Book of Proverbs, Maxims and Familiar Phrases* (New York: Macmillan, 1948).

Other excellent sources are:

Hoyt, Jehiel Keeler. *Hoyt's New Cyclopedia of Practical Quotations.* compl. by Kate Louise Roberts. New York: Funk & Wagnalls, 1922.

Oxford Dictionary of Quotations. 3d ed. London, New York: Oxford University Press, 1979.

Evans, Bergen. *Dictionary of Quotations.* New York: Delacorte Press, 1968.

Adler, Mortimer J., and Van Doren, Charles, eds. *Great Treasury of Western Thought: A Compendium of Important Statements on Man and His Institutions by the Great Thinkers in Western History.* New York: Bowker, 1977.

It saves time if you always check the arrangement in quotation books. When looking for quotations by a specific person, it's easier to use a book arranged by author or speaker; at other times you might need sayings on a particular subject, so an alphabetical list by subject is the most useful. Good quotation books have indexes covering the approaches not used in the basic arrangement.

CHAPTER 29 SCIENCE AND TECHNOLOGY

Science, as the last and probably endless frontier, boasts a staggering amount of published information. Listed here are general works, broad in scope. Not listed are the thousands of books on specific areas within the field of science.

Malinowsky, Harold Robert, and Richardson, Jeanne M. *Science and Engineering Literature: A Guide to Reference Sources.* 3d ed. Littleton, Colo.: Libraries Unlimited, 1980.

Grogan, Denis Joseph. *Science and Technology: An Introduction to the Literature.* 3d ed. Hamden, Conn.: Linnet Books, 1976.

Since this subject is complex and has so many subjects within subjects, once again the recommendation is to use guides to the literature. The two above are good examples.

GENERAL WORKS

McGraw-Hill Encyclopedia of Science and Technology. 5th ed. New York: McGraw-Hill, 1982. 15 vols.

This international reference work is comprehensive and scholarly, though it is aimed at the intelligent layman. There are introductory survey articles for each branch of science as well as articles on more specific topics. Bibliographies follow the longer articles. Biographies are not included. Volume 15 is the index to this indispensable set, and most important in such a changing field, the set is kept up-to-date by an annual, the *McGraw-Hill Yearbook of Science and Technology.*

Van Nostrand's Scientific Encyclopedia. 6th ed. Princeton, N.J.: Van Nostrand, 1982. 2 vols.

A single alphabetical arrangement covering all science from aeronautics to zoology. There are articles on the centipede, measles, nitric acid, and, for the airplane buff, a discussion of "wing stress analysis."

Lapedes, Daniel N., ed. *McGraw-Hill Dictionary of Scientific and Technical Terms.* 2d ed. New York: McGraw-Hill, 1978.

In this work, definitions of almost 108,000 terms from science and technology are clear and concise. Each term is identified according to its field of science or technology.

The Way Things Work. New York: Simon & Schuster, 1971.

Much of this is on an advanced level, but the clear language (translated from the original German) and the illustrations help. Its subtitle is *An Illustrated Encyclopedia of Technology,* and the book deals with a variety of subjects, such as color television, pumps, dry ice, mirrors, cameras, and fire extinguishers. See the text and the illustration on pages 164 and 165 for a sample of the format used for each subject.

Diagram Group. *Comparisons: of Distance, Size, Area, Volume, Mass Weight, Density, Energy, Temperature, Time, Speed and Number Throughout the Universe.* New York: St. Martin's Press, 1980.

Offers graphic presentations of measurable phenomena and makes comparisons between like and like and like and unlike.

SUBJECT AREAS

What follows are a few titles that can only suggest the many wonderful reference sources in the sciences. Checking library catalogs and the guides to the literature under *specific* subject headings within science and technology will reveal many other useful books.

Weast, Robert C., ed. *Handbook of Chemistry and Physics.* 63d ed. Boca Raton, Fla.: CRC Press, 1982.

An indispensable tool for chemists and physicists, this is a ready reference book of chemical and physical data.

Menzel, Donald H. *Field Guide to the Stars and Planets.* The Peterson Field Guide Series. Boston: Houghton Mifflin, 1975.

A guide by the director of the Harvard College Observatory that includes information on stars, planets, the moon, satellites, comets. The book is well illustrated with "sky maps" and such and describes features like Halley's comet and an eclipse of the sun and the moon. Here is an example of this small book's pithiness:

Aberration of Light. A person walking rapidly through a heavy rainstorm with the drops falling straight downward, will have to tilt his umbrella slightly forward to compensate for his own motion (Fig. 61). In the same way and for the same reason, an astronomer on the rapidly moving earth must tilt his telescope slightly forward in the direction of the earth's motion in order to have the starlight fall exactly down the center of his tube. As a result of this motion, the apparent position of a star does not ordinarily coincide with its true position. We term this phenomenon the *aberration* or "wandering" of light. The maximum shift from true to apparent position is 20″.47.

Fig. 61. Aberration of light

Henderson, Isabella Ferguson. *Henderson's Dictionary of Biological Terms.* 9th ed. New York: Van Nostrand Reinhold, 1979.

The "pronunciation, derivation, and definition of terms in biology, botany, anatomy, cytology, genetics, embryology and physiology."

Challinor, John. *A Dictionary of Geology.* 5th ed. New York: Oxford University Press, 1978.

Defines terms and examines concepts. Many entries have quotations illustrating meanings. There is even a word, "clunch," which is defined as "an old local name for various stiff clays."

Grzimek, Bernhard. *Grzimek's Animal Life Encyclopedia.* New York: Van Nostrand Reinhold, 1972–1975. 13 vols.

Each volume in this profusely illustrated set has chapters written by scholars treating zoological families, orders, etc. Volumes cover lower

WHY DOES A SHIP FLOAT?

According to Archimedes' principle, a body which is wholly or partly immersed in a fluid undergoes a loss in weight equal to the weight of fluid which it displaces. An aluminium cube with sides 1 ft. in length weighs about 168 lb. (Fig. 1a). A cubic foot of water weighs about 62 lb. If the aluminium cube is immersed in water (Fig. 1b), its weight has apparently decreased to 106 lb. This is because the cube displaces a cubic foot of water and thereby undergoes a loss in weight equal to the weight of this displaced water. The upward force due to *buoyancy* in this case is equal to 62 lb. and acts at the centre of gravity of the displaced volume of water. If a body, on being totally immersed in a fluid, would displace a volume of fluid whose weight is greater than that of the body concerned, then that body will float on the fluid. Floating merely means that the body sinks into the fluid to such a depth that the displaced volume of fluid weighs exactly as much as the whole floating body. In that case the upward force (buoyancy), which is equal to the weight of the displaced fluid, is in equilibrium with the weight of the body. A 1 ft. wooden cube weighs about 50 lb. It will float in water; the submerged part of the cube displaces a volume of water weighing 50 lb., so that the upward force is 50 lb. and thus counter-balances the weight of the cube (Fig. 2). Hence the displacement of a floating object is equal to its weight.

This is the elementary principle of floating. However, a ship must additionally have stability, i.e., it must be able to right itself after being swung to an inclined position by an external force such as wind pressure. A ship is said to "heel" when it leans over to port or starboard (Fig. 3a); the term "trim" refers to the longitudinal position of a ship in relation to the waterline: the ship is said to be trimmed by the head (as in Fig. 3b) or by the stern, according as the head or the stern lies deeper down in the water. Stability is especially important with regard to the danger of capsising. Fig. 4a shows the ship in its normal position. Its weight can be conceived as a downward force acting at its centre of gravity S. The counterbalancing upward force acts at the centre of buoyancy W, which is the centre of gravity of the displaced volume of water. Normally the points S and W are located on the same vertical line. When the ship heels over (Figs 4b and 4c), the centre of buoyancy shifts to a different position (marked W^1), and the upward force acting here strives to rotate the ship around its centre of gravity S. The intersection M of the line of action of the upward force A with the ship's axis of symmetry is called the metacentre. If the metacentre is located above the centre of gravity S of the ship (as in Fig. 4b), the ship will return to its normal upright position; it is said to be in stable equilibrium. On the other hand, if the metacentre is below the centre of gravity S (Fig. 4c), the ship is in unstable equilibrium and will capsise when it heels over.

FROM: THE WAY THINGS WORK

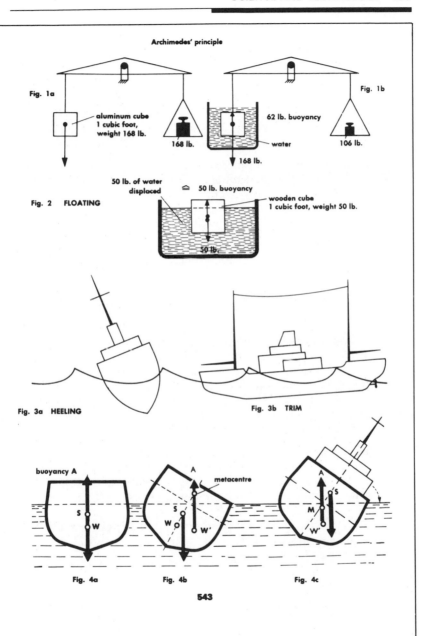

Archimedes' principle

Fig. 1a

aluminum cube
1 cubic foot,
weight 168 lb.

168 lb.

62 lb. buoyancy

water

Fig. 1b

106 lb.

168 lb.

Fig. 2   FLOATING

50 lb. of water
displaced

⇌ 50 lb. buoyancy

wooden cube
1 cubic foot, weight 50 lb.

50 lb.

Fig. 3a   HEELING

Fig. 3b   TRIM

buoyancy A

A

metacentre

S

W

S

W   W'

A

S

M

W'

Fig. 4a

Fig. 4b

Fig. 4c

543

animals, insects, fishes, mollusks and echinoderms, reptiles, birds, and mammals.

MEDICINE

Blake, John Ballard, and Roos, Charles. *Medical Reference Works.* Chicago: Medical Library Association, 1967–1975. Three supplements.

Lists more than 3,000 reference titles in a classified arrangement under general medicine, special subjects, and, in earlier volumes, history of medicine. For in-depth research.

Medical Books for the Lay Person. Boston: Boston Public Library, 1976.

Lists books on various aspects of medicine, health, diet, and exercise. Works are chosen for the nonexpert.

Berkow, Robert, and Talbott, John H., eds. *Merck Manual of Diagnosis and Therapy.* 13th ed. Rahway, N.J.: Merck, Sharp & Dohme Research Laboratories, 1977.

Diseases are described under main headings like "Neurologic Disorders," "Pediatrics," and "Genetics." Entries include definition or description, etiology, symptoms and signs, diagnosis, prognosis, and treatment. Brief discussions for quick reference.

Physician's Desk Reference. Oradell, N.J.: Medical Economics Co., 1947 to date. Annual.

Information on about 2,500 drugs and products of drug manufacturers. Has sections by brand names and generic names, and a six-color section of pictures identifies about 1,000 capsules and tablets. *PDR* gives a drug's composition, action, use, dosage, side effects, etc.

Physician's Desk Reference for Nonprescription Drugs. Oradell, N.J.: Medical Economics Co., 1980 to date. Annual.

A companion to the above title, this offers essential information on nonprescription drugs.

American Medical Association. *American Medical Directory.* Chicago: American Medical Association, 1906– . Biennial.

Directory of Medical Specialists. 19th ed. Chicago: Marquis Who's Who, 1979. 3 vols.

The above two titles offer information on physicians, with each entry providing education, experience, status, and other data relating to professional qualifications.

BIOGRAPHY

Gillespie, Charles C., ed. *Dictionary of Scientific Biography.* New York: Scribner, 1970–1980. 16 vols.

Scholarly articles on approximately 5,000 scientists of the world from ancient to modern times. Each article has a bibliography of major writings by and about the scientist. Living scientists are not included.

American Men and Women of Science. Physical and Biological Sciences. 15th ed. New York: Bowker, 1982. 7 vols.

These volumes offer short biographies of living Americans who are prominent because of research, achievement, or position. All the physical and biological sciences as well as mathematics, engineering, and computer science are represented. There is also a volume covering the *Social and Behavioral Sciences.*

Asimov, Isaac. *Asimov's Biographical Encyclopedia of Science and Technology.* Garden City, N.Y.: Doubleday, 1982.

Biographies are not in alphabetical order. They're arranged chronologically to show the influence of outstanding scientists upon their followers. Covers scientists from the age of Greece to the space age. Below, an example of the detailed but informal style, the beginning of the biography of American physicist Robert H. Goddard.

[1083] **GODDARD,** Robert Hutchings
American physicist
Born: Worcester, Massachusetts, October 5, 1882
Died: Baltimore, Maryland, August 10, 1945

Goddard, the son of a machine shop owner, was raised in Boston, a sickly boy whose thoughts turned inward toward what seemed fantasy in those days. His family returned to Worcester when he was sixteen and he went to the Polytechnic Institute there, graduating in 1908. He received his Ph.D. in physics at Clark University in Worcester in 1911. He taught at Princeton but returned to Clark in 1914 and remained there for nearly thirty years.

He had a mind daring enough for a science fiction writer, and he was firmly grounded in science, to boot. While still an undergraduate, he described a railway line between Boston and New York in which the trains traveled in a vacuum under the pull of an electromagnetic field and completed their trip in ten minutes. He called it "Traveling in 1950," but, alas, the railroad trip still took four hours and more when 1950 actually rolled around.

INDEXES AND ABSTRACTS

Here is a *partial* list of what's available in science and technology:

Applied Science and Technology Index
Biological Abstracts
Biological and Agricultural Index
Chemical Abstracts
General Science Index
Index Medicus
Science Abstracts
Science Citation Index

CHAPTER 30   *SPEECHES*

Oratory, that old-fashioned form of communication, continues to inspire, incite, or alienate listeners. Speeches are another approach to history.

Sutton, Roberta Briggs. *Speech Index*. 4th ed., rev. and enl. New York: Scarecrow, 1966. Supplements, 1966–1970, 1971–1975.

The work indexes collections of famous orations and speeches. It is arranged by author/speaker, subject, and type of speech.

Peterson, Houston. *Treasury of the World's Great Speeches*. Rev. and enl. ed. New York: Simon & Schuster, 1965.

A few of the speeches included in this world history collection are:

Sermon on the Mount
Napoleon Bids Farewell to the Old Guard
John F. Kennedy's Inaugural Address
Martin Luther King, Jr., "I have a dream . . ."

Hurd, Charles. *A Treasury of Great American Speeches*. New York: Hawthorn Books, 1959.

Texts of speeches reflecting American history are preceded by brief "news stories" that set the scene and describe the circumstances. When pertinent, a "sequel" describes what happened after the speech was given. Includes Patrick Henry—naturally—and many others such as Oliver Wendell Holmes, Billy Sunday, Woodrow Wilson, and J. Robert Oppenheimer.

The New York Times Index

The newspaper often prints the full texts of contemporary (though now perhaps historical) speeches and documents, which may later be included in anthologies. (See page 69 in Newspaper and Magazines for full details on this index.)

Vital Speeches of the Day. New York: City News Publishing Co., 1934 to date. Biweekly.

This magazine prints the full texts of important contemporary speeches given by leaders in all fields. It carries the slogan "Best thought of the best minds on current national questions." The cover of each issue carries the table of contents and indicates the wide variety of speakers.

Manning, Beverley. *Index to American Women Speakers, 1828–1978.* Metuchen, N.J.: Scarecrow Press, 1980.

This work indexes by author, subject, and title the speeches by women that have been recorded in collected works, and at conferences, conventions, and hearings.

CHAPTER 31 — *SPORTS AND RECREATION*

Remember that this is a brief general list of only a few of the books that have been written about almost every sport or game you can think of.

Menke, Frank G. *Encyclopedia of Sports.* 6th rev. ed. New York: A. S. Barnes, 1978.

A reference book that has records, history, and rules of a wide variety of sports, including, to name just a few, baseball, croquet, polo, tennis, and weight lifting. It also has miscellaneous information, such as a list of stadiums with their seating capacities. Here is an excerpt from the colorful history of billiards:

> The championship matches in the early part of the century were social affairs approximating the atmosphere of the opera, held in ballrooms of large hotels with spectators of both sexes attending in formal clothes. Four thousand people witnessed Hoppe's first match in this country upon his return from winning the 18.1 balk-line title abroad, and several years later he was to give a "command performance" at the White House.
>
> A generation earlier George F. Slosson numbered among his pupils President Grant and King Edward VII of England, who once, as Prince of Wales, met Slosson in Liverpool with his private railroad car when he arrived with another pupil, the famed Adelina Patti. Other pupils included Mark Twain, Henry Ward Beecher, Robert G. Ingersoll, Charles A. Dana, and John McGraw.

and some incidental background on bobsledding:

> The bobsled was developed from the sled of ancient times, which was merely a strip of animal skin stretched between smoothed strips of wood acting as runners. The first step in this evolution was the toboggan. It was conceived and developed about 1890 by a group of thrill-seeking American

and English vacationers in Switzerland who were looking for something more daring than plodding through the Swiss Alps on snowshoes.

They laid out a course on the mountains around St. Moritz and were soon hurtling down the snow-clad slopes.

It soon was discovered that the toboggan was too safe for this particular brand of daredevils, so they came up with the idea of mounting the toboggan on sled-like runners. This produced speeds far in excess of what the toboggan was capable of doing, but the light weight of the toboggan-sled, combined with the excessive speeds, caused the sled to lose its course and there were many serious accidents and some deaths.

Arlott, John, ed. *The Oxford Companion to World Sports and Games.* New York: Oxford University Press, 1975.

This *Oxford Companion* offers an introduction to sports and games that "are the subject of national and international competition," and though it does not print the complete rules of each game, it does have a digest of them. Does not include blood sports or board games.

The Baseball Encyclopedia. 4th ed., rev. and expanded by Joseph L. Reichler. New York: Macmillan, 1979.

A compilation listing season-by-season and lifetime statistical records of everyone who has played major-league baseball. It covers the game from the beginning and gives data on pitchers, players, managers, World Series, and All-Star games. The total picture of the game.

Hollander, Zander, ed. *The Modern Encyclopedia of Basketball.* New York: Four Winds Press, 1973.

Basketball started one day in 1891 when "Doc" Naismith nailed a peach basket at each end of a gymnasium and tossed his gym class a soccer ball. Historical and contemporary information is included in this comprehensive book.

Treat, Roger. *The Official Encyclopedia of Football.* 16th rev. ed. New York: A. S. Barnes, 1979.

Includes information on players, coaches, teams, and leagues, a year-by-year history, and a description of the evolution of the game.

Hindman, Darwin A. *Kick the Can and Over 800 Other Active Games and Sports for All Ages.* Englewood Cliffs, N.J.: Prentice-Hall, 1978.

Describes games and how they are played. They are grouped according to type (tag games, alertness games, combat games), and there is also an index.

Foster, Robert Frederick. *Foster's Complete Hoyle*. Rev. ed. Philadelphia: Lippincott, 1963.

An encyclopedia of indoor games—especially card games and games of chance. Hoyle gives the rules and techniques of everything from bridge and poker to dominoes and checkers. It even explains (under the heading "Juvenile Games") old maid, pig, and go fish.

This book is the origin of the phrase "played according to Hoyle," meaning, of course, played in accordance with the rules of the game. The book includes many versions of solitaire in case you're bored with the one you know and states that even in this game there is an "opponent":

> BY Solitaire or Patience is meant any card game that can be played by one person. His opponent is the luck of the shuffle—or any personification thereof he chooses to pose, as Beelzebub.

Torbet, Laura, ed. *The Encyclopedia of Crafts*. New York: Scribner, 1980. 3 vols.

Lists individual crafts, in dictionary arrangement, and the terms, materials, tools, etc. of each. There are numerous line drawings and diagrams.

Scott's Standard Postage Stamp Catalogue. New York: Scott Publications, 1867 to date. Annual.

An encyclopedia of philately giving illustrations, description, denominations, and value of major stamps of all countries.

> One of the most interesting foreign postmarks was devised in France, during the siege of Paris by the Prussian Army in 1870. Paris was cut off from the outside world, and carrier pigeons and large postal balloons provided the only means of communication. Letters that traveled by balloon were postmarked Par Ballon Monté, "carried by balloon."

Krause, Chester L., and Mishler, Clifford. *Standard Catalog of World Coins*. 7th ed. Iola, Wis.: Krause Publications, 1980.

A catalog of national coin issues. Offers documentation of the world's coinages from the 1760's to the present day.

Reinfeld, Fred, and Hobson, Burton. *Catalogue of the World's Most Popular Coins*. 9th ed. Garden City, N.Y.: Doubleday, 1976.

This source lists coins with illustrations of each. Value in U.S. dollars is given for each, and when coins are not silver, their composition is given. Some early American coins were for odd amounts, such as the half cent, half dime, three cents, and twenty cents coins.

Kirschner, M. J. *Yoga All Your Life*. New York: Schocken Books, 1977.

Offering an alternative (or a supplement) to more violent exercise, this excellent little book is an example of the wide variety of books on health. It describes yoga breathing and relaxation and the postures (exercises) are illustrated with line drawings.

CHAPTER 32   *THEATER, FILM, AND TV-RADIO*

THEATER

"Drama—what literature does at night." So said critic George Jean Nathan. When the play's your thing, some things to consult are:

Whalon, Marion K. *Performing Arts Research: A Guide to Information Sources*. Detroit: Gale Research, 1976.

An annotated guide to encyclopedias, directories, indexes, bibliographies, reviews, etc.

Encyclopedia of World Theater. New York: Scribners, 1977.

This is an English-language work based on a German work, *Friedrichs Theaterlexikon*, which has brief entries for actors, playwrights, directors, designers, types of drama, and theatrical institutions.

Shipley, Joseph Twadell. *Guide to Great Plays*. Washington, D.C.: Public Affairs Press, 1956.

The guide lists by author great plays of all times. It gives a digest of each play in addition to information on famous productions, casts, and reviews.

Hartnoll, Phyllis. *Oxford Companion to the Theatre*. 3d ed. London, New York: Oxford University Press, 1967.

Like other *Oxford Companions*, this is a one-volume work arranged in dictionary form. It is international in scope and includes articles on subjects such as Jewish theater, makeup and lighting, and individuals such as Russian dramatist Anton Chekhov and black Shakespearean actor Ira Aldridge.

Campbell, Oscar James, and Quinn, Edward G., eds. *The Reader's Encyclopedia of Shakespeare.* New York: Crowell, 1966.

An excellent one-volume source of information on Shakespeare. Arranged in dictionary form, it discusses actors, characters, adapters, etc. For each play it considers sources, plots, stage history (productions), and selected criticism. The smallest details are given. Even Crab, the dog in *The Two Gentlemen of Verona,* is given an entry.

Rigdon, Walter, ed. *Biographical Encyclopedia and Who's Who in the American Theatre.* New York: James H. Heineman, 1966.

An informative work containing biographical information on contemporary actors, producers, directors, etc. It also has a list of productions with opening dates, numbers of performances, and lists of awards. In addition to information about people, the book has a list of "theatre building biographies." Here is a sample:

> **OLYMPIA,** east side of Broadway between 44th and 45th Sts. Owner, Oscar Hammerstein. Architect, J. B. McElfatrick and Son. The complex consisted of a music hall, a concert hall, a theatre, a roof garden, etc. Opening of what was called the LYRIC THEATRE, November 25, 1895, with *Excelsior, Jr.* The **MUSIC HALL,** opened with Yvette Guilbert, December 17, 1895.
> MUSIC HALL re-opened as:
> NEW YORK THEATRE, April 24, 1899, with *The Man in the Moon*
> LYRIC THEATRE, reopened as:
> CRITERION THEATRE, August 29, 1899, with *The Girl from Maxim's*
> VITAGRAPH THEATRE, February 7, 1914, as a cinema theatre
> CRITERION THEATRE, September 11, 1916, with *Paganini*
> Demolished 1935
>
> **PALLADIUM,** 254 W. 54th St., between Broadway and 8th Ave.
> **(See GALLO THEATRE)**

Gassner, John, and Quinn, Edward G., eds. *The Reader's Encyclopedia of World Drama.* New York: Crowell, 1969.

A one-volume book with emphasis on drama as literature. It has information on plays and playwrights from all countries and has an appendix containing "basic documents in dramatic theory."

Hochman, Stanley, ed. *McGraw-Hill Encyclopedia of World Drama.* New York: McGraw-Hill, 1984. 5 vols.

This international reference work covers dramatists and the literature of the theater. There are entries for terms, movements, and genres; and for playwrights, the entries include biographical data, a brief critique, synopses of plays, and bibliography.

THEATER REVIEWS

The New York Times Directory of the Theater. New York: Quadrangle/
The New York Times Book Co., 1973.

This is an index to theater reviews published in *The New York Times* during the period 1920–1970. There is a section at the front listing major theater awards, with reprints of *New York Times* articles announcing those awards. There are separate indexes by title and personal name.

The New York Times Theater Reviews, 1920–1970. New York: The New
York Times, 1971.

Related to the above title, this work contains actual reprints, in chronological order, of *Times* reviews. There are appendixes listing awards and prizes, and productions and runs by season, and indexes of titles, production companies, and personal names.

Samples, Gordon. *How to Locate Reviews of Plays and Films: A Bibliography of Criticism from the Beginnings to the Present.* Metuchen,
N.J.: Scarecrow, 1976.

This is an annotated guide to indexes, checklists, and bibliographies of reviews and critiques of plays and films. It is a useful tool, even though there are some inaccuracies.

FILM

Lyon, Christopher, and Doll, Susan, eds. *Macmillan Dictionary of Films
and Filmmakers.* London: Macmillan, 1984. 4 vols.

An international set in four volumes covering films, directors/filmmakers, actors and actresses, and writers and production artists. This scholarly work gives detailed information and, when appropriate, includes bibliographies, review references, and information on published screenplays.

Armour, Robert A. *Film: A Reference Guide.* Westport, Conn.: Greenwood Press, 1980.

Each chapter in this book has a bibliographic essay on some aspect of film—history of film, production, actors, directors, reference books and periodicals.

Bawden, Liz-Anne. *The Oxford Companion to Film.* London: Oxford University Press, 1976.

Like all *Oxford Companions*, this has an alphabetical arrangement, with articles of varying lengths. It covers producers, actors and actresses, film terminology, and outstanding films.

Halliwell, Leslie. *The Filmgoer's Companion.* 6th ed. New York: Hill and Wang, 1977.

A very useful guide, the work's emphasis is on British and American films, but it does include some entries for films of other countries. Articles on actors and actresses, directors, well-known films, and terms. Also lists films by topic—all-star films, horror, death, airplanes, etc.

———. *Halliwell's Film Guide: A Survey of 8000 English-Language Movies.* New York: Scribner, 1981.

A work that gives brief synopses and information for thousands of movies. Short entries include year first shown, running time, color, film company, cast, production personnel, and critical comment.

The New York Times Directory of the Film. New York: Arno Press, 1971.

The directory is a personal name and corporate name index from the work listed below and gives reference to the date and page in *The New York Times.* Lists awards and yearly ten best films.

The New York Times Film Reviews, 1913–1968. New York: The New York Times and Arno Press, 1971–72. 10 vols. and supplements.

Photographic reprints of film reviews that have appeared in *The New York Times* are presented along with related information on awards. Reviews are by some of the most famous critics, such as Alexander Woollcott, Brooks Atkinson, Howard Taubman, Clive Barnes.

TV-RADIO

McCavitt , William E. *Radio and Television: A Selected, Annotated Bibliography.* Metuchen, N.J.: Scarecrow, 1978.

Offers more than 1,000 selected books on radio and television, arranged by topics.

Terrace, Vincent. *The Complete Encyclopedia of Television Programs, 1949–1979.* 2d rev. ed. South Brunswick, N.J., and New York: A. S. Barnes, 1981.

Lists more than 2,000 programs, giving description, length, date, cast and personnel, and network.

Brown, Les. *The New York Times Encyclopedia of Television.* New York: Times Books, 1977.

Articles in the encyclopedia cover a wide range of TV topics: stars, programs, technology, laws, networks, ratings, foreign broadcasting systems, public and cable television.

Dunning, John. *Tune In Yesterday: The Ultimate Encyclopedia of Old-Time Radio, 1925–1976.* Englewood Cliffs, N.J.: Prentice-Hall, 1976.

More than 1,000 radio shows are listed alphabetically, and there is also an index. Descriptions include history of the show, personnel, sponsors, dates, popularity, and so on. Here is the beginning of the entry for Jack Armstrong:

Jack Armstrong, the All-American Boy

Jack Armstrong, the All-American Boy, one of the greatest, longest-running juvenile adventures of all radio, was first heard on CBS from Station WBBM, Chicago, on July 31, 1933. Created by former journalist Robert Hardy Andrews, Jack Armstrong was cast in the Frank Merriwell mold—a super-athlete whose last-of-the-ninth efforts saved games for Hudson High School and glorified team athletics. The series began at Hudson High, where Jack was the prime color-bearer and his cousins were also enrolled as students. Jack's athletic powess gave rise to the famed school song, which became the series theme and is still fondly remembered:

Wave the flag for Hudson High, boys,
Show them how we stand;
Ever shall our team be champions
Known through-out the land!

CHAPTER 33 WOMEN'S STUDIES

Our consciousness having been raised, there is a mushrooming literature on a subject well worth studying.

Ballou, Patricia K. *Women: A Bibliography of Bibliographies*. Boston: G. K. Hall, 1980.

An annotated bibliography of books, pamphlets, essays, journal articles, and dissertations produced since 1970.

Krichmar, Albert. *The Women's Rights Movement in the United States 1848–1970: A Bibliography and Sourcebook*. Metuchen, N.J.: Scarecrow, 1972.

A topically arranged bibliography on the political, legal, religious, economic, educational, and professional status of women since 1848.

———, et al. *The Women's Movement in the Seventies: An International English-Language Bibliography*. Metuchen, N.J.: Scarecrow, 1977.

This work is arranged geographically with subject indexes and many annotations.

Stineman, Esther. *Women's Studies: A Recommended Core Bibliography*. Littleton, Colo.: Libraries Unlimited, 1979.

Lists topics as they relate to women—anthropology, autobiography, business, history, literature, medicine and health, politics, sports, and the women's movement.

Ritchie, Maureen. *Women's Studies: A Checklist of Bibliographies*. London: Mansell, 1980.

This work is arranged by subject with an author index and a key word index. Under "Area Studies" are listed many books that deal with women in geographic areas—Asia, Arab countries, Europe, etc.

Haber, Barbara. *Women in America: A Guide to Books.* Boston: G. K. Hall, 1978, 1981.

A guide to books from 1963 to 1975, with an appendix of books published from 1976 to 1979. The arrangement is by subject.

Rosenberg, Marie, and Bergstrom, Leonard. *Women and Society: A Critical Review of the Literature and a Selected Annotated Bibliography.* Beverly Hills, Calif.: Sage Publications, 1975.

Arranged by subject, such as women in history, women in philosophy, economics, literature, etc., this review has several indexes. There is an index by author/organizations, an index of persons not cited as authors, an index of journal issues entirely devoted to women, and indexes by place and subject (see page 182). This work is supplemented by:

Een, JoAnn D., and Rosenberg-Dishman, Marie. *Women and Society, Citations 3601–6000.* Beverly Hills, Calif.: Sage Publications, 1978.

Hinding, Andrea, and Chambers, Clarke A. *Women's History Sources.* New York: Bowker, 1980. 2 vols.

Subtitled *A Guide to Archive and Manuscript Collections in the United States,* the first volume has collections arranged by state and city; volume two is an index.

INDEX

Women's Studies Abstracts. Rush, N.Y.: Women's Studies, 1972 to date. Quarterly with annual index.

Abstracts articles from a wide range of periodicals, along with some books and pamphlets.

[168] WOMEN AND SOCIETY

1980. Reed, Evelyn. PROBLEMS OF WOMAN'S LIBERATION: A MARXIST APPROACH. New York: Pathfinder Press, 1970. Discussion of matriarchal periods in history, how women have been subjected in the past, and prospects for the future.

1981. Reimar, Robert Fernandez, ed. CASA DE LAS AMERICAS [Home of the Americas], Havana (Mar.-June 1971). Issue devoted to women includes articles on black women in Cuba since Castro's rise to power, women in Brazil, and Vietnamese women.

1982. Stephens, Winifred. WOMEN OF THE FRENCH REVOLUTION. London: n.p., 1922.

1983. Tatarinova, Nadezhda. WOMEN IN THE USSR. Moscow: Novosti Press, n.d. 110 pp. Summary of women in the Soviet economy, highlighting changes since the Russian Revolution in women's participation in political and public life.

1984. Weinstein, James. THE DECLINE OF SOCIALISM IN AMERICA, 1912-1925. New York: Monthly Review Press, 1967. See his chapter on "Women and Socialism."

1985. "Women in Revolution," WOMAN: A JOURNAL OF LIBERATION, vol. 1, no. 4 (1969), pp. 2-32, 64. Issue devoted to women in Asia, Cuba, France, and Vietnam.

1986. WOMEN OF VIETNAM. Nos. 1, 2, 3, and 4. Hanoi: Vietnam Women's Union, 1967. Series of pamphlets on women in the revolution, Ho Chi Minh on the emancipation of women, and illustrations of changes in the lives of women in North Vietnam.

1987. Yetman, Norman. LIFE UNDER THE PECULIAR INSTITUTION: SELECTIONS FROM THE SLAVE NARRATIVE COLLECTION. New York: Holt, Rinehart and Winston, 1970. Many selections by women slaves before and after abolition.

I. Women as Colonists and Pioneers

It is particularly intriguing that social and economic historians of the past century have overlooked women, for during that time one of the most impressive social and economic facts has been the rapid change in the part women have played in the society and the economy.
                                                            —*Ann Firor Scott*

The power of a woman is in her dependence, flowing from the consciousness of that weakness which God has given her for her protection.
                                                            —*The Congregational Clergy of Massachusetts*

1988. Acrelius, Israel. A HISTORY OF NEW SWEDEN OR THE SETTLEMENTS ON THE RIVER DELAWARE. Stockholm: Harberg and Hassellberg, 1759. The part women played in the settlements is discussed throughout the book.

1989. Adams, James T. THE FOUNDING OF NEW ENGLAND. Boston: Atlantic Monthly Press, 1921. Women in the founding of the early colonies.

1990. Augur, Helen. AN AMERICAN JEZEBEL: LIFE OF ANNE HUTCHINSON. New York: Brentano, 1930. A biography of the early colonist in the Massachusetts Bay Colony who was exiled to Rhode Island, and

PART IV

EVALUATING INFORMATION

CHAPTER 34 CRITICAL THINKING

Well, now that we have discussed the tremendous resources available in libraries and some excellent reference books in various fields, it's time for this advice: Don't believe everything you read. *Finding* the information is not the most important part of research; what you *do* with it is. In the research process, searching for information should lead us to the really interesting part—the challenge of dealing critically and creatively with information.

The search, of course, is not an end in itself. The reason some students and researchers find the process of using an index, getting a magazine article, and feeding it (almost unchanged) back to a professor or reader (who has probably read the same newsmagazine) to be a boring experience is that it *is* boring. It describes a process that does not seem to be related to the person or to real life. Our preoccupation with procedures can make us forget the reasons for searching—to learn, to make informed decisions, to evaluate applications of knowledge, and to find truth.

"Sponge" readers are those who totally accept anything in print or computer printout. They do not think about what they read. Critical reading is critical thinking, and the critical reader evaluates both the ideas presented and the manner of their presentation. A critical reader asks questions. Are the ideas valid? Who is the author? An area that particularly lacks critical evaluation seems to be criticism itself. Who are those interpreters and book reviewers? No matter how bizarre a criticism of Shakespeare or an interpretation of art, some readers, finding it in print, appear to buy it all. Is Mona Lisa really smiling because she's pregnant?

There are certain attitudes we can take that best prepare us for critical thinking and are useful throughout the search process as well as during the use or communication of information. These attitudes include: *intellectual curiosity*, asking questions about who, what, where, when, and how; *personal honesty and objectivity*, a readiness to accept truth based on objective factors even if it challenges an old belief or, frequently, the idea we thought we were pursuing when we began our research; *open-mindedness and respect for the viewpoints of others*, listening to other views and carefully considering differing points of view; *flexibility*, a willingness to change a belief if sufficient evidence warrants it; *skepticism*, questioning and refusing to believe everything we hear or read; *persistence and orderliness*, following a line of reason to its conclusion and seeking to resolve discrepancies, giving each view a fair chance.

Part of attaining these attitudes is knowing and understanding ourselves. Everyone has prejudices and blind spots. Recognizing these is the first step toward not letting them get in the way of our objectivity. Holding beliefs and ideas in abeyance while we consider other views does not in itself constitute giving them up. Trying to keep an open mind and seeking other views encourage critical thinking.

Critical thinkers are able to:

Identify main issues: The main points of a paper or argument may be perfectly clear, or hidden in obscure language, or possibly never stated at all. Until the main ideas have been identified, the searcher cannot begin to test them.

Recognize underlying assumptions: Analysis of ideas must go beyond the argument to the assumptions upon which the major points are based. Some assumptions are generally accepted; others are subject to doubt or may be untenable.

Evaluate evidence: One must test claims to see if they are true. This involves discovering if the facts are relevant, if the facts support the conclusions drawn, if the data are adequate (are there enough?), and if important data have been omitted.

Evaluate authority: Who is the author, and what are the author's qualifications? Who is the publisher, and does the publisher have a point of view?

Recognize bias: Listen for the drums of propaganda, and be aware of emotional appeals, labeling, and name-calling.

Understand the problems of language: Recognize generalities, ambiguities, vague terms, clichés, and equivocations, and question definitions.

Relate information to ideas: This has some of the elements of evaluating evidence. A connection must be made between information, facts, figures, however correct, and the way they contribute to ideas or concepts. Otherwise, information is never used to reach a conclusion.

Some of the works already described in this book will help in the critical process. In addition to *Who's Who* (for geographical areas and in certain fields), there are directories for professions, sources on scholars and writers, and master biographical indexes. Articles in en-

cyclopedias are signed with names or initials that are identified somewhere in the set (usually in the first or last volume). Katz's *Magazines
for Libraries* (New York: Bowker, 1982) and Farber's *Classified List of
Periodicals for the College Library* (Westwood, Mass.: Faxon, 1972) describe the political stances of journals. (See also the sources in this
book that list journals, in the section "About Magazines" on page 67.)
Editor & Publisher International Yearbook describes newspapers and
identifies political affiliations, if any. Reviews for books, films, plays,
or art can also assist the critical process.

Though one must view criticism critically, book reviews are extremely useful for determining the value of a source. *Book Review Digest* and *Book Review Index* are two aids to finding reviews; others are
listed in the section on Books and Literature under "Criticism," on
page 91.

Remember, even the best and most reputable source can have a mis-
take in it. It's a good idea to check a "fact" in three sources and, if they
don't agree, to check further.

Reference books can be evaluated by consideration of their authority, purpose, scope, and proposed audience:

Authority: Again, who is the author of the work itself or the individual article within the work, and what are his or her qualifications?
What sources did the author use? Are they primary or secondary
sources, are they well chosen, are they recent, up-to-date titles,
and does that matter in this topic? After researchers have been ex-
posed even briefly to a subject field, they begin to recognize certain cited authors as authorities. And appraising sources,
footnotes, and the writer's bibliography can be a test of the accuracy and authority of a book or article. Who is the publisher? A
reader can begin to appreciate the personality of a publisher by a
look at the *Literary Market Place* and *Writer's Market*, which describe what kinds of things they publish and what they require
from an author. Check *Publishers' Trade List Annual* for the catalogs of some publishers to see what other materials they have in
print.

Purpose: Does the work fulfill its stated purpose (as stated, for example, in the introduction, preface, subtitle, etc.)? Does it claim to
be exhaustive information on the subject, encyclopedic information? Is it limited to a certain time period?

Scope: Does the coverage live up to the stated purpose? What is the
actual extent of the material given? For example, does it cover one
nation or all nations, one time period or several? Check the index
and table of contents to investigate a work's coverage further.
What has the author given that can't be found elsewhere? Once
again, what is not included as well as what is included should be
considered.

Audience: Is the work aimed at a child or an adult, a lay person or an expert? If it's meant for a beginner, it will be written in a language and format suitable for that level. Much more is expected of work claiming to be for the expert. (Format and presentation of material are also factors in finding the right reference book. There are times when the information hunter wants only a graph or chart, not a chapter.)

PRIMARY/SECONDARY SOURCES

This is an important concept in research. A primary source is an original manuscript, document, or eyewitness account. A secondary source is a work based on primary sources, distilling them and perhaps drawing conclusions from them that were not visible in the original primary source. An account of the Battle of Wounded Knee in the words of a participant is a primary source; an account of the battle in a contemporary encyclopedia of American Indians is a secondary source. The United States Constitution is a primary source; a work written today on the forming of the Constitution is a secondary source, but the author would certainly draw heavily on primary sources in the process of writing such a book. One kind of source is not *necessarily* better than another. A useful book might be made from only derivative material, but an authority would be suspect if no primary sources were cited.

Furthermore, an eyewitness account can be distorted, a memoir can contain an error, and sometimes a secondary source, giving a retrospective view, can present more truth, but probably only after the author has carefully scrutinized the primary sources. Some research may be on topics or events so new that, strictly speaking, there are no primary sources available yet. Perhaps an author is involved in producing a primary source. Perhaps you are.

Evaluation adds an analytical dimension to the intellectual process of research. It requires a certain tough-mindedness that overcomes our blind spots and our laziness, and it requires a commitment to seek reasons and to judge impartially—even if that means doing still more research.

PART V

ORGANIZING AND COMMUNICATING INFORMATION

CHAPTER 35   *ON WRITING A PAPER*

WRITING GUIDES

Ernest Hemingway is quoted as having said, "Easy writing makes hard reading." So perhaps it's a good thing for readers when writers find writing difficult. It is an exact art, and fortunately several excellent writers have published some excellent advice on writing and choosing the right word.

Barzun, Jacques. *Simple & Direct.* New York: Harper & Row, 1975.

A brisk—and funny—guide to effective writing. The author teaches by making choices, translating hundreds of examples into the language he calls "simple and direct."

Bernstein, Theodore. *Dos, Don'ts & Maybes of the English Language.* New York: Times Books, 1977.

With wit and urbanity, the author of *The Careful Writer* (see page 50) examines words that plague writers and readers.

Safire, William. *On Language.* New York: Times Books, 1980.
———. *What's the Good Word?* New York: Times Books, 1982.
———. *I Stand Corrected.* New York: Times Books, 1984.

Drawn from the author's *New York Times* column, examples of the use and misuse of language are accompanied by letters from readers. Safire attacks the fuzzy thinking that inhibits communication.

Strunk, William, and White, E. B. *The Elements of Style.* 3d ed. New York: Macmillan, 1979.

E. B. White's version of his former professor's "little book" on the use of language. A slim volume covering a lot of territory in an interesting and lively way.

Zinsser, William K. *On Writing Well: An Informal Guide to Writing Nonfiction.* 2d ed. New York: Harper & Row, 1980.

This book is an outgrowth of an extremely popular Yale course on writing nonfiction. The author believes that there is no subject that can't be made accessible if the writer goes about his work with humanity and cares enough to write well—"the race is not to the swift but to the original." Lots of good advice and humor.

For now here are a few writing reminders:

Keep your writing clear and straightforward. Be accurate and honest. Somewhere in the first paragraph or beginning of the paper make a concise statement of your subject and what the reader can expect from your paper; follow this with some orderly progression of the material (perhaps chronologically, perhaps by subject—for example, U.S. history by the date of events or by topics like government, economics, social history), and conclude the paper with a summary of ideas. It is recommended that you make an outline before you start to write, but if you are the sort of person who gets hung up on such a procedure, forget it, and use whatever method is comfortable.

If you have even the tiniest amount of natural curiosity, the researching of a subject will lead to an interest in it, so don't resist the task. Keep an open mind, try to have a genuine involvement with the topic (even if it's assigned and not your choice), and the resulting attitude will allow you to *develop enthusiasm, deal creatively with the material*, and give free play to your imagination.

PUBLISHING AND MARKETING GUIDES

If you're making the effort to do research, why not share it by publishing? Getting something published also takes effort, but there are excellent guides.

Literary Market Place. New York: Bowker, 1940 to date. Annual.

Lists book publishers and magazines with addresses, editors' names, and brief information on what kinds of things they publish. Also lists book clubs, agents, awards, etc.

International Literary Market Place. New York: Bowker, 1965 to date. Biennial.

Arranged by country, this guide gives brief information on publishers, describing what kind of material they publish. Also lists book clubs, major booksellers, major libraries, translation agencies, and so on.

Writer's Market. Cincinnati, Ohio: Writer's Digest, 1930 to date. Annual.

Describes a wide range of markets—book publishers, magazines, consumer publications, scriptwriting, trade, technical and professional markets, regional sources, gag writing, and greeting card publishers.

Fredctta, Jean M., and Brady, John, eds. *Fiction Writer's Market 1982/83.* 2d ed. Cincinnati, Ohio: Writer's Digest, 1981.

Offers advice on writing techniques followed by market information for books and magazines. Also lists awards, writers' organizations, etc.

Other useful guides are:

Writer's Handbook. Boston: The Writer, 1936 to date. Annual.

International Directory of Little Magazines and Small Presses. Paradise, Calif.: Dustbooks, 1954 to date. Annual.

Directory of Publishing Opportunities in Journals and Periodicals. 4th ed. Chicago: Marquis, 1979.

Meyer, Carol. *The Writer's Survival Manual: The Complete Guide to Getting Your Book Published Right.* New York: Crown, 1982.

Artist's Market. Cincinnati, Ohio: Writer's Digest, 1981.

Photographer's Market. Cincinnati, Ohio: Writer's Digest, 1983.

There are also many guides to publishing in particular fields, such as business, education, and history. Check library catalogs or the *Subject Guide to Books in Print* for these.

CHAPTER 36   *STYLE MANUALS*

Like most things, if an article or paper is worth doing, it's worth doing with style. It's essential that footnotes and bibliographies be consistent and complete so readers can find again a source quoted or cited. A few examples of footnotes and bibliographic citations are shown in the next chapter, but to handle such matters comprehensively and precisely, the following "style manuals" offer guidance in the preparation of manuscripts and the correct citing of works consulted.

Campbell, William Giles. *Form and Style: Theses, Reports, Term Papers.* 6th ed. Boston: Houghton Mifflin, 1981.

Jordan, Lewis. *The New York Times Manual of Style and Usage.* New York: Quadrangle/The New York Times Book Co., 1976.

Skillin, Marjorie E., et al. *Words into Type.* 3d ed. Englewood Cliffs, N.J.: Prentice-Hall, 1974.

Turabian, Kate L. *A Manual for Writers of Term Papers, Theses, and Dissertations.* 4th ed. Chicago: University of Chicago Press, 1973.

University of Chicago Press. *The Chicago Manual of Style.* Chicago: University of Chicago Press, 1982.

Van Leunen, Mary-Claire. *A Handbook for Scholars.* New York: Knopf, 1978.

Also, many professions have their own requirements and publish their own style manuals, such as those put out by the Modern Language Association and the American Psychological Association.

CHAPTER 37 FOOTNOTES AND BIBLIOGRAPHY

FOOTNOTES

A footnote is an explanatory or bibliographic comment or note at the bottom of a page.

An explanatory footnote is used to free the text of incidental material and still amplify the discussion for the reader who might be interested. The following explanatory footnote was indicated in *The Modern Researcher* in a discussion of the Mohammedan and Christian calendars:

2The Moslem year is computed from the Hejira, or Flight of Mohammed, in A.D. 622. Since it is a lunar year, it is shorter than ours, and this accounts for the fact that 622 plus 1156 equals more than 1743.*

*Jacques Barzun and Henry F. Graff, *The Modern Researcher* (New York: Harcourt, Brace, 1957), p. 116.

In the writing of any paper, many ideas and facts are borrowed from others, and the use of bibliographic footnotes enables the writer to give recognition to important sources and to establish the validity of a statement. If footnotes are not used, the borrowed idea or fact becomes stolen. Honesty is the scholarly policy. After the first reference to a work has been cited in full, *Ibid.* (Latin, *Ibidem*, in the same place) may be used, but only when the next reference is to the same work with no other work intervening.

1Lewis S. Feuer, *The Conflict of Generations: The Character and Significance of Student Movements* (New York: Basic Books, 1969), p. 11.
2*Ibid.*, p. 41.

If there is a second reference to a work already cited in full but with other references intervening, *op. cit.* (Latin, *opere citato*, in the work cited) is used with the author's name.

¹Lewis S. Feuer, *The Conflict of Generations: The Character and Significance of Student Movements* (New York: Basic Books, 1969), p. 11.
²Dorothy Day, *The Long Loneliness* (New York: Harper, 1952), p. 39.
³Feuer, *op. cit.*, p. 50.

Instead of *op. cit.*, the author's name and a shortened title may be used:

³Feuer, *The Conflict of Generations*, p. 17.

If more than one work by the same author has been cited in the footnotes, then the title of the work would also have to be included in subsequent footnotes to make the reference clear:

¹Martin Luther King, Jr., *The Trumpet of Conscience* (New York: Harper & Row, 1968), p. 70.
²Martin Luther King, Jr., *Where Do We Go from Here: Chaos or Community?* (New York: Harper & Row, 1967), p. 35.
³King, *Trumpet of Conscience*, p. 99.
⁴King, *Where Do We Go from Here?*, p. 50.

Each footnote is indicated by the number at the end of the statement to which it refers. Footnotes in a book may be numbered serially either on each page, or by chapters, or for the entire book. Footnotes may also be numbered and listed consecutively on a separate page at the end of a report or paper. The numbers calling attention to the footnotes are written slightly above the line and should not be enclosed in parentheses or followed by a period or any punctuation. The main body of a typed report or paper should be double-spaced, but the footnotes should be single-spaced, except on a manuscript that is to be set in type.

BIBLIOGRAPHY

The bibliography is a list of every work cited in the text or in the footnotes plus other pertinent sources. A bibliography must include every work referred to in a report or paper, but it may also include works that contributed to the writer's ideas or conclusions but were not cited in the text. Padded bibliographies are ridiculous and only reveal a mind that thinks quantity, not quality. Do not list every work consulted. List only those that made a real contribution to your paper.

The form of the bibliography differs from that of the footnotes. The list is arranged alphabetically by the author's last name, it does not include parentheses, and periods, not commas, are used between each part of the entry. The author's last name is against the left-hand margin, and any succeeding lines are indented three spaces. For magazine articles, the inclusive pages of the article should be given, and for newspaper articles, the page on which it begins and pages on which it may be continued (separated by a comma, as in the sample headed "Newspaper" below).

Books

ONE AUTHOR

Footnote:
¹Lewis S. Feuer, *The Conflict of Generations: The Character and Significance of Student Movements* (New York: Basic Books, 1969), p. 14.
Bibliography:
Feuer, Lewis S. *The Conflict of Generations: The Character and Significance of Student Movements.* New York: Basic Books, 1969.

TWO AUTHORS

Footnote:
²Charles Judah and George Winston Smith, *The Unchosen* (New York: Coward-McCann, 1962), p. 17.
Bibliography:
Judah, Charles, and Smith, George Winston. *The Unchosen.* New York: Coward-McCann, 1962.

THREE AUTHORS

Footnote:
³Hans H. Landsberg, Leonard L. Fischman, and Joseph L. Fisher, *Resources in America's Future* (Baltimore: Johns Hopkins Press, 1963), p. 2.
Bibliography:
Landsberg, Hans H.; Fischman, Leonard L.; and Fisher, Joseph L. *Resources in America's Future.* Baltimore: Johns Hopkins Press, 1963.

MORE THAN THREE AUTHORS

Footnote:
⁴James Westfall Thompson *et al.* [or James Westfall Thompson and others], *The Civilization of the Renaissance* (New York: Ungar, 1959), p. 69.
Bibliography:
Thompson, James Westfall; Rowley, George; Schevill, Ferdinand; and Sarton, George. *The Civilization of the Renaissance.* New York: Ungar, 1959.

EDITOR

Footnote:

⁵Herbert Mitgang, ed., *Lincoln as They Saw Him* (New York: Rinehart, 1956), p. 3.

Bibliography:

Mitgang, Herbert, ed. *Lincoln as They Saw Him.* New York: Rinehart, 1956.

Magazine

Footnote:

⁶Kenneth L. Woodward, "Seances in Suburbia," *McCall's* (March 1970), p. 70.

Bibliography:

Woodward, Kenneth L. "Seances in Suburbia." *McCall's* (March 1970), pp. 70–71, 149–51.

Newspaper

Footnote:

⁷J. Anthony Lucas. "The Drug Scene: Dependence Grows," *The New York Times,* January 8, 1968, p. 22.

Bibliography:

Lucas, J. Anthony. "The Drug Scene: Dependence Grows." *The New York Times,* January 8, 1968, pp. 1, 22.

Encyclopedia

Footnote:

⁸Harold E. Driver, "Indian, American," *Encyclopedia Americana,* 1969, XV, 27.

Bibliography:

Driver, Harold E. "Indian, American." *Encyclopedia Americana.* 1969. Vol. XV.

ENCYCLOPEDIA *(Unsigned Article)*

Footnote:

⁹"Ironwood," *Encyclopedia Americana,* 1969, XV, 467.

Bibliography:

"Ironwood." *Encyclopedia Americana.* 1969. Vol. XV.

This explanation of footnotes and bibliography offers only the simplest examples to give a basic idea of forms. There are other ways of arranging research references, and some disciplines and publishers require the use of a specific style manual. See "Style Manuals," page 194.

CHAPTER 38   *SAMPLE TERM PAPER*

SAMPLE PAPER SHOWING THE USE OF REFERENCE BOOKS

The following paper is an example of how to use the information found in reference books. It is an oversimplification meant only to illustrate the use of a few sources.

OUTLINE

Paper on Nonviolence

I.   Introduction and Purpose

II.   Definition of Nonviolence
            Satyagraha translations

III.   Some Practitioners of Nonviolence
            Jews, early Christians, Godwin,
            Shelley, Thoreau, Tolstoy, Gandhi,
            Martin Luther King, Jr.

IV.   Visible Reasons for Resorting to Violence
            Definition of violence
            Deprivation and poverty, frustration,
            slow process of government, brutality

V.   Invisible Reasons for Violence
        (Psychological)
            Fear, conscience, attitudes
            Treatment of persons as things

VI.   Violence Harms Self as Well as Others

VII.   Persuading the Enemy
            Gandhi's philosophy
            Understanding others
            Treating persons as humans

VIII.   Nonviolence as Action

IX.   Conclusion

<u>Remember</u> <u>When</u> <u>Mace</u> <u>Was</u> <u>a</u> <u>Spice</u> <u>in</u> <u>Mother's</u> <u>Kitchen?</u>

Nonviolence. It sounds like a recommendation not to do anything, doesn't it? Or worse, it sounds like consent to evil, or withdrawal. Maybe the "non" started as a sly, semantic trick perpetrated by the violent as a subtle put-down. In any case, it is a philosophy that is currently out of favor. Violence is in.

The purpose of this paper is to redefine nonviolence as an action. This is not a comprehensive study of the philosophy. The hope here is to serve as a catalyst for a consideration of nonviolence as a positive force and to argue that violence is a negative force whose chief reality is self-destruction.

> The paragraph above is a statement of the theme.

The message of <u>satyagraha</u> has been diluted and confused in the passage from Gandhi's word to our word "nonviolence." <u>Satyagraha</u> has been more correctly translated as "strength of truth," "force of soul," "steadfastness for truth," "grasp of truth," "truth force," and "creative force." These stronger definitions better represent the two principles in the practice of <u>satyagraha</u>--to adhere to the truth and to defend it to the utmost by voluntary suffering. It is in these stronger terms that the word "nonviolence" is used in this paper.

As an extreme opposite of violence, nonviolence
implies the same force as violence, but it is transformed
into a moral force. The nonviolent seek not to destroy
the enemy but to convert him. Gandhi is quoted: "I
seek entirely to blunt the edge of the tyrant's sword,
not by putting up against it a sharper-edged weapon,
but by disappointing his expectation that I would be
offering physical resistance."[1]

Found through the *Readers' Guide to Periodical Literature* under the
heading nonviolence.

NONFERROUS metals. See Metals. Nonferrous
NONSENSE verse
    See also
    Mother Goose
NONVIOLENCE
    Gandhi: the heritage of non-violence; symposium. UNESCO
        Courier 22:4-32 O '69
    What role for non-violence today? excerpts from Gandhi's truth.
        E. H. Erikson. Cur 112:42-7 N '69
NON-WAGE payments
    NRPA's personal security program; including life insurance benefits.
        D. D. Magee. il Parks & Rec 4:73-4 S '69
NOONAN, Joseph
    Something new. Cath World 210:78-9 N '69

The idea of nonviolence is an ancient concept,
though it did not always have a name and was not always
a clearly defined philosophy to those who practiced it.

In A.D. 37-41, the Jews are said to have practiced
nonviolence in resistance to Roman Emperor Caligula's

1 René Habachi, "The Heritage of Non-Violence,"
UNESCO Courier (October 1969), p. 13.

determination to force the Jews to erect his statue in the Temple at Jerusalem.[2] The Sermon on the Mount is usually considered a nonviolent philosophy, and early Christians refused to pay taxes to support heathen temples.[3]

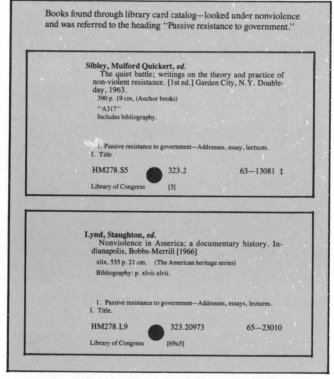

Books found through library card catalog—looked under nonviolence and was referred to the heading "Passive resistance to government."

Sibley, Mulford Quickert, *ed.*
    The quiet battle; writings on the theory and practice of non-violent resistance. [1st ed.] Garden City, N.Y. Doubleday, 1963.
    390 p. 19 cm. (Anchor books)
    "A317"
    Includes bibliography.

    1. Passive resistance to government—Addresses, essay, lectures.
    I. Title

HM278.S5   323.2   63—13081 ‡

Library of Congress   [3]

Lynd, Staughton, *ed.*
    Nonviolence in America; a documentary history. Indianapolis, Bobbs-Merrill [1966]
    xlix, 535 p. 21 cm. (The American heritage series)
    Bibliography: p. xlvii-xlvii.

    1. Passive resistance to government—Addresses, essays, lectures.
    I. Title.

HM278.L9   323.20973   65—23010

Library of Congress   [69u5]

[2] Mulford Q. Sibley, ed., The Quiet Battle (Chicago: Quadrangle Books, 1963), pp. 111-15.

[3] Staughton Lynd, ed., Nonviolence in America: A Documentary History (New York: Bobbs-Merrill, 1966), p. 11.

The eighteenth-century philosopher William Godwin in his <u>An Enquiry Concerning Political Justice</u> (1793) asserted that the best way to effect a revolution in any political system was to change through persuasion the opinion on which all government is founded. Godwin probably influenced his son-in-law Percy Bysshe Shelley, who wrote <u>The Masque of Anarchy</u> after reading about peaceful demonstrators being fired upon by British troops.[4]

Early American history is filled with incidents of the use of nonviolence, as in the life-style of the Quakers[5] and in the life of Henry David Thoreau, who had

Thoreau quotation from *The Oxford Companion to American Literature* and not footnoted because essay is famous and found in many sources.

Civil Disobedience, essay by Thoreau (q.v.), originally delivered as a lecture, and first printed as 'Resistance to Civil Government' in Elizabeth Peabody's *Aesthetic Papers* (1849).

Asserting that 'That government is best which governs not at all' and that 'Government is at best but an expedient,' the author points to such injustices and abuses as the prosecution of the Mexican War, the treatment of native Indians, and the institution of slavery. To co-operate with government, even to

[4] Sibley, <u>op. cit</u>., pp. 21-24.

[5] Lynd, <u>op. cit</u>., pp. 3-21.

refused to pay taxes and in his essay on civil disobedience states: "Under a government which imprisons
any unjustly, the true place for a just man is also in
prison." The essay later influenced Gandhi.[6]

> The *Reader's Encyclopedia* and footnoted because of claim to have
> influenced Gandhi.
>
> **Civil Disobedience** (1849). An essay by Henry David THOREAU. Its
> major premise is "that government is best which governs least." Thoreau
> asserts that a man's first loyalty is to his own nature; true to himself, he
> may then be true to a government. The essay influenced Gandhi's doctrine
> of passive resistance.

Three well-known advocates of nonviolence in more
recent times are Leo Tolstoy, Mohandas K. Gandhi, and
Martin Luther King, Jr. The list, of course, is much,
much longer.

Even some historical figures commonly associated
with rebellion have spoken out against violence. The
theme of alienation is important to current theories
of nonviolence. Albert Camus, writing of this psychological state, believed in a life committed to becoming
more humane and thereby more human and more alive as a
person. "For Camus, physical violence is the supreme
evil, but he does not rule out its use entirely; violence must be used only to reduce or forestall far more

[6] William Rose Benét, The Reader's Encyclopedia
(New York: Crowell, 1965), p. 202.

worse violence in the immediate future, as a last,

desperate resort, if no nonviolent means are available."[7]

> Using the index to the *International Encyclopedia of the Social Sciences*
> the reader is referred to the heading "Civil Disobedience" among other
> headings. Note the "see also" reference to "violence."
>
> Nonviolence
>   civil disobedience 2:473, 474, 478
>   community disorganization 3:167
>   Indian political thought 7:178
>   pacifism 11:353 fol.
>   race relations: world perspectives
>   13:275
>   see also Violence

Even Marx had a tempered view:

> The more dubious and uncertain an instrument of
> violence has become in international relations,
> the more it has gained in reputation and appeal
> in domestic affairs, specifically in the matter
> of revolution. The strong Marxist rhetoric of the
> New Left coincides with the steady growth of the
> entirely non-Marxian conviction, proclaimed by
> Mao Tse-tung, that "Power grows out of the barrel
> of a gun." To be sure, Marx was aware of the role
> of violence in history, but this role was to him
> secondary; not violence but the contradictions
> inherent in the old society brought about its end.
> The emergence of a new society was preceded, but
> not caused, by violent outbreaks, which he likened
> to the labor pangs that precede, but of course do
> not cause, the event of organic birth. In the same
> vein he regarded the state as an instrument of
> violence in the command of the ruling class; but
> the actual power of the ruling class did not con-
> sist of or rely on violence.[8]

[7] Christian Bay, "Civil Disobedience," International
Encyclopedia of the Social Sciences, David L. Sills, ed.,
(New York: Macmillan, 1968), vol. 2, pp. 478-79.

[8] Hannah Arendt, On Violence (New York: Harcourt Brace
Jovanovich, Inc., 1970), p. 11.

The visible reasons for resorting to violence are many and dramatic. Violence is, of course, as old as its opposite. The Oxford English Dictionary uses two and one-half pages to show the use of the word in its

Because the writer is stating that violence is old and is then going on to define the word, the *Oxford English Dictionary* is used since it emphasizes the historical development of words.

various forms, going far back in time. The OED defines "violence" as the exercise of physical force so as to inflict injury on, or cause damage to persons or property . . . treatment or usage tending to cause bodily injury or forcibly interfering with personal freedom.

And there are subtler meanings that can only be hinted at here. There is, for example, the theory that secret thoughts can do violence or even that "haste is violent in the dimension of time. We have our own natural rhythms and we develop harmoniously and gently only if we conform to them."[9]

Book found through library card catalog.

Régamey, Raymond, 1900—
    Non-violence and the Christian conscience [by] P. Régamey. With a pref. by Thomas Merton and a foreword by Stanley Windass, [New York] Herder and Herder [1966]
    272 p.   22 cm.
    Bibliographical footnotes.

    1. Passive resistance to goverment.   I. Title.
    BT736.6R413   1966   261.7   66—22610

    Library of Congress   [677]

[9] Pie Régamey, O.P., Non-Violence and the Christian Conscience (New York: Herder and Herder, 1966), p. 169.

One of the chief visible reasons for violent action
is poverty and deprivation. Collective violence is
likely to occur in a nation in which most citizens feel
deprived and feel they have exhausted constructive means
available to them and lack nonviolent opportunities to
act on their anger. The slow process of government, that
unoiled, unwieldy machine that doesn't work fast enough,
is another visible reason for violence. Government may
not recognize a problem, or if it does, there remains the
gap between the recognition of need and the accomplishment
of change. Violence is often used to call attention to a
problem ignored and to goad those in power to change their
attitude.

The situation is further complicated by the fact
that nonviolence sometimes begets violence. An insensitive,
established power will sometimes not distinguish between
peaceful and nonpeaceful tactics. A sit-in is not the
same as burning a bank. If a peaceful tactic brings
brutal repression, it tends to radicalize the nonviolent
movement.

The frequently vivid contrast between what is taught
in schools and homes and the actual state of affairs in
the world causes a frustration that leads to violence.
And since short-term goals are often achieved by violence,
this tends to reinforce such a pattern of behavior.

The belief that the end justifies the means is
another factor of violence. The process of violence,
like all action, changes the world, but the nonviolent

believe that the most probable change through that process is to a more violent world; the end is overwhelmed by the means. The advocates of violence contend that a period of temporary violence is necessary to accomplish goals. The risk they face is that violence might become a habit. As Hannah Arendt observed, even revolutionary Frantz Fanon admitted that "'unmixed and total brutality, if not immediately combatted, invariably leads to the defeat of the movement within a few weeks.'"[10]

> Non-violence is not always the heading used, as seen in the catalog card headings. But the library catalog will refer the reader to the heading used—such as "Passive resistance to government."
>
> And, as indicated in some of these examples, it is useful to check under opposite headings ("violence") and related headings ("terrorism"). These will often be suggested in "see also" references.
>
> Other headings may be searched depending on the direction the material is taking ("colleges and universities" for campus disorders).

The accusation that violent behavior is easier in the sense that it does not practice the disciplines of love and does not restrain itself from the thing it opposed in the first place--the forced role under

[10] Arendt, op. cit., p. 14 footnote.

another's opinion--calls for a look at the invisible
reasons for violence.

The blunted conscience, the unacknowledged and
unconscious conflicts that explode and generate wars,
and fear that causes hate and killing are viewed as
psychological reasons for violence.[11] Most important,
warped attitudes leading to the treatment of persons
as things are a large factor in violent behavior.
Violence forces people to act in a way they would not
freely choose and so it destroys them as persons.
Violence produces resentments that work havoc on personality. Treating others as things allows the
offender to kill them because they are not viewed as
human. Without mutual recognition of humanity, no
love is possible. Here is Robert Brustein, former dean
of the Yale School of Drama, writing in The New York Times:

> The moral superiority of the peace movement
> is vitiated by those who urge us to "bring
> the war home," for they are asking us to be-
> come one with the very thing we oppose. We
> must beware of those who call others "pigs,"
> just as we must beware of those who call
> others "effete impudent snobs"--both are
> dehumanizing the opposition in preparation
> for committing inhuman acts against it.[12]

If one believes, as the practitioners of nonviolence do, that every act that harms others harms
the self as well, one must focus on the quality of
life as it is lived as well as on intermediate goals.

[11] Régamey, op. cit., pp. 136-74.

[12] Robert Brustein, "Topics: A Matter of Accountability," The New York Times, April 18, 1970, p. 28.

Gambling—Dominican Republic, Ap 29
BRUSTEIN, Robert (Dean). See also Colls—US—
Student Activities. Ap 18. US—Pol—Fringe Pol
Movements. Ap 18 in Ap 18 par. US Armament—
Draft, Ap 18 in Ap 17 par
BRYAN, D. Tennant. See also Associated Press, Ap 22

The reference to the quotation on the opposite pages can be found in the *New York Times Index*. Shown here is the author entry, which refers the reader to the subject headings under which the complete citation will be found. Also shown is the entry as it appears under one of the subject headings "Colleges and Universities—U.S.—Students' Activities and Conduct."

school and hs educ in urban areas as way of solving open admissions
problems without diluting acad standard, Ap 26,IV,13:4
•*Research:* **See also** Science — US, Ap 23,30
•*State Aid.* **See** subhead US — Finances, Ap 17
•*Student Activities and Conduct.* **See also** Med—NYC, Ap 19. NYC —
Environmental Problems (General), Ap 20, 23. US—Environmental
Problems (General) Ap 20,21,23,24 in Ap 17 par
Prof S W Page lr on New Left on campus scores faculty who participate
in campus agitation, calling them seducers of naive students whom they
use in quest of their power goals, Ap 17,36:3; Dean R Brustein article says
youthful radicals must be held accountable for their actions and warns
against concept that idealistic goal justifies any behavior, Ap 18,28:3; Calif
Gov Reagan calls for 'blood bath' to deal with campus demonstrators if
necessary, s to pol

```
The journey, not the arrival, matters.  Frequent

resorts to violence continually lessen the distinction

between when it is "necessary" and when it is not,

and violence risks becoming a way of life as casually

donned as a garment:


        So pride is their chain of honour,
        violence the garment that covers them,
        their spite oozes like fat,
        their hearts drip with slyness.  Ps 73:6
```

Found through Cruden's *Complete Concordance to the Old and New Testament.*

Because violence is in disharmony with what is best in self, it finally cuts itself off from humanity. In an article in The New York Times Magazine, Irving Howe said:

> The life of the political terrorist is overwhelmed by loneliness, not merely because he can no longer trust completely friend or comrade, but because he cuts himself off from all movements and communities in which choices can be weighed. Staking everything on the act, he blocks off all that comes before it and all that comes after. Deciding whom to smite, he replaces God. Choosing whom to punish, he replaces the justice (be it good or bad) of society. And since the conflicts of social classes must be bent on his will, he replaces history, too. The terrorist carries a moral burden only saints or fanatics would undertake--worst of all, fanatics mistaking themselves for saints.[13]

The Reader's Guide indexes The New York Times Magazine so this is found through that guide (violence has a see also reference to "terrorism"); and it is also found in The New York Times Index. Example of author entry from The New York Times Index 1970 which refers the reader to the subject headings under which the full citation will be given—"News—U.S.," and "U.S. Politics Fringe Political Movements."

[13] Irving Howe, "Political Terrorism: Hysteria on the Left," The New York Times Magazine, April 12, 1970, p. 25.

A principal tactic of nonviolence is persuading the opposition. This calls, first of all, for a recognition of the fact that the role of the doubter and the challenger is not the only one in the human drama. Therefore, the role is not forced on anyone. Gandhi sought to convert, not force. His pervading mood was a spirit of giving the opponent the courage to change. The willingness to convert rather than to force is backed by a view of each person as human, not as thing. There is truth in the old cliché that one can best understand another by putting oneself in his place and proceeding from that insight. This point is made by the experience of a man who won the friendship of eagles and other wild animals and succeeded in getting a hen to snuggle down affectionately on the head of a fox. He said:

> I have no mysterious "fluid"; quite simply
> I have always tried to put myself in the place
> of the animal I studied, and first of all to
> see how it looks upon the world that surrounds
> it. . . . The universe has a very different
> meaning for each of them; it is not the same for
> the tortoise, the heron, the lizard, the eagle. . . .
> To understand a given animal is to carefully
> reconstitute its universe, its way of living,
> in order to perceive as clearly as possible
> the significance to itself of what it does
> and expresses.[14]

Finally, nonviolence is not passive, it cries for action. If you act contrary to justice and I remain silent, it is I who am unjust. We are guilty if we

14 Régamey, op. cit., p. 173.

whispered when we should have shouted. Many instinctive abdicators call themselves nonviolent, a view that lacks an appreciation of peace as an action. Even the peaceful Gandhi "believed in nonviolence, but also held that violence is better than cowardice."[15]

Nonviolence as an active force is not easy. Martin Luther King, Jr., said: "A . . . point that characterizes nonviolent resistance is a willingness to accept suffering without retaliation, to accept blows from the opponent without striking back."[16] But given the "strength of

> Book found through card catalog under "King, Martin Luther" as a subject rather than as an author (subject cards behind author cards).

truth" it is possible for the action of nonviolence to be, as Staughton Lynd says, "the vision of love as an agent for social change." Let us hope that Plutarch is right when he says: "Perseverance is more prevailing

[15] Joan V. Bondurant, "Gandhi," The World Book Encyclopedia, 1968, VIII, 25.

> *The World Book Encyclopedia* cited in footnote because claim that Gandhi held that violence is better than cowardice might be questioned.

[16] Negro Heritage Library, A Martin Luther King Treasury (Yonkers, N.Y.: Educational Heritage, 1964), p. 71.

than violence; and many things which cannot be overcome when they are together, yield themselves up when taken little by little." Nonviolence claims to break the

Found in Bartlett's *Familiar Quotations* and not cited because easily found in most general quotation books. (The quotation is also indexed under "Perseverance" and can be located in the Index to Authors under "Plutarch."

Viol of her memory, 955b
  violet and vine, 642a
Viola, notes *v.* fiddles bass, 505a
Violate agreements, 972a
Violations, security against future *v.*, 426a
Violence, age of comfort and *v.*, 999b
  and injury to humanity, 100a
  and injury to willow, 100a
  blown with restless *v.*, 271b
  covereth the mouth of the wicked, 24a
  dictatorship maintained by *v.*, 957b
  nation at mercy of *v.*, 1013a
  never by *v.* constrained, 189a
  not by force or *v.*, 465b
  overcome *v.* without *v.*, 1082b
  perseverance more prevailing than *v.* 136b
  truth not permit *v.*, 897a
Violent and sudden usurpations, 480b
  death of slaveholder, 684a
  delights have violent ends, 224b

circle of ever-increasing violence; it says that the important thing is not the visible success of one's life but its quality.

Our obligation here is to be truly alive, to learn to love, whether this obligation is seen from a humanist view, as a supernatural gift of God, or as a simple dictate of conscience. It is difficult. There will be times of failure.

That then is the plea. To be alive, active, and nonviolent. And if you aren't--well, how would you like a punch in the nose . . . ?

BIBLIOGRAPHY

Arendt, Hannah. On Violence. New York: Harcourt Brace Jovanovich, 1970.

Bay, Christian. "Civil Disobedience." International Encyclopedia of the Social Services. New York: Macmillan, 1968.

Brustein, Robert. "Topics: A Matter of Accountability." The New York Times, April 18, 1970, p. 28.

Cornell, Thomas C., and Forest, James, eds. A Penny a Copy: Readings from the Catholic Worker. New York: Macmillan, 1968.

Finn, James. Protest: Pacifism and Politics. New York: Random House, 1967.

Gurr, Ted Robert. Why Men Rebel. Princeton, N.J.: Princeton University Press, 1970.

Habachi, René. "The Heritage of Non-Violence." UNESCO Courier (October 1969), pp. 13-17.

Howe, Irving. "Political Terrorism: Hysteria on the Left." The New York Times Magazine (April 12, 1970), pp. 25-27, 124-28.

Lynd, Staughton, ed. Nonviolence in America: A Documentary History. New York: Bobbs-Merrill, 1966.

Negro Heritage Library. A Martin Luther King Treasury. Yonkers, N.Y.: Education Heritage, 1964.

Régamey, Pie. Non-Violence and the Christian Conscience. New York: Herder and Herder, 1966.

Sibley, Mulford Q., ed. The Quiet Battle. Chicago: Quadrangle Books, 1963.

Selected
Bibliography

Barzun, Jacques, and Graff, Henry F. *The Modern Researcher.* 3d ed. New York: Harcourt Brace Jovanovich, 1977.

Cheney, Frances Neel, and Williams, Wiley J. *Fundamental Reference Sources.* Chicago: American Library Association, 1980.

D'Angelo, Edward. *The Teaching of Critical Thinking.* Amsterdam: Gruner N.V., 1971.

Ennis, Robert H. "A Concept of Critical Thinking," *Harvard Educational Review,* Vol. 32 (Winter 1962), pp. 81–111.

Leidy, W. Philip. *A Popular Guide to Government Publications.* 4th ed. New York: Columbia University Press, 1976.

Moorehead, Joe. *Introduction to United States Public Documents.* 2d ed. Littleton, Colo.: Libraries Unlimited, 1978.

Gates, Jean Key. *Guide to the Use of Libraries and Information Sources.* 5th ed. New York: McGraw-Hill, 1983.

Prakken, Sarah L., ed. *The Reader's Advisor: A Layman's Guide to Literature.* 12th ed. New York: Bowker, 1974, 1977. 3 vols.

Sheehy, Eugene P. *Guide to Reference Books.* 9th ed. Chicago: American Library Association, 1976. First Supplement, 1980, Second Supplement, 1982.

Stevens, Rolland, and Walton, Joan M. *Reference Work in the Public Library.* Littleton, Colo.: Libraries Unlimited, 1983.

Walford, A. J. *Guide to Reference Materials.* London: Library Association. Vol. 1, 4th ed., *Science & Technology,* 1980. Vols. 2 and 3, 3d ed. *Social & Historical Sciences, Philosophy and Religion and Generalities, Languages, the Arts and Literature,* 1975.

The author wishes to thank the following publishers for their kind permission to quote from works held in copyright:

p. 40: Arthur Kopit entry, copyright © 1984, Marquis Who's Who, Inc. Reprinted by permission from *Who's Who in America,* 43rd edition.

p. 46: "Guitar" excerpt from *Funk & Wagnalls New Standard Dictionary of the English Language* (Funk & Wagnalls), copyright © 1969 by Harper & Row, Publishers Inc. Reprinted by permission of the publisher.

p. 46: *The Random House Dictionary of the English Language,* copyright © 1969, 1967, 1966 by Random House, Inc. Reprinted by permission.

pp. 46 and 48: *Webster's Third New International Dictionary,* copyright © 1981 by Merriam-Webster, Inc., publisher of the Merriam-Webster ® Dictionaries. Used by permission.

p. 48: *The American Heritage Dictionary of the English Language,* copyright © 1969, 1970 by American Heritage Publishing Co., Inc.

p. 51: *A Dictionary of Contemporary American Usage* by Bergen and Cornelia Evans. Copyright © 1957 by Bergen Evans and Cornelia Evans. Reprinted by permission of Random House, Inc.

pp. 59–61 and 64–65: *Reader's Guide to Periodical Literature,* copyright © 1984 by H. W. Wilson Co. Reprinted by permission of the publisher.

p. 80: *Architecture Through the Ages* by Talbot Faulkner Hamlin, published by G. P. Putnam's Sons, Inc. Copyright © 1953. Used by permission.

p. 87: *Cambridge History of English Literature* by A. W. Ward. Copyright © 1927. Published by G. P. Putnam's Sons, Inc. Used by permission.

p. 87: *The Oxford Companion to American Literature* by James D. Hart. Copyright © 1965 by Oxford University Press, Inc. Reprinted by permission of the publisher.

p. 87: *The Oxford Companion to English Literature,* edited by Sir Paul Harvey, 4th edition. Copyright © 1964. Published by The Clarendon Press, Oxford, England.

p. 88: *Literary History of the United States* by R. E. Spiller, W. Thorp, T. H. Johnson, H. S. Canby, and R. M. Ludwig. Copyright © 1963. Published by Macmillan Publishing Co., Inc.

p. 89: *Cyclopedia of Literary Characters,* page 690 ("The Member of the Wedding," Principal Characters List), edited by Frank N. Magill. Copyright © 1963 by Salem Press Inc. Reprinted by permission of the publisher.

p. 91: *Book Review Digest,* copyright © 1984 by H. W. Wilson Co. Reprinted by permission of the publisher.

p. 96: *Market Guide* (1984), page II–134. Reprinted by permission of The Editor & Publisher Co.

p. 99: *The Book of Days: A Miscellany of Popular Antiquities,* edited by Robert Chambers. Originally published by W. & R. Chambers, Ltd., London. Reprinted by Gale Research Company, Detroit, Michigan, 1967.

p. 100: *Chase's Annual Events 1984.* Published by Contemporary Books, Inc., 180 North Michigan Avenue, Chicago, Illinois 60601. Copyright © by Contemporary Books, Inc. Used by permission.

p. 103: *The New American Guide to Colleges* by Gene Hawes, Columbia University Press, New York, copyright © 1966.

p. 112: *An Encyclopedia of World History* by William L. Langer, 5th edition. Copyright © 1940, 1948, 1952, renewed 1968, 1972 by Houghton Mifflin Co. Reprinted by permission of Houghton Mifflin Co.

pp. 114–115: *Dictionary of Events: A Handbook of Universal History* by G. P. and G. H. Putnam. Copyright © 1927 by G. P. Putnam and G. H. Putnam. Published by G. P. Putnam's Sons, Inc. Reprinted by permission.

p. 117: *What Happened When* by Stanford M. Mirkin. Copyright © 1966 by Stanford M. Mirkin, published by Ives Washburn, Inc.

p. 118: *The Encyclopedia of American Facts and Dates,* 7th edition, page 416, edited by Gorton Carruth (T. Y. Crowell). Reprinted by permission of the publisher.

p. 119: *Documents of American History,* edited by Henry Steele Commager, 9th edition. Copyright © 1974. Published by Prentice-Hall, Inc., Englewood Cliffs, N.J. Used by permission.

p. 121: "There Was A Young Fellow From Trinity" from *One, Two, Three . . . Infinity* by George Gamow. Copyright © 1947, 1961 by George Gamow. Copyright renewed © 1974 by Barbara Gamow. Reprinted by permission of Viking Penguin Inc.

p. 123: *Mathematics for the Million* by Lancelot Hogben, by permission of W. W. Norton & Co. and George Allen & Unwin Ltd. Copyright © 1937, 1940, 1943, 1951 by W. W. Norton & Co., Inc. Copyright © renewed 1964 by Lancelot Hogben. Copyright © 1967, 1968 by Lancelot Hogben. Illustration copyright © 1967 by Pan Books, Ltd.

p. 126: *Ethnic Information Sources of the United States,* edited by Paul Wasserman and Alice Kennington. Copyright © 1976, 1983 by Paul Wasserman. Reprinted by permission of Gale Research Company, 2nd edition, Gale Research, 1983, p. 60.

INDEX